The Prac...

Getting great results from
the six days *between* music lessons

Mother,
Merry Christmas
Love,
Tony

Philip Johnston

PracticeSpot Press

www.practicespot.com

Published by
PracticeSpot Press
52 Pethebridge Street
Pearce ACT 2607
AUSTRALIA

Ver. 1.03

Cover design by Whizzbang Art

ISBN 0-9581905-0-X

Acknowledgements

To my students, past and present, who have been part of more than a decade of study, experimentation and laughter that has made this book possible—but who also had to put up with being guinea-pigs for all the not-so-good ideas that *didn't* make it into this edition.

Also with long overdue thanks to my parents, Christine and Merv, who have been tireless sources of encouragement and inspiration on every step of my various mad adventures.

And a special thanks to my wife Katherine, who continues to be both my muse and greatest source of delight—for her constant support, her unconditional faith, and for being oxygen for the fire whenever I come bouncing into the room with "I've had a great idea!". Katherine, none of this—*none of this*—would be possible without you.

Contents

Introduction: The 0.3% syndrome

As music teachers, we're usually very careful to walk students through things that are new. We don't introduce scales to students simply by tossing a scales manual to them and wishing them good luck—instead, we discuss the whole process with the precision of a pet store owner giving instructions for the care of a new kitten. Do this. Don't do that. Watch out for these. Pay special attention to those. We take this time because our students have years of scales ahead of them, and we know how ugly things can get later if they mess it up now.

It's not just scales that receive this special treatment. We'll give similar in-depth introductions to every landmark technique as it appears. As a result, violin students aren't just slapped on the back at the end of one lesson and told to "have a go at some vibrato this week"—their teacher will have plenty to say first about how they should proceed with this new adventure. This care and attention doesn't feel like wasted time, because it all goes to developing a crucial skill, and the time allocated is proportional to that importance.

Well, before we congratulate ourselves on what wonderful Sherpas we are for our students, there's one skill that we normally provide no guidance for whatsoever. The student is sent home to figure it out as best they can. Worse still, this skill just happens to be an order of magnitude more important than anything else we could show them:

Practicing.

I'm not belittling the importance of vibrato or scales in saying this. It's just that without effective practicing, there is no vibrato development, and scales are stillborn. New pieces will remain uncharted, old pieces will remain unpolished, and the lessons themselves will stagnate.

If practicing fails, then the lessons fail. It's that simple, and it's that important.

So while we fuss about far less critical issues, such as whether trills begin on the top or the bottom note, it's as though we assume that the instruction "please practice" is magically imbued with explanations as to what's involved. Perhaps it's because we have practiced so many times ourselves that the whole process feels self-evident. No explanations necessary. So get on with it already, our students know what to do.

No they don't.

And worse yet, as teachers we can often be confused too.

This book is dedicated to equipping you with hundreds of ideas for turning practice into a powerful tool—helping students get more done in less time, and ensuring that they use the right techniques for the right problems. It will also provide an analysis of common practice flaws, together with tactics for combating them. But none of this is going to work if you simply read the book, and then try to squeeze the new ideas into the same amount of time that you currently allocate to discussing practice.

For the transformation to be complete, you need to accept that from now on, in every lesson you need to dedicate some serious time to teaching practicing. Introducing new practice techniques. Outlining what specific problems these new techniques are designed to fix. Analyzing the practice that took place this week. Planning the practice that will take place next week. Warning of potential practice traps. And showing them a way out of the traps that they already fall victim to.

Remember, if practicing fails, then the lessons fail. Why? It's simple arithmetic:

You see your students for *one* lesson each week.

That half hour lesson represents 0.3% of the student's time in those seven days. Zero point three percent. And that's rounding *up*. A mere thirty minutes in a week containing 168 hours.

This means that for a staggering 99.7% of the time, *music students are responsible for their own destiny*. It's no surprise then that the great leaps forward don't happen during lessons. They're most likely to happen *between* lessons, because that's where your students are almost all of the time.

This book is dedicated to helping your students get the most out of the time when you *can't* be with them...

...so that they can get the most out of the time when you can.

...To the barricades

"Time has no divisions to mark its passage, there is never a thunderstorm or blare of trumpets to announce the beginning of a new month or year. Even when a new century begins it is only we mortals who ring bells and fire off pistols."

Thomas Mann (1875–1955), German author and critic

The Practice Revolution: Chapter 1

• The Quantity Myth
• The Revolution Begins

1. ...To the barricades

1.1 The Quantity Myth

For too long, music teachers have been obsessed with *how much* practice students do. Seminars and online newsgroups around the world are filled with suggestions for getting students to do more, and lamentations about students who never seem to do enough. It then often becomes the first question asked at each lesson—usually couched in terms of "How did your practice go this week?"—but we're not really fishing for a report on the success of the practice when we ask this. We want to know how much *time* they spent, and how regularly that practice took place. As the teacher, give me a big number, tell me it happened seven times in the week, and I'll be smiling already.

In this way, practice has been regarded simply as a barometer of *dedication*— a tangible way for students to demonstrate how serious they are about their music lessons. They tithe time, not money, as a regular gesture of good faith to the institution that is their teaching studio, and to the parents who make those lessons possible.

And once the number of minutes spent practicing has been noted, there's not usually much attention paid to how productive that time actually was.

Following this logic, many parents and teachers will assume that a student who is spending thirty minutes every day is twice as dedicated as one who spends fifteen. And if they're not practicing at all...gee...then lessons are obviously a complete waste of time. They better quit.

If you ever have doubts about the prevalence of this perception, try asking a parent how they think their child's music lessons are going. The answer will usually be in two parts—first a subjective assessment of progress:

"They seem to be going really well"
"Struggling at the moment"
"Enjoying it!"
"Second half of this year has been better than the first"

And then they'll reinforce their conclusion with evidence expressed in terms of how much practice their child is doing:

"They're practicing every day! I don't even have to ask"
"It doesn't matter how much I nag, they won't even open their instrument case"
"They practice most days, but rarely for more than twenty minutes"

So how are lessons going? Sounds as though you can answer that with a simple number. They're going *20 minutes of practice, three times a week.* (not going so well) They're going *practice every day, from four to half past four.* (Good lessons!) They're going *no practice at all, apart from a ten minute panic session on the day of the lesson* (Baaad lessons!)

It's madness. There are two fatal flaws in this approach, and together, they have been wrecking music lessons since before your favorite composers were born.

First of all, this time-obsession approach has the student (and their family!) focussing on the minute hand of the clock, rather than outcomes. Students shouldn't practice just to pass time, students practice so that they can master certain skills by next lesson—skills that otherwise may have taken many weeks or months to acquire. Practice is a means to an end, and not an end in itself. And most alarming of all, as the "Common Practice Flaws" section of this book illustrates, if time is the only consideration, it's possible for a student to spend a lot of time practicing, and actually make their playing *worse*. So it's not a given that just because they are telling you Big Numbers when they answer "How did your practice go this week?" that they have been helping their playing any.

Secondly, an obsession with how much practice is being done sets up as the Most Important Issue the one part of music lessons that is often in trouble. Problems with practice is the single biggest reason that lessons fail. You might have a student who is progressing well, looking forward to lessons, performing well at recitals and exams, improving with both their reading and rhythmic skills, excited about the future and engaged in the present—but has an on-again-off-again attitude to practicing at home. In fact some weeks they don't do any. Despite the profile which clearly paints a picture of a student who is getting a lot from their lessons, because their practice is not so good, they are told regularly that what they are doing is "just not good enough". Even if we temper that by acknowledging how well they are playing, they are still left in no doubt that according to the most important yardstick, they are failing.

A month or two of that, and you can watch everything else dry up. As a student, it's very hard to be enthusiastic about music lessons when you know that the focus of the lessons themselves is going to be on the one thing that is *not* going well. And suddenly, an exciting and excited music student has been struck down, consigned to the great Graveyard of lessons that didn't quite work out.

Shame on us. It's like taking a car to the wreckers just because the glove box doesn't close properly.

This is particularly destructive if there is no understanding as to *why* practice is sometimes missing. In the absence of any genuine analysis of what causes the lack of practice, it's all too easy to declare that the student is "not dedicated". *Dedication often has nothing to do with it.* As we'll see later in the book, there are many reasons students avoid practice, from reading difficulties, to an impossible environment at home, to inadequate project management skills...each of which is completely independent of dedication, and each of which needs to be handled uniquely.

Not only that, but if you can maintain the fundamentals that are going so well in lessons, and combine that with an understanding of what is genuinely preventing practice, you'll eventually end up with a student who practices of their own accord anyway—without the need for constant intervention from the adults in their life. And one of the great battlegrounds surrounding music lessons is removed.

We don't get this wrong because we're bad people. In fact it's usually an indicator that we take what we do very seriously, and that we believe the student should too. We also know as experienced teachers that it is a very rare student indeed who can progress to anyone's satisfaction if they are doing no practice at all. The understanding is that Time is the most valuable asset the student has, and that they should be spending plenty of it in the practice room—otherwise they are selling themselves and their lessons short.

It's precisely *because* Time is the most valuable asset that students have that we should be focussing instead on how we can help them get more done in *less* time. Instead of thinking up ever more creative ways to get our students to do more practice, we should be thinking up ever more efficient methods of practice, so that whatever practice they do actually *works*. The irony is that in shifting the obsession away from how much practice students do, and towards how we can help them practice better, students end up spending more time practicing anyway—because they get more out of it.

1.2 The Revolution Begins

Of course it's not quite as simple as that. Even if practicing were reframed so that outcomes become more important than time spent, without time spent, there are no outcomes. This means that there will still exist the basic ages-old tension between teacher and student—the desire on the teacher's part for the student to always come to lessons prepared, colliding head on with the desire on the student's part to do as little practice as they can get away with.

The beauty of the Practice Revolution is that it defuses this tension. And it does so in a way that has the student concentrating harder and practicing more efficiently than ever before. Not because it's magic, but simply because it restructures the institution of practice to allow human nature to work *for* you, instead of constantly fighting against it.

Here's how it works.

Your students are interested in doing less practice, if at all possible. You want them to be ready for their next lesson. But because of the attitude shift at the core of the Practice Revolution, you don't need to be particularly interested in how *long* it actually takes them to get the job done each week. As long as the outcomes are satisfactory, it's actually their business—and only their business—how long they spent doing it. Just as if we worked in a conventional office job, and we are to submit a report by Friday, our boss doesn't care whether it takes us twenty minutes or twenty hours, as long as it's a good report, and it is delivered on time. In fact, if your boss were to ask you "how is your report coming along", he or she would look at you very oddly indeed if you answered "Great! I've been spending half an hour on it every day".

Because *time spent* is now seen as a separate issue from *outcomes achieved*, you can direct your energies towards helping your students get more done in less time.

In other words, you're on their side. They want to do less practice, and you're going to help show them how to do exactly that.

The secret is in *how* they practice. Your job is to help your students become so efficient when they practice that they can get more done in ten minutes than they used to be able to in two hours. To help you with this, this book will take a fresh look at the institution of practicing, regarding it not as a single entity, *but as a set of tools.* Each tool is designed to solve a particular problem—some are great for learning brand new pieces, others are designed for helping nervous students through the few days before a major recital, others are designed to help students create compelling dynamics for a previously bland performance. And like any tools, you need to use the right tools for the right job. It's no good trying to hammer in a nail with a screwdriver, and it's a waste of time trying to speed a piece up with a practice technique that was designed for *memorizing* pieces.

So why would your students be excited about this?

Look at it from their point of view. After years of being chained to a clock, as they complete the daily chore that is their practice, you are coming to them with a new model.

> *"Here's what I need you to do this week. I don't care how long it takes you, which means that if you can practice so effectively and efficiently that you can knock it all off in two days, great. Enjoy the five days off.*

> *The only thing is that if you genuinely want to get it all done in the shortest time possible, you'll need to be smart about **how** you work. I have some suggestions if you're interested."*

If they're interested? Of course they're interested—you're about to teach them some tactics that will enable them to spend *less* time practicing. And so we end up with a student who is motivated by the idea of more free time if they work well, is now very interested in learning how to work efficiently in the pursuit of that end, and no longer watches the clock while they work. All because they're not done until the job's done...but they are as soon as it is.

Sounds like a good outcome all round.

But there's one more benefit to all this, although you have to keep it a secret from your students:

Students who are practicing efficiently and without watching the clock *end up doing more practice anyway*. It's just that they don't notice, and more importantly, they don't mind.

We should probably start at the very beginning.

Giving Better Instructions

"Today, communication itself is the problem. We have become the world's first overcommunicated society. Each year we send more and receive less."

Al Ries, Chairman, Trout & Ries Advertising Inc

The Practice Revolution: Chapter 2

• The words with the power to shape their week
• The importance of being specific • Challenges, not requests • Making sure you've been heard
• Giving them ownership over the instructions •
Involving parents in the process •

2. Giving Better Instructions

2.1 The words with the power to shape their week

It all starts here. Before the weekly journey On Their Own has even begun. The final 120 seconds of your student's music lesson—that twilight during which the next student is arriving, books are being collected and instruments packed away.

"How was Sally today?"
"Great, excellent work this lesson. The new piece is really coming along. Scales too."
"Good to hear. That's the stuff Sally. I'm proud of you. Come on, home time—no, you can carry your own books, let's go. Same time next week?"

Yes, same time. And besides which, now only half of your attention is on Sally and her parent. The rest is on the student who has just come in.

In the middle of this wind-down, there will be a moment, unremarked upon and seemingly unremarkable, when you'll give practice instructions for the week to come. A note jotted in Sally's book. A sound-bite given as she pulls the studio door shut behind her. It's an event that seems innocent enough—one more instruction after half an hour filled with directives.

It's not at all innocent. In fact, it's the most important thing you have said in the entire lesson. For the next six days, *everything* your student works on—or doesn't—will be shaped by what you just said.

The next time a Sally closes the door, ask yourself this just before the next lesson starts:

Would you bet your car that her understanding of what she should do this week is the same as yours?

Because if the answer to that question is "um...no...", then you have no right to be annoyed with her next lesson if she falls short of your expectations.

It just may be that they were never *her* expectations in the first place.

So long before we examine the mechanics of effective practicing, the subtleties of motivation techniques, or the role of parents, we have to start with something much more fundamental.

Communication.

Ensuring that your practice instructions are powerful springboards for the week ahead—directions that are precise, easy to absorb, fun to work with, and impossible to ignore.

2.2 The importance of being specific

It's going to come as a shock to a lot of teachers, but one of the first things that cripples practice is lack of precision when instructions are given.

It feels absurd—and almost insulting—to point this out, because so much of what we do as music teachers is actually nit-pickingly precise. After all, the twenty-five minutes before practice instructions are given is taken up by the music lesson itself—a time usually filled to bursting with directions so detailed that they can sound downright *bossy*:

"Start your crescendo at bar 24, but don't actually arrive at a genuine forte until bar 29. Let go of the B flat after three and a half beats. No...four is not "near enough"...um, no, neither is three...uh huh, yes your school teacher may have told you that, but we don't round down fractions in music...it has to be exactly three and a half.

Why? Because it just sounds better that way, don't lecture me about integers, just do it. Where were we...play this section staccato, except for the last three notes—you have to observe the slur. Change your pedal now. Rotate your wrist to reach the G. Use your fourth finger on the Ab the first time, and your third finger the second time...oops, watch out for the key signature change. Five flats to remember now, instead of only three. That's better. Ok, from the top again—did I mention the crescendo at bar 24?, yes well I don't think you should do it again on the repeat..."

Wow. And that's just for the first page. It's a lot to remember for any student, but it probably all had to be said.

23

I'm prepared to concede that the information we give *during* lessons is a carefully thought through litany of "when" "what" and "how"—every last moment of the student's piece is analyzed, corrected and polished. We give directions accurate to fractions of a beat, as we become precision watchmakers, insisting that our students scrutinize their work through the same powerful lenses we use.

However, at the end of the lesson—in that moment during which we explain what the student needs to work on at home— things are usually very different.

We abandon our watchmaker's tweezers and eyepieces, and brandish blunt and rusty shovels instead.

Far from giving instructions that are detailed and precise, our here's-what-you-are-supposed-to-work-on-this-week requests are more often like this:

"Learn page three of your new piece"
"Memorize the Waltz"
"Do some work on that tricky bit in the center of the piece"

Now at first glance, there seems to be nothing wrong with these instructions, and as a teacher, it can seem that no additional information is required. It's clear that the student should come back next week with page three *learned*, the waltz *memorized*, and the tricky bit in the center of the piece *fixed*. (That's what you asked for, wasn't it?)

And more to the point, if the student doesn't come back with all of that, they'll be in trouble. It's their job this week—their part of the tuition bargain.

But put yourself in your student's shoes for a minute, and look at just the first of these instructions:

"Learn page three of your new piece"

Now let's see. "Learn"? What does that mean? Have I "learned" it once I can play it up to tempo with no breakdowns...or when I can first lurch through it from beginning to end without startling the cat? If I am a pianist, does "learned" mean hands separate or together? Should I "learn" dynamics and fingerings, or are the notes enough?

Does "learned" imply "memorized"? Or is it a rough sketch with most of the essentials in place? Does a "learned" piece have to be of a uniform high standard throughout? Or do I just have to demonstrate that I have some idea as to what's going on in the score?

And perhaps most vexing—does "learned" after only a week imply a necessary lower quality than "learned" with a one month deadline?

Taken alone, these ambiguities may appear to be worthy of concern. But there are more powerful forces at work that will soon have you appreciating the full dangers of the open ended nature of these requests.

As a student, there are two things that will be important to me as I practice this week—and every other week. The first is to make sure my teacher is not unhappy with my progress next lesson (even the most recalcitrant of students would rather have "good" lessons than "bad" ones).

And the second is not to do any more practice than I absolutely have to in the pursuit of that first end.

Reconciling these two concerns can cause problems…particularly if the practice instructions are open to interpretation.

As a student, I am going to dance in the grey areas caused by sloppy definitions. In fact, I am highly likely to hereby define "learn" to mean "be able to approximately play most of the notes from beginning to somewhere near the end, without needing to stop for directions too many times". I'm not going to worry about trivial extras such as rhythms, dynamics, fingering or tone production. (Those things seem to me to come under the category of "polish"—and I wasn't asked to "polish"!) That way I can stay faithful to my teacher's request, while still keeping my own practice to an acceptable minimum.

Next lesson rolls around, and I'll be feeling ok. I've not only done some practice during the week, I've actually finished all the jobs that were asked of me. As I put my books on the music stand and tune my instrument, a feeling of well-being pervades—my teacher is smiling at me, and all is well.

It's not going to last long.

As the lesson progresses, it becomes clear that there is a yawning gulf between what I have produced, and what my teacher was expecting. It probably won't be far into the lesson before I am asked whether I have done any work on this piece or not.

That question is NOT going to go down well with me. After all, I was asked to "learn" the piece, and I did. Not only did I give up some of my free time to comply with that instruction, but now I'm being given a hard time about it! Well, we'll just see how much practice I do *this* week. Apart from anything else,

25

if my silly teacher wanted dynamics included as part of "learning" the new piece, they should have said so, instead of suddenly changing the rules on me. It's bad enough I wasn't allowed to round three and a half beats down to three…

As the student, I'm still out of line about the double dotted half note. It is worth three and a half, and three was never going to be good enough.

But as to my practice efforts this week, I'm within my rights. I was given instructions, followed them to the letter… and was then told off as a result. There is a range of possible expressions you could use to describe how I would feel about that, but "highly motivated!" is really not one of them.

So how do you solve this problem?

2.3 Challenges, not requests

The core of the problem is actually in the language used—there is an over reliance on verbs that are at best vague, and at worst, actively ambiguous.

Unless you have actually established a lexicon that defines for all students what "Learn" or "Improve" or "Spend some time on" actually means in terms of practice sessions, they will always be open to abuse from unmotivated students, and misinterpretation from even your most genuine pupils. So don't use them.

It's time to replace the standard requests with something much more tangible. Something that can't be argued with.

Instead of lodging a request, issue a *challenge*—a clearly defined and objective test that the piece *needs to be able to pass at some stage before the next lesson*. Once defined, this test would always have identical requirements, whether it were undertaken in your studio, or in the student's living room. In other words, they can replicate it next time they see you, creating a powerful feeling of unity between what goes on at home, and what happens in the lesson.

The idea is that once they can pass this test, they're ready for the lesson. Better still, they can attempt the test at any time during the week to see how the piece is progressing, knowing that until they have passed the test at home, there's still work to be done before they show the piece to their teacher. They can't fudge on your expectations, because the rules of the challenge are clearly defined.

One example, instead of "Learn Page 1":

"The challenge: To be able to play Page 1, from beginning to end THREE TIMES IN A ROW, with no false notes, and correct fingerings throughout. While you are allowed to pause to consider the next note where needed, the entire challenge needs to be completable with six minutes."

Ok, so as the student, I am allowed to compromise rhythm a little with this challenge (so I can stop and figure out whether that next note is really still an E flat or not), but the six minute rule means that I cannot sit and contemplate too many notes in that fashion. So I know straight away that sight reading it at my next lesson is out of the question. This immediately changes my assumptions about the sort of practice I will need to do.

The requirement for "Three times in a row" also rules out the possibility of simply being happy with fluking it once—my practice is going to have to produce a high degree of consistency in the final result, or I won't be able to perform the challenge in front of my teacher. So if I have one glorious shining moment on Tuesday, during which I finally played page one right through with no errors, I won't rest on my laurels. It might have been nice to get from beginning to end like that, but the challenge demands more.

I also know that at the next lesson, instead of my teacher's question being "did you work on the piece this week", it will be "On which day did you pass the test for the very first time?". So I cannot relax after I have "done some practice"—I have a job to do, and I'm not done until it's been completed.

There is a flip side though…while I'm not done until I've completed the job, I *am* finished as soon as I have. This is actually very good news for me. It means that in theory, if I work so well in the first three days of the week that I complete the challenge with days to spare, then I can reward myself with a couple of days of lighter practice (or no practice whatsoever!). Knowing this will have me concentrating harder when I do practice—the trade-off being that if I work well, I can be doing something more fun sooner.

The point at the center of this (and The Practice Revolution will stress it over and over) is that practice is there to achieve specific goals, not simply pass time. How long it takes is actually irrelevant.

2.4 Making sure you've been heard

There can be a big difference between a student having *heard* their instructions for the week ahead, and a student having *listened* to them.

When students arrive at a lesson, protesting that they were only supposed to prepare half of their new piece (instead of the whole thing PLUS the first page of another one!), they're not always trying to take advantage of your fading memory. The indignation that you see is sometimes genuine—sometimes the student will swear on their grandmother's headstone that you asked for only half a page, however awkwardly that may collide with the reality *you* remember. So defining a task clearly for the student is actually only half the battle.

Communicating it is the other.

Most of the communication normally centers on the student's notebook. They bring it to the lesson, and you then write down the practice instructions at the end of the lesson. It's actually a good system—as long as the student actually *reads* what you write at some point.

If you're feeling brave, and want to find out for yourself how frequently your notes go unread, try sending home books with pages sticky-taped together, or with a nonsense limerick instead of instructions, and see how many students come to their next lesson without having noticed.

See. I told you.

So how can you ensure the message actually gets through?

The problem is not in the medium. It's in the message. The notebook's fine (although there is a much more effective option outlined in Chapter 14 of this book)—but it has to be handled a little differently.

Here's how to make sure they hear you...and that they have listened to what they heard.

2.4.1 Write it in their book—but make it memorable to read

Simply writing the information on their page is not enough. You're not putting pen to paper here just to get an idea off your chest—you have to construct something that students will willingly absorb, and then retain.

As any children's book editor will tell you, it all starts with carefully chosen words. There's no point in encouraging the child to "Be vigilant in your quest not to allow accidentals to escape undetected". But you can probably ask them to "Watch out for sharps and flats ".

Similarly, you wouldn't insist that "Appropriate consideration is to be given to the implications of an overambitious tempo", when "Don't play too fast!" will do the job.

If badly selected vocabulary can stop them from comprehending what you write, poor handwriting can actually stop them from even looking at it in the first place. The doctor's prescriptions or florid scripts that we usually use as handwriting may be fine for writing essays or shopping lists, but will actively repel the eyes—and attention—of young readers. In other words, if you expect them to read it, make it easy for them to read. Print, not cursive. Big letters. Short sentences. Indents to structure subtasks. Underlines for key features. White space between paragraphs. The extra couple of seconds that you take to craft how the message looks will enormously increase the chances that they will actually attempt to absorb the meaning, rather than simply look at the words.

Group similar instructions inside boxes, or diamonds, or four-leaf-clovers, or roadsigns...whatever. It all helps the student feel as though they won't be drowning in words when they look at what you had to say.

If you have any sort of artistic bent, include pictures! For example, if you want to reinforce the idea that forgetting to check the fingering in the middle of page 4 will produce a *disaster*, don't just rely on the word—draw a picture of an asteroid hurtling towards a fleeing violin student. The pictogram will not only make the message more fun to read (and therefore more likely to be read in the first place), it will actually help the central message become adhesive.

2.4.2...and checking that your efforts were actually read

So how will you know if the instruction has been read? There's a simple technique that will let you see at a glance whether the book was opened during the week or not—it's a bit like the sticky-tape trick in reverse.

At the end of the lesson, produce a smiley-face sticker, *but don't give it to the student*. Give it to their parent. The student will end up with it eventually, but there is something simple they have to do for you first.

When the student gets home, they have to read the instructions through with their parent, at which point the sticker will go at the bottom of the page. Next lesson, you'll see that sticker and know that the instruction review took place.

This trick won't guarantee that they will *follow* the instructions, but at least you will know that the directions were checked out in the first place.

2.4.3 Have them retell their instructions back to you at the end of the lesson

The problem with simply writing down or telling students their practice instructions is that the communication only flows in one direction. All the student has to do is nod and say "ok" at the right times, and you can be left with the impression that they know exactly what to do.

The reality can be quite different.

Some students will nod and say "ok" because they have taken everything on board. Others will nod and say "ok" even if they didn't understand a word you said.

And worse still, some students will nod and say "ok" while they are actively not listening to you in the first place. (Such students have probably had plenty of practice in dealing with their parents in the same fashion!)

All of this means that as a teacher, you have no way of honestly knowing whether the instructions were absorbed—so you really shouldn't be too surprised or disappointed if they don't deliver. And their failure to deliver can have nothing whatsoever to do with how dedicated they are.

A very simple technique to ensure that they did listen is to ask them to *explain to you*—and their parents—exactly what their task this week is. Then you can gently push them for some more information, just to confirm that their understanding is actually three dimensional.

For example, you may want to ask *how* they propose going about completing the task by next week. Not only will their answer reveal the extent of their comprehension of the requirements of the job, but it will also provide a useful opportunity to examine the pros and cons of some different possible strategies for getting the job done. (There is much more on this later in the book)

You might also ask when in the week they think they will have completed the set challenge for the very first time. In answering that, they end up constructing a projection of the successfully completed job—making the subtle but vital psychological shift from "*if* I get all this done by next lesson" to "*when* I get this all done...".

Probably the easiest way to engineer this retelling of instructions is to have them explain the task to their parents when they get home—particularly if their parents were not able to be at the lesson.

2.4.4 Have a set ritual for giving instructions—the Chair of the Week Ahead

Because the next six days—not to mention the tone and success of next lesson—depend on the student understanding and following your instructions, you want to guarantee that they are paying close attention when you give them.

It's worth highlighting the moment in which instructions are about to be given...lending the occasion an air of a little pomp and regality.

One tactic is to have a Special Chair—one that the student only gets to sit in when they are about to get practice instructions. Play a little fanfare, insist on complete silence in the room. The Practice Instructions are about to be given. Everything to do with the week ahead—the instructions, the retelling, the discussions about how—all take place while the student is in that chair.

It won't take them long to learn that this chair determines not only the week ahead, but the tone and success of the next lesson. (They'll also know that they tend to get asked a LOT of questions about the job ahead when they are sitting in this chair).

In short, there's no way they will confuse the ceremony of Giving Practice Instructions with a regular moment from the rest of their lesson. Make the moment formal enough, and it will be hard for them not to listen. (There's something about ceremony, fanfares and litany that make human beings curious—and when people are curious, they listen harder)

It doesn't have to be a chair. It could be a hat they have to wear, a place in the room they have to stand, or the fact that they have to close their eyes. As long as it's something out of the ordinary, you'll have their attention.

2.5 Giving them ownership over the instructions

One of the easiest ways to convince someone else to adopt an idea *you've* had, is to help them feel that it was *their* idea. People don't need to be persuaded about a plan that they believe was theirs to begin with...in fact, they are likely to be champions for it, particularly if it looks like they might be also getting some of the credit. Presto—you have an instant ally, without even needing to mount an argument.

It's a tactic that is used by shrewd power brokers in committees all around the world. (In fact, if you have ever been on a committee, unless you are the one occasionally doing it, it's probably been done to you.)

A substantial part of getting students to do the practice you need them to is convincing them that the tasks to be practiced are good ideas. In other words, to convince them that the vision for the week ahead is worth pursuing. You can either expend some serious energy with a PR campaign for *your* idea, telling them what a fabulous difference your instructions will make to their piece this week...

...or you can make the whole thing *their* idea. It's not as Machiavellian as it sounds—in fact, it's a great way to promote harmony as well as boost motivation.

Instead of simply telling them what they need to work on, make a list—with the student—of the various problems that need to be solved in their pieces at the moment. Perhaps the dynamics are directionless in this one. Or the tempo is only half what it should be in that one.

Then, armed with that list, ask them to tell you what they will be practicing this week. Have them detail exactly what they are hoping to achieve. They have free choice as to what this is, but the recent discussion you had about problems in their pieces will have put those issues at the front of their minds. Whatever their practice intentions for the week, they are highly likely to include a reshaping of dynamics for the first piece, and a speeding up the second piece.

Of course, these issues were really *your* issues. It's a variation on the Henry Ford principal of "You can have whatever color you like as long as its black"—your student is highly likely to be "choosing" from within the framework of the limited agenda you set for them. If you listed for them "bad fingering" as an issue of concern, you can bet it will come up in their practice intentions somewhere.

And if it doesn't, you can always steer it:

"Sally, this plan looks like a good one—but didn't I hear you saying earlier today that you wanted to improve your fingering in the minuet? I thought that was a great idea at the time...did you also want to include that in your practice plan too?"

Oh yes. How did I overlook that. Silly me, you're right, it was a good idea I had. Add it, make it so.

It's as though you have given them a steering wheel...but then ensured that they are driving a train. They'll be busy turning the wheel and "steering" the train, but you will have laid out the tracks for them in advance.

Everyone's happy—they have a feeling of ownership over what has to be done this week. You have been able to set the agenda to reflect what needs to be done.

2.6 Involve parents in the process

There is an entire chapter later in this book devoted to the role of parents, but at the very least, they need to be well informed each week as to what the tasks for the week are. The heart of the Practice Revolution is a shift away from practicing based on time, towards practicing to get particular jobs done—as the principal supporters of the student, parents absolutely need to know what these jobs *are*.

There are a number of ways you can do this. You can create a special section in the notebook that the parent needs to read and sign each week —candid notes about the task ahead, together with details of the practice techniques that the child should be using to complete the task. If you have your own studio web site (see chapter 14 for details on how to do this), parents can pop into their child's web page at any time in the week, and see the practice instructions for themselves. They can also send you messages with any problems or breakthroughs they may have observed, ensuring that you can hit the ground running next lesson.

Another technique is to have a debriefing at the end of every lesson, in which you go through—with the parent—exactly what is required of the week that's coming up. Encourage the parents to follow up on this by talking to their child about it in the car on the way home. A well-planned practice week with a clear understanding of the task at hand is half the battle won before the first note is even played.

And the other half of the battle? Most of the rest of the book is dedicated to winning that, but before we go any further, we need to spend some time looking at why these battles are so often *lost*.

Common Practice Flaws

"He is verye often drunke and by means there of he hathe by unorderlye playing on the organs putt the quire out of time and disordered them."

From the archives of Lincoln Cathedral,
relating to Thomas Kingston, organist, 1599-1616

The Practice Revolution: Chapter 3

• Chopping Wood with a Spoon • Shiny object polishers • Sheep counters • Speed Demons • Gluttons • Drifters • Skimmers • Clock-watchers • Autopilots • Pattern Practicers • Always from the Top • Bad Bricklayers • Map ignorers • Red Light Runners

3. Common Practice Flaws

3.1 Introduction

No matter how effectively we communicate what needs to be done, sometimes students arrive at lessons with their pieces in exactly the same tangle they were in the week before. It's easy at that point to start lecturing them about practicing harder, but here's the shock—and it lies at the core of the Practice Revolution:

Often these students *have* been practicing.

It's just that how they have been working *doesn't work*, meaning that extra practice is not going to fix the problem. If I'm trying to start a fire by banging two logs together, working harder at it is not going to get my dinner cooked any sooner. In exactly the same way, it's possible for students to be tremendously busy, and get nothing done, particularly if their practice method was doomed from the start.

Worse still, if these practice flaws go uncorrected, the student will quickly learn that practicing doesn't make any difference anyway—so they might as well not bother. The subsequent lack of practice is not a comment about their dedication to music lessons, but rather an indication of disenchantment with a process at home that was failing them.

The flip side though is exciting for any teacher.

If you can eliminate these flaws from the practice process, practice suddenly becomes more productive, the student gets more done in much less time, lessons are better, and the student is then motivated to do more practice anyway.

So before we launch the Practice Revolution with some new approaches to old problems, we need to know what the old problems are. You have to be able diagnose practice flaws as surely as a doctor can identify medical maladies.

This chapter outlines the most common practice flaws—what they are, how to spot them, what causes them, and how to get rid of them.

3.2 Chopping wood with a spoon

Defining this practice flaw

There is a huge variety of tasks that teachers can set for their students each week, and there is an even bigger array of possible practice techniques available to students as they complete those tasks. The difficulty can lie in *selecting the right practice technique for the right task.*

Some students make the match very well, others get it right some of the time, while some seem to constantly get it hopelessly wrong, applying inappropriate practice techniques to the problem at hand—trying to Chop Wood with a Spoon.

For example, practicing with a metronome is a perfectly valid practice technique, and might be an excellent idea for a student who is struggling with keeping a constant tempo in a piece that otherwise wants to run away. Whenever they feel the metronome "dragging", it will be like an alarm going off—their very own personal Acceleration Detector, and they'll ease up on the tempo a little.

> Of all the practice flaws, Chopping Wood with a Spoon is the most important to eliminate.
>
> So much so that the second half of this book has been dedicated entirely to solving this problem.

However, despite the fact that the metronome works so well for *that* scenario, using a metronome would be a complete *disaster* for a student whose problem is that they are meeting a piece for the very first time, and is *not coping with an unfamiliar key signature.* The metronome will force them to deliver notes on time, every time, ready or not. And sometimes they just won't be ready, so they'll play their best guess at that time.

If they spend enough time working with the metronome like this, they will almost certainly deeply embed some reading errors, wasting plenty of lesson and practice time later on as you work together to dislodge them.

Of all the practice flaws, Chopping Wood with a Spoon is the most important to eliminate. So much so that the second half of this book has been dedicated entirely to outlining the common practice tasks, and then

37

providing lists of techniques for each task that will get the job done, together with warnings about the techniques students *shouldn't* use.

How to tell if your student may be practicing this way

This can be a tough one to diagnose. Because there are so many possible weekly tasks, and also so many potential practice techniques, the symptoms produced by bad pairings can vary quite wildly. At its simplest though, you'd be looking out for a discrepancy between *how hard* a student reported working, and the *quality* of the results they produced. If it seems that they are putting in a lot of time for little gain, then you can be certain that the way they are currently practicing doesn't work.

This could indicate that the practice technique is inappropriate for the task, or it could simply be a demonstration that they weren't being rigorous enough in the application of an otherwise perfectly valid technique.

To distinguish between the two, the next step would be to conduct a review of *how* they practiced this week, and *assess that for suitability* against the job they had to complete. Armed then with their job in one column, and the practice techniques they used in the other, you'll quickly be able to tell whether their week was sabotaged by poor technique selections (Don't worry if you don't know how to do this yet - you will be able to by the time you have read chapters 6-12 of this book ☺), or whether the conversation needs to be about the way the techniques were applied.

Another reason that this can be tough to diagnose is that there are *degrees* of inappropriateness—it's not always as clear cut as a choice between a Great Practice Technique and a Hopelessly Mismatched Practice Technique. Sometimes you'll need to intervene, not because the technique they chose was a disaster, but because it was simply *less than ideal*—after all, they still would have had to have done more practice than otherwise should have been that case to achieve the result. It's their time we're talking about saving here.

Taking the analogy of chopping wood a little further, it's therefore not always so hard to identify when they are Chopping Wood with a Spoon. It can be a little tougher though if they have been Chopping Wood with a *Bread Knife*. (It will do the job, but it takes a long time!). It can be tougher still if the tool they chose was a *Blunt Saw*. And once the distinctions are between different types of axe, it can be very difficult to be certain about which one to use.

38

But then again, by the time things have evolved to the point where the problem at hand is which *type* of axe was being used by your woodchopping student, then there really isn't much of a problem in the first place.

Why students practice this way, and why it doesn't work

There are two reasons that students will use the wrong practice technique for the job at hand.

The first is that students often have no idea which practice technique *would* be appropriate. Sometimes they only know a total of two or three practice techniques in the first place, and so they have to use them for everything. So if their job this week is to memorize a piece, unless you have specifically taken them through some practice techniques that are designed to help them memorize pieces, they'll have to make up their own way of handling the problem. We can hardly blame them if they get things wrong in those circumstances.

The second reason can be that they *don't understand the nature of their job this week* well enough to select the appropriate technique. In other words, they can't select the cure, because they're not quite sure which disease they are dealing with in the first place. This can be easily corrected with clearer instructions, and by the student understanding the basic categories into which practice requests fall.

Tips for correcting this practice flaw

• Read the second part of this book. It provides an analysis of those basic categories into which practice requests fall, and then takes you on a guided tour of practice techniques that specifically target each category. Before you can arm a student with a list of possible ways of working, that list needs to be clear in your own mind first. (You'll also end up adding your own techniques to the list provided here, and there's nothing wrong with that.)

• Before each week of practice begins, have the student tell you what their task for the week is (so you can be sure there is no misunderstanding), and then have them take you on a guided tour of *exactly* how they propose to work this week to complete that task. If that guided tour throws up practice techniques that just don't seem right for the job, now is the time to let them know. Don't wait until they have wasted hours of practice time with techniques that were never going to help in the first place.

• At first, your students will very much be dependent on your recommendations as to the best way to practice. But eventually, you want them to be able to select the right tools for the job automatically. It's worth spending some lesson time quizzing them on practice techniques—ask them *"Let's imagine your job was to speed this piece up. How many different practice techniques can you name for me that are especially designed to target this?"* The chapter later in this book on "Speeding up Pieces" will talk about Metronome Method, Chaining, Interpolated Eighth Notes, Spurts, Visualization, Halflight Technique and much more...but that information is only useful if those techniques occur readily to your student too. (And if they know what on earth you are talking about!)

• The easiest way to have your student enthusiastically looking for the most effective practice technique is to remind them that choosing the *wrong* practice technique will result in them needing to do loads of extra practice. Any student who is interested in doing less practice (which is most students) will find the idea of being able to minimize practice through efficient practice absolutely fascinating—even if it seems to be for all the wrong reasons.

3.3 Shiny Object Polishers

Defining this practice flaw

Students who Polish Shiny Objects may well be practicing regularly and at length, but spend all their practice time working on things that they can already play well, while very little (if any) attention is given to weaker sections. The choice of what to work on is governed entirely by how good the section already sounds, and therefore any overlap between what they did and goals that were set for the week will be purely co-incidental.

We've all heard the joke that banks are only prepared to lend you money

> Polishing Shiny Objects is one of the most common practice flaws, but here's the shock—it's a monster that *teachers* actually create.

once you can prove you don't need it. Well, students who Polish Shiny Objects will only practice sections once they are certain the section doesn't need work in the first place.

The end result is that the good bits get even better, while the bad bits continue to disappoint, resulting in huge (and growing!) inconsistencies in the quality of the student's performance. Students working this way are often not ready for their lessons, as they will omit any tasks that require a focus on "bad" bits—or at the very least defer them indefinitely.

How to tell if your student may be practicing this way

If the good bits seem to be reaching ever new dizzying heights of perfection, while the bad bits continue to limp, then the student is probably Polishing the Shiny Objects when they practice. To be absolutely certain, have the student *keep a log* of what they actually work on when they practice, together with how long they spend on each section. Even knowing that the whole reasons the log is there to check up on practice imbalances, they'll find it hard not to play favorites.

Why students practice this way, and why it doesn't work

Polishing Shiny Objects is one of the most common practice flaws, but here's the shock—it's a monster that teachers actually create.

Here's how it works, and it all begins with best of intentions.

When we teach, we spend a lot of time establishing *standards* in the minds of our students, so that they will recognize good playing when they hear it. It's a worthwhile aim, but it can have an unintended and devastating impact on practicing.

Students learn from us that a performance that continues without breaks is better than one that needs to stop frequently for directions. They're told that a performance that is clean and precise is better than one that is leaking wrong notes like an old roof in a thunderstorm. They're told that good intonation is preferable to bad intonation. And they're told that a performance that is at the indicated tempo is more satisfying for the audience than one that drags along at half pace.

We usually do a pretty good job explaining all of this—so much so, that

41

our students (hopefully) will come to adopt these values for themselves. After all, we don't want our student recitals being dominated by performances that are filled with wrong notes, bad intonation, and half-tempos that make the student sound as though they are being overwhelmed technically.

Of course, the three values listed above are just a tiny fraction of those that our students end up taking on board. Good posture is better than bad posture. A clear and engaging dynamic plan is better than a flat performance. Even semiquavers are better than uneven ones. Good fingering is preferable to bad fingering. You could fill a page right now with such guidelines (every teacher's list is slightly different), and if your students adhere to your pointers when they perform, there's no doubt that they'll sound much better.

Now the trouble begins.

Given the focus on these values, it makes sense that as a music student, *your playing self-esteem will be linked to how often you get these things right.* So for example, you'll feel better about your playing—and yourself—if you are producing beautifully even semiquavers than if they are lurching around like Addams Family relatives. Why? Because your teacher has instilled in you the value that even playing is superior to uneven playing.

So ask yourself this. If it's time to practice, and you are given the choice between practicing a section that is already beautifully even, and one that is a mess, which one are you likely to spend time with?

The section that makes you feel good about your playing? *Or the section that actively reminds you of your shortcomings?*

And if you then have the choice between practicing a piece that's in C Major that you are already delivering fluently, and another that is brand new, and filled with more accidentals than a Schoenberg arrangement of Flight of the Bumblebee, which one are you more likely to spend time with? The piece that makes you sound fluent and adept? Or the piece that will force you to crawl along at 5 bpm while you squint at the music, trying to figure out which notes to play?

This is the logic behind one of the most common of all practice flaws— the tendency for students to practice things they can already play well, while avoiding the things that they are not good at.

From the student's perspective, practicing only the good bits keeps everyone at home happy. Their parents will be able to hear the required half hour of daily practice taking place...and what's more, the student is sounding great the whole time!

In fact, the student might be sounding *so* good that their parents may even take the time to mention how well their practicing is going—reinforcing the behavior in the process. The student's doom is assured.

So how do you combat this? Obviously you don't want to be teaching without creating a set of values. Those values are a road map for the rest of your student's musical life, and are among the most important things they will learn from you. It *is* important to perform evenly, and perform with compelling dynamics, and perform without the sort of intonation problems that make audiences squirm.

But that's the key word. *Perform.* You want your *performance* to be filled with these qualities, but it's unreasonable to expect them all to be there from the very first time you ever play the piece. In fact, you should assume that things are going to be a little bumpy when the piece is brand new.

This is not a license for the student to abandon all these qualities. Practicing will still be very much about the pursuit of these ends. But their practicing cannot simply be a hunt for sections that are *already* filled with these qualities— otherwise they'll just run up and down on the spot.

Tips for correcting this practice flaw

• Before anything else, there are two things that you have to let your student know.

First of all, *it's ok to sound bad while you're practicing.* It's not an aim, but it is an expected consequence of working with something that's brand new. The world's greatest dancers, when taken through a brand new work, will mess things up while they come to terms with choreography that they have not worked with before.

Taking this a step further, you end up with the second directive, and it's advice so important that your student should probably engrave it on their instrument:

If your practice is sounding great all the time, you're practicing the wrong bits.

Practice is a tool that helps you turn bad bits into good bits more quickly— it's not a device for turning up evidence on how well you are already playing.

43

In other words, it's a tool for repair, not self-congratulations.

• Make parents aware of this only-practice-the-good-bits syndrome. If they hear the same section delivered flawlessly for twenty minutes, they need to quietly pop in to the practice room, praise the great playing, but suggest that there are other sections that now need more work. More than that, even if the student has been mixing up the sections, but twenty minutes have passed without them sounding like they are really struggling with *something*, then the student is probably cruising through "safe" passages.

• Move from a practice model that is based around *time* to one that is based around *outcomes* (that's something you should be doing anyway!). The student then comes into each practice session knowing that they have a list of specific problems to fix, and that as soon as their list for the day has been taken care of, they can stop practicing. They also know that *until* they have dealt with the problems on that list, they *can't* stop.

As a result, they're unlikely to waste their own time by practicing things that have nothing to do with the task at hand. It would be like being given the chore of mowing the lawn—with the promise of being able to take the rest of the day off once the job is complete—and them procrastinating by doing some weeding instead. It's not going to happen.

• Have the student break their piece up into sections, and then *rank* those sections from worst to best. The rule then is that they are only allowed to practice whichever section is *worst* on the list. After a while, that section will have improved to the point where it is no longer the worst section, at which point the student will switch to whatever the new worst section is. They continue leapfrogging in this fashion until the "worst" section is really not so bad after all.

• For hard-core serial basket-case no-hope offenders, photocopy their music, and actually cut out the "good bits" from that photocopy. With scissors. I'm serious. The only music you'll send them home with are the sections that need work—even if they have the work memorized, this is a powerful and tangible reminder of what they really should be focussing on.

44

3.4 Sheep Counters

Defining this practice flaw

Sheep Counters practice simply by playing targeted sections over and over and over and over again, with the hope that sheer repetition will eventually lead to improvement. All tasks for the week are dealt with in this blunt-instrument fashion, independently of what the unique demands of those tasks might

> **...students who rely on repetition *alone* had better plan on doing plenty of practice.**
>
> **They'll need to, because their chosen practice method is horribly inefficient.**

actually be, and practicing takes on all the charm and creativity of working on an assembly line.

How to tell if your student may be practicing this way

Because repetition reinforces behavior without assessing the *appropriateness* of that behavior, Sheep Counters will often have errors in their piece which are heavily resistant to being dislodged. They've been "practiced in" by the repetition.

But the simplest way to confirm that you are in the presence of a Sheep Counter is to ask them to describe to you how they are planning on practicing this week. Most Sheep Counters will limit their replies (just as they limit their practice) to "I'll play it over and over again until I get it".

In fact, most Sheep Counters simply cannot think of any other way of working.

Why students practice this way, and why it doesn't work

This practice flaw is another example of the student's intentions being good, but missing something in the delivery.

Most of us have impressed on students the importance of repetition when practicing—that it's not enough to play something once or twice, and then magically expect mastery to somehow follow. The question then logically follows from the student:

If once or twice is not enough, then how many is sufficient?

"Lots!" is the answer we give. And if lots is good, then lots plus a few more is even better.

As a student, your practice session therefore starts by choosing a section in the piece, and then thinking of a nice big number. You're then supposed to play through the chosen section that many times.

It's a very simple formula, and is not necessarily entirely bad advice, as most teachers are aware of the power of repetition in any skill building process. But if repetition is the *only* practice tool in your student's shed then there's trouble ahead.

There are four problems that will emerge sooner or later for students who rely solely on repetition when they practice.

The first problem is that repetition is a *blunt* tool, particularly if used alone. This means that while repeating a section until you've worn grooves into the keys may eventually deliver a degree of proficiency through sheer brute force, the whole process will take much longer than it needs to. The student who uses repetition *in conjunction* with other more targeted practice techniques will reach the same level of proficiency much sooner. (There are plenty of such techniques outlined later in this book).

In other words, students who rely on repetition alone had better plan on doing plenty of practice. They'll need to, because their chosen practice method is inefficient.

The second problem is that repetition is *blind*. It does not help the student discover better ways of doing things, nor will it help students detect problems in their playing. Instead, it simply reinforces what they are *already* doing.

So if a student repeats a section and uses bad fingering every time, not only will the repetition fail to detect the problem, *it will actually deeply imbed the incorrect fingering into the piece*—and you'll need a crowbar to dislodge it next lesson. Often, they actually would have been better off not practicing the section at all.

The third problem, often underrated, is just how *boring* a repetition-only approach is. I call these students "Sheep Counters" because playing a section through one hundred times is not enormously different to counting sheep, and we all know what that's used for.

So if the student comes to you complaining that their practice feels like shovelling snow or washing dishes, it might not just be an attitude problem on their part. No amount of positive thinking is going to have a student looking forward to practicing when they know their practice is simply going to consist of the same passage played five hundred times in a row. It's the reason joggers prefer to plan scenic outdoor routes, rather than simply running endless laps of their living room.

The final problem is that repetition directs the student's energies towards *keeping count*, rather than an awareness of how the piece is responding to practice. The student will be highly aware that this is the fifteenth playthrough, but may not be noticing the direction their playing has been heading in since the *seventh* playthrough.

Has this fast section actually been becoming more difficult, simply because the sheer number of repetitions has made relaxation of the hand almost impossible? Is there a fingering half way through the piece that needs some special attention? (Since giving such attention wouldn't count towards the overall repetition total, it can feel to the Sheep Counter like a waste of time. In fact, our repetition-obsessed student probably wouldn't even *consider* stopping to look at a specific trouble spot like that).

At its worst, it means you could ask the student *"So how is your practice going?"*, and they'll reply that they have no idea, but that they are up to 85 reps. Problem is, at their next lesson, it won't be the number of reps that is relevant— it will be how the section *sounds*. Which means that "85 reps" doesn't tell them anything about the health of their piece. It just tells you that whatever they have been doing in that section anyway is now much more strongly ingrained than it ever was before.

This may or may not be good news.

And if it's *not* good news—if they've been busy repeating errors all week— then you have the unenviable task of telling them that their practice this week has been worse than a waste of time.

In which case, don't be surprised if they do no practice the following week.

So what can you do to combat this?

Tips for correcting this practice flaw

• The first thing is to make the student aware of the problem by hitting the nerve that they are most likely to respond to:

Tell them that if they are going to practice simply by playing the same thing over and over and over, then they must LOVE practicing.

Why? Because by working this way, they will need to do five times as much practice as they need to to get the result they are after.

Now that you have their full attention (nobody wants to do five times as much practice as they need to!), you can introduce them to some specific techniques that are better suited to solving the problems in their piece. You're not trying to eliminate repetition altogether—in fact some of the techniques outlined later in this book have strong elements of repetition built into them. You're just trying to introduce some healthier variety into their practice diet.

• Having established the possibility that there are faster ways of doing things than simply repeating a bit over and over, set aside some time in a lesson for an illustration.

Choose a short section of music for them to learn—just a couple of lines will be plenty. Using a *mix* of practice techniques from the "Learning the New Piece" section later in this book, issue the student a challenge:

Their job is to learn this section so that they can play it back to you flawlessly from memory, but with as few playthroughs as possible. (In fact if they use the Tabletop Challenge method from that same chapter, they may be able to do this *without playing it through at all!*).

This will introduce them to two ideas. First of all, that there are alternatives to simply playing things over and over again. And secondly, that these alternatives are more effective than sheer repetition, and will therefore need *less* practice to yield the same result. Most students will regard anything that requires LESS practice as being a very good idea indeed.

3.5 Speed Demons

Defining this practice flaw

Simply put, Speed Demons practice too fast, too often. They make the migration to full speed playthroughs long before they know the piece well enough to do so, and in so doing, fail to lay the technical foundations necessary for controlled and musical at-tempo performances in the future.

How to tell if your student may be practicing this way

Students will always have trouble doing things in lessons that they have not practiced at home first. So the

> When the notes are flying past at Mach 3, mistakes can be almost impossible to spot...
>
> ...which gives the student the delicious illusion of the *absence of errors.*

next time you are suspicious that you might have a Speed Demon on your hands, ask them to play the piece for you v-e-r-y s-l-o-w-l-y.

If this absolutely confounds the student, you can safely assume that they have probably rarely (or never!) tried it slowly before. You can then apologize, and have a conversation about what tempo *would* feel comfortable.

They will usually demonstrate their practice tempo at that point.

Because the default tempo for Speed Demons is "as fast as possible", they will often tend to play too fast in lessons as well, and you can be fairly confident that students who are tough to slow down when you're working with them will be hitting the accelerator hard at home too.

The toughest to identify can be those Speed Demons who *only speed when they think nobody is listening.* In other words, they'll be perfect angels in the lesson, always trying to play slowly, but the instant they get home their practice is all about car chases and land-speed-records.

Why students practice this way, and why it doesn't work

It's not news to teachers that a lot of students practice too fast, but the real question is *why*.

Students are not simply being wilfully disobedient. There are plenty of attractions in practicing fast—as teachers our job is first to understand what those attractions are. Cleverly modified practice instructions can then rob those attractions of their appeal.

So why is it that all students (go on, admit it...you too sometimes!) practice too fast on occasions? What makes it irresistible?

The first great lure of practicing fast is for those students who are impatient to have the piece sounding the way it was presented *when they first heard it*. They may well have been told to practice their "Presto the Porcupine" at a slothful Largo, but they certainly weren't *shown* the piece at a slothful Largo. This can be very frustrating for the student—they didn't sign up for this piece in the first place only to be told that they had to play it slowly. (If they wanted to play slowly, they would have asked for "Andante the Aardvark") But it's ok, you can't be with them twenty-four hours a day...and when you're not watching, this piece is going to be at *least* presto, irrespective of whether that's good for the piece or not.

It comes back in part to the point made earlier about students wanting to feel good about their playing. They might have first seen "Presto the Porcupine" at a student concert, and if they're like most kids, the reason they remembered the performance is because of how fast it went.

In fact, it might be the *only* thing they can remember about the performance. Keen to relive that glory now for themselves, they'll play it as fast as they can, every time. *Hey look at me! I can do it too!*

They're not practicing—they're *pretending* to be that performer they saw, just as surely as if they were waving a stick around and pretending to be a Jedi Knight. They're not being a bad student, they're being an entirely normal child, and the aspiration at the center of the behavior is actually worth encouraging. You're actually seeing the embryo of a highly motivated student...as soon as a student thinks *"I wish I sounded like that"*, you have a powerful foundation for them to do whatever you ask.

Practicing at performance tempo can have some hidden appeals for more patient students too. When the notes are flying past at Mach 3, mistakes can be almost impossible to spot, which gives the student the delicious illusion of the absence of errors. If you asked them "did you notice anything wrong?", they can honestly say no, because they were so busy concentrating on not falling off during their roller-coaster ride that they simply didn't have time to notice *anything*.

That, of course, is very different from whether or not there actually *was* anything to notice in the first place. It is for this reason that I sometimes refer to practicing too fast as an anaesthetic—it dulls the perception of the pain of mistakes for students, but does nothing to target the cause of the pain itself. In other words, the mistakes are very much intact at the end of such sessions, but students don't have to confront that unpleasant reality.

A third reason students practice fast *is to get to the end of their practice session sooner.* This is particularly the case for students who are given the directive to "play the piece x times every day". At Andante, that might take 15 minutes.

Play it prestissimo though, and your job is complete in only 6 minutes. Woo hoo! To agree to play slowly under such a system is therefore to unnecessarily sacrifice free time—meaning that if prestississississississimo is at all possible, they'll try it. (They could finish their practice session in only 2 minutes if they play fast enough!)

Tips for correcting this practice flaw

• Instead of simply asking for "slow" practice (which is open to interpretation), *define exactly what "slow" is* in Beats Per Minute. Tell your student that their practice session has not begun until they've set their metronome to that speed. And tell their parents that unless they hear the metronome going then none of the practice counts.

Or—to frame it more positively—tell your student that slow practice with the metronome counts DOUBLE. Which means that if they agree to practice that way, they only have to do half as much practice. It's not a capitulation for you—it's a bargain. 15 minutes of careful slow practice is worth 30 minutes of frenzied prestissimo any day.

• Discuss with them the mechanics of *why* practicing fast can feel so rewarding. The lure is less great once the magic has been stripped away, and the best way to strip away magic is with an explanation of the process behind it all.

Remind them then that because this lure can be strong, when they are by themselves practicing, it will be VERY tempting to play fast all the time.

There's nothing stopping them...except for the little voice in their head that is telling them that practicing fast is actually *hurting* their piece.

Where did that little voice come from? You just put it there ☺

• Help them to realize that they won't be condemned to playing slowly for the rest of their lives by building a *structure* for them that helps them progress towards playing fast. One powerful method for doing this is using the Metronome Method (outlined later in this book in the "Speeding the Piece up" section). Paradoxically, this then uses their desire to play fast as an incentive to stick to a structure that will have them playing slowly 80% of the time.

• And for the constant offenders—have their parents create a Slow Practice Money Jar. Every time they hear their child practicing fast, they take ten cents from the jar. Every time they get right through a practice session with nothing but slow, careful practice, they put *in* ten cents.

The student can keep whatever is left at the end of the week. (It's a variation on the "swearing" jars that some people try to keep to tone down their language—and parents can substitute lollies for money if they're more comfortable with that)

3.6 Gluttons

Defining this practice flaw

Gluttons are students who try to digest too much at once when they practice. Instead of working on bite-sized sections of a piece, they'll try to work on the whole piece. And instead of working on one or two specific issues within the piece at a time (for example, spending ten minutes carefully working out a good fingering), they'll try to fix *everything*

> Gluttons end up feeling like a novice juggler, hurling a dozen eggs into the air at once.
>
> It's not just that they drop some—with an overload like that, they're very likely to drop *all* of them.

simultaneously. Like most people who try to do everything at once, they often end up running around like headless chickens and having very little to show for their efforts.

How to tell if your student may be practicing this way

Gluttons are not always easy to spot, although they can tend to become overwhelmed by practicing and by the demands of each weekly target (you would be too if you tried to cram your entire week of work into each practice session).

They will also often complain that there is too much to get right, and that while they were trying to put in all the dynamic, articulation, rubato, fingering, intonation, balance, posture and tone color changes you recommended last lesson, they suddenly found to their horror that they couldn't even play the notes any more. They can feel like the Dutch boy at the dike, running out of fingers to plug the leaks.

Gluttons can also have trouble memorizing pieces, because while working on the whole piece at once can be great for getting a rough sketch of the entire work (and it can actually be quite valuable in creating a sense of unity within works), it is a very inefficient way of absorbing and retaining details in the score. Details such as what note comes next.

Probably the safest way to identify a glutton is to have them keep a record of what they work on each day. You'll be able to see at a glance whether or not they are trying to process too much at once.

Why students practice this way, and why it doesn't work

Unlike many of the other practice flaws, Gluttony can actually affect students who are very clear about their goals for the week. In fact, Gluttons are usually painfully aware of exactly what's required by next lesson.

With the student being under pressure to cover a lot of ground in only seven days, it can be enormously tempting for them to try to cover *everything* every time they practice. The desire to be comprehensive may well be praiseworthy, but unchecked it can lead to some classic practice disasters.

A quick example. If the job was to learn a brand new piece in one week, a lot of Gluttons will practice by starting at the *beginning* of their piece, and soldiering on until they get to the *end*. Then they'll go right back to the beginning, and they'll lather, rinse and repeat until the practice session is over. Students working this way will often complain that by the time they get to the end of the piece, they can't remember how the beginning went— like painting the Sydney Harbour Bridge, by the time the painters get to the end, the beginning needs painting again. This is a particularly bad variation of the "Sheep Counters" flaw outlined earlier, and has a work-put-in to results-yielded ratio that doesn't bear thinking about.

Even students who already practice their pieces in bite-sized chunks can be tempted to try to do too much at once. Not too much in terms of number of bars attempted, but too much in terms of number of *concepts* targeted. For example, some students will read through the list of a dozen points you made last lesson about a particular section in their piece, and then try to implement *all dozen points* straight away. Every one of them, right now, and they end up feeling like a novice juggler, hurling a dozen eggs into the air at once. It's not just that they drop some—with an overload like that, they're very likely to drop *all* of them.

This everything-at-once approach won't work for music students in their daily practice any better than it works non-musicians in their daily lives. The human mind can do all sorts of extraordinary things like invent spaceships, write plays or remember birthdays, but it has enormous trouble giving intense concentration to more than one thing at a time. (It also has enormous trouble coping with large amounts of unsorted information in one hit—which is exactly what attempting all of a brand new piece at once is doing.)

As ever, there's more to fixing this problem than just politely asking students to avoid the trap.

Tips for correcting this practice flaw

• The first thing you have to do is force students to confront the reality of the sheer inefficiency of Gluttony as a practice tactic. Begin with a simulation of the problem in action—an illustration that should stick in the student's mind.

The aim of the exercise is to memorize a phone number...but this is no ordinary phone number. Apart from having no discernible pattern, it's 20 digits long. Here, I'll even give it to you: 18574039022871997482

Now try to "teach" the number to the student by rattling it off as fast as you can to them, and then have them repeat it back to you straight away. All of it. One-eight-five-seven-four-oh-three-nine-oh-two-two-eight-seven-one-nine-nine-seven-four-eight-two.

Got that? They won't have either. That's ok. Read it out a second time. And a third time. Because there is so much information to process, you could quite safely read it out fifty times, and they still won't have mastered it—not because they are stupid, but because it's an ineffective way of working. Our braings just aren't wired to cope with 20 unrelated pieces of information in a string.

Not only that, but there is very little chance of retention of the bits that they think they do know. So if you repeat the exercise tomorrow, it will almost be like starting again.

Now give them a brand new 20 digit phone number. This time, you're not trying to teach all of it to them at once—*you're just rehearsing the first seven digits*. Read them out. Have them repeat those digits. Have them write them out. Have them tell you every *second* number.

Have them tell it to you *backwards*. Have them *sing it* to the tune of a nursery rhyme. Have them *write it out* ten more times, but each time using a different colored pencil. Have them *vary the pace* at which they read the numbers back to you. Have them tell you the numbers as many times as they can in *thirty seconds*. Have them actually *dial it* on a phone (with the receiver down!).

Have them *draw objects* that correspond to the numbers—triangles for three, pentagons for five, dots for one and so on. Have them *whisper it*, have them *yell it*, have them write it with the hand they *don't normally write with*. Have them *explain patterns* in the number to you, or *add it* all together, or *subtract each number from 10* and give you that phone number instead (an inverse phone number!)...

...at the end of ten minutes of mayhem, they will know those seven digits. They'll remember them tomorrow too, even if they don't do any more work on it today.

And you will have made your point. Sure, they've only dealt with roughly a third of the job (which they will be quick to protest). But they have dealt with it effectively—by targeting it and nothing else—that they now know it so well, *they won't need to work seriously on it again this week.* All they'd need to do in their next session is conduct a cursory revision of this first set, and then get on with targeting the second set.

• If you expect your students to deal with things in bite-sized chunks, then you should help by creating those chunks *for* them. Break the piece up into sections, and clearly mark those sections.

If the problem was trying to cope with too many instructions at once, then get them to use the Practice Hats strategy to deal with the issues one at a time (see the practice flaw "Red Light Runners" for more on Practice Hats)—specify exactly which hats they should be using, and when.

• Create a rule that forbids them from going on to a new section until a set amount of time has elapsed—or better still, until they have achieved a particular result for that section. Remind them that if they are just plowing on regardless of this rule, they are not actually practicing. They're just playing stuff.

• For students who need a more tangible reminder, teach them how to use *blinkers* (those peripheral vision blocks that horses wear in the city so that they are not startled or distracted by things going on around them). Have them stick pieces of paper over every part of the page EXCEPT the section they are actually supposed to be working on. *If they can't see it, they're not supposed to play it.* Once that section's done, they move the blinkers and reveal a new section—but the old section will now be covered up.

• Have them choose a very small section, and then turn over an egg-timer as they start to work on it. Tell them that for the next three minutes they will ONLY be working on that section. Most students will be amazed at how long that three minutes takes, indicating to you—and more importantly to them—just how soon they normally move on to greener pastures.

You can then combine this with a simple calculation:

If they are trying to cover one section or issue in fifteen minutes, they get to spend 900 seconds on that one item. (And as we'll see later in this book, if they're working intelligently, 900 seconds is a long time!) If, however, they try to cover *ten* different things in the same time, no matter how efficient the practice techniques they select, they'll only have 90 seconds to spend on each. Despite the fact that they practiced for fifteen minutes, each section will sound like it only had ninety seconds of practice...

...because each section actually only had ninety seconds of practice.

3.7 Drifters

Defining this practice flaw

Drifters may well be prepared to do plenty of practice, but they work without any clue as to what they are trying to achieve. They'll wander aimlessly from piece to piece, blissfully uninterested in how their efforts are contributing to the bigger picture (bigger pictures such as being ready for next lesson, or preparing for an upcoming recital).

They just practice, working on

> Each day is a fresh roll of the dice, meaning that it's possible sometimes for Drifters to achieve *nothing* when they practice—despite having been furiously busy the whole time.

whatever they feel like, trusting that everything will be just fine if they simply *persist*. Their practicing has an air of tranquility that belies the dangers that lurk beneath.

How to tell if your student may be practicing this way

When asked *"So how did you go this week?"*, drifters will tend to answer with an honest *"I don't know"*. They're not being difficult - it's just that because they are working with the absence of goals, they have no reference point to help them answer such a question.

Not only that, Drifting lends itself nicely to not paying too much attention to what you're actually doing while you're working, so quite apart from being unable to assess the *impact* of their practice, they often won't even be able to provide a summary of what *elements* their practicing consisted of in the first place. This makes discussions about the effectiveness of specific practice techniques almost impossible. There are no patterns to analyze, no "typical" pitfalls to warn them about.

To make things even more difficult, Drifters can feel very comfortable with the way they work, as their brand of practicing rarely produces challenging moments for them at home. In fact, whenever the going gets tough, they can easily react by switching to something else—like water, they'll follow the path of least resistance. As a result, drifters can easily turn into students who Polish Shiny Objects (see earlier in this chapter)

Why students practice this way, and why it doesn't work

Part of the challenge of practicing by yourself is learning to cope with the freedom of being able to work on *whatever* you like, *however* you like.

So a student could play some scales for a while—up and down and up and down and up and down—then fiddle with their new piece, then play through some old pieces, before finishing with some sight reading. All done, and a good day at the office it was too.

Or was it? At first glance, that seems like a practice session that covers plenty of ground, but in reality, the student may have been one of many Drifters who arbitrarily choose tasks as they work, resulting in a "make-it-up-as-you-go" approach to practicing. *Today I feel like playing this bit. And today my favorite number is "6", so I'll play this bit six times. I think one of my scales is A Major, so I'll play that a couple of times while I'm at it. And come to think of it, that Musette I used to play last year had some A's in it, so I think I'll play that for a while too.*

Oh dear. Each day is a fresh roll of the dice, meaning that it's possible sometimes for Drifters to achieve *nothing* when they practice, despite having been furiously busy the whole time.

And to make things even worse, the Drifter is often not likely to register this approach as a problem in the first place, because as far as they are concerned, they have been working hard. They *have* been! (Let's give them some credit here) They've just given up half an hour of their time to practice, and were concentrating hard throughout. The assumption at their end would be that by doing this every day, *they'll automatically be ready for their next lesson.*

All of this means that when the student is *not* ready for their next lesson, it hits the Drifter particularly hard, and the whole idea of practicing in the first place suddenly becomes a whole lot less attractive—especially if they have then also been on the receiving end of a lecture about how they should practice harder. Once a student has learned that practicing doesn't necessarily prepare them adequately, they're not likely to be wasting time on it in the future.

Sadly, it doesn't always occur to them that it's the *way* they practice that doesn't work, and that a condemnation of practicing as an *institution* is making the error of deriving a general conclusion from a specific disaster.

The problem here is not the level of industry of the student, but simply the absence of goals from the process. If a student has no sense of what they are trying to achieve, then they shouldn't be surprised when they achieve nothing.

That's easy enough to say. Getting your students to understand it can be another thing entirely. What your Drifters need to do is forget about practicing for a while, and listen to the following story.

The Gardener: An illustration of Drifting in Action

Imagine for a moment that one of the local kids has offered to do some gardening for you for $5 an hour. Sounds good—you can kick back with a good book, and let them get on with making your yard look good.

At the end of the day, if your gardener was leaning on their shovel, perspiring and red-faced from five hours of exertion in the garden, it would be reasonable to assume that there are going to be some improvements to the garden somewhere. After that much effort there *has* to be.

Not necessarily. Before you get too excited about how great the backyard is going to look now, let's spend a moment or two looking at exactly how that time was spent.

• The first hour and a half was the most exhausting. The kid spent the whole time moving a large rock around the yard, only to end up putting it back where it used to be, because it looked better there after all.

• Then two hours were spent digging holes. Not digging holes for anything in particular, like planting a tree or burying compost...just digging...holes. Wherever. Your rose garden. The vegetable patch. The lawn. Some of them were in your *neighbor's* yard.

•And then they spent another hour and a half *counting weeds*. That's right. One-thousand-two-hundred-and-fifty-seven, one-thousand-two-hundred-and-fifty-eight...and then writing those numbers down in a book.

That's five hours gone, and the only change to the backyard is that it is now pock-marked with random holes, a rock is where it always was, your neighbour is banging angrily on your front door, and there has been a weed census. (For the record, there were one-thousand-four-hundred-and-thirty-two weeds, but knowing that really doesn't help the garden look better) The kid might have worked hard, but I'm not sure this is worth $25.

Two things would strike an observer of this little scene:

1) That the same result (for what it's worth) could easily have been achieved in a fraction of the time.

2) That the absence of a plan does not only mean that good things *don't* happen (No weeding, pruning or watering took place)—it can mean that bad things *do*. (Your garden didn't used to have pock marks throughout, but now it does)

In other words, *working without a goal can actually be* **worse** *than not working at all*. Your mistake was in not giving the gardener a clear target—get rid of the weeds in the vegetable patch, clear the dead leaves from under the big tree, trim the hedge. And move that rock to the back fence.

Instead, in the absence of a defined goal, the default instruction becomes "Do whatever you like in the garden", so you really can't complain when they do exactly that. Hey, maybe for another $5 an hour, they'll agree to fill those holes back in again...

There can be an even more insidious side-effect for students who practice without goals. Apart from ensuring practice sessions are a huge waste of time, the absence of a goal can also leave a student with the dangerous *perception* that the institution of practice itself is pointless. And you know something? Without a goal in place, they are absolutely right—by definition! Having no goal renders whatever you are doing as literally *pointless*!

You then are in the impossible position of having to ask your student to sacrifice their valuable time each day to do something pointless...and there is nothing in this book that will help you win that battle.

Fortunately, there is plenty you can do to help your students avoid the no-goal practice trap, but with younger students in particular, you'll need to provide some extra help.

Tips for correcting this practice flaw

• Create "Random Goal Checks". You'll need parents' help with this—their job is to wander into the practice room at random, stop the student, and ask them to explain EXACTLY what they are hoping to achieve with the practice they are doing right now. Fluffy answers such as "to get better" are not good enough, and will need prompting for more detail.

If they don't have a quick and highly specific answer for that question, the practice session actually stops until the parent and child can come up with a goal:

"To be able to play these four bars without the music"
"To be able to get the fingering for this run right five times IN A ROW"
"To work out a bowing for this passage"
"To speed this section up from 125bpm to 140 bpm"
"To create a dynamic plan for the development section that works"

At its core, it forces the student to answer questions that they should *always* know the answer to:

*"**Why** am I practicing right now?"*
If they don't know, they shouldn't be practicing until they do.

• Instead of just giving the student goals for the week, break those goals down into daily goals. It's a lot easier for the student to answer the question "Why am I practicing right now?" if the answer has been given to them already. And if necessary, break that daily goal down again into three or four mini-goals.

As well as providing a clear reason to practice, the student ends up with a tangible feeling of progress as they complete each task.

Older or more advanced students should also break down their goals in this fashion, but can be encouraged to work them out for themselves.

• It keeps coming up in this book, but goal-less students are yet another reason to set up a model of practice that is based around completing specific tasks, rather than working for a set amount of time. This change in approach will *guarantee* that the student is practicing with a goal, because under these rules, without a goal to reach their practice session can never actually end. No student is going to feel comfortable proceeding without knowing where the exit is!

• Have your student keep a special type of practice log. Instead of recording how much practice they did, or what type of practice they did, simply have them record what *breakthroughs* they made each day. What can they now do that they couldn't do when the practice session started?

You then put pressure on them to be able to write something *fresh* for each day—which will ensure that each day there is something to write.

3.8 Skimmers

Defining this practice flaw

Skimmers will practice a section until they experience their very first taste of success with it, and then will prematurely declare it "cured" and move on to something new. They do this without regard for how many unsuccessful attempts it took to play the section, and therefore of the odds of reproducing the little miracle at their next lesson.

As soon as the Skimmer has got a section right a couple of times, it can be very easy for them to start thinking "Ok, great. I've got that now, let's move on."

No they haven't, and no they shouldn't.

How to tell if your student may be practicing this way

Students who Skim when they practice will often complain that their playing in the lesson does not accurately reflect how well they normally play. They have a distorted perspective of the degree of mastery they have over their repertoire, and feel "unlucky" when they mess up.

A practice diary of a Skimmer is filled with dozens of different sections tackled—and ticked—each day. They will often perceive their practice as being highly productive as a result, and of all the practice flaw types, can feel the most deeply disillusioned when things don't go according to plan in the lesson itself.

Why students practice this way, and why it doesn't work

Sooner or later, every student will interrupt a lesson to protest "but it sounded much better at home!". We've all heard it plenty of times. The thing is, the piece probably *did* sound much better at home—but contained in this statement are the seeds of the Skimming practice flaw.

In going to such pains to inform you that their playing sounded better at home, the student is not making any statements about *when* it sounded much better, nor are they making any claims about *how often* it sounded better. In fact they're not giving you any sort of useful comparison between how it usually sounds at home, and what you just heard.

The comparison they are making is between what just happened (which probably had a few mistakes in it) and some Great Shining Moment earlier in the week when they played it through with no errors.

What they really mean therefore is "Compared with my personal best, that wasn't so good", which is a different statement entirely, and it doesn't carry with it the illusion that at-home playthroughs always go well. Compared with our personal bests, what we just did is rarely going to measure up—such is the nature of personal bests.

So what lies behind this complaint, and what does it have to do with practicing?

Once students are given a clear goal for the week, it falls to them to determine when that goal has been realized, at which point they'd be free to move on to something else. Because the tasks are usually related to the development of a skill, rather than (say) the production of a physical item, there is no automatic and clearly predefined completion point. As we so often remind our students, however good they become at a particular skill, they can always get better, so they're never truly finished.

This absence of a natural "I've got this now!" point means that students have the freedom to determine their own criteria for declaring closure. And all too often, such declarations of competence are made too early, because the criteria were not rigorous enough. As soon as a student has got a section right a couple of times, it can be very easy for them to start thinking "Ok, great. I've got that now, let's move on." No they haven't, and no they shouldn't.

It's perhaps easiest to demonstrate why with a scenario that takes place outside of music lessons. Let's imagine that the student's task was to develop a backhand in tennis—a similar premature declaration of competence could happen once the tennis pupil has put two backhands successfully into play for the first time. It does not take into account that these two shots might have been sitting amongst five hundred *unsuccessful* shots.

In other words, it's not whether you got it right once or twice when practicing, it's whether or not you can get it right *when you really need it*. If I am playing someone whose backhand record is two from five-hundred, I'm going to be hitting it to their backhand a lot.

The practice flaw of moving on prematurely is dangerous partly because it does not adequately prepare the student for lessons, but mostly because it sets up a collision between a student's expectations and reality. Because they can remember getting page three of their piece right a couple of times at home, they are fully expecting that it should be no problem in the lesson—having conveniently forgotten just how many times they *didn't* play it properly. When the section collapses during the lesson, they feel frustrated and betrayed, and will make the celebrated protest "it sounded much better at home".

What they're not admitting to is that there were plenty of occasions on which it also sounded *exactly* like that at home...and more occasions still on which it actually sounded *worse*.

Tips for correcting this practice flaw

• The next time the "but it sounded much better at home" protest arises, take a moment and ask them *why* they think that was the case. Describe to them the mechanics of the problem outlined above, and decide together that it's not fair to claim "it sounded much better at home" until it sounds much better at home *every* time.

Then take this a step further and recommend they undertake a Survey at home to find out how often the piece really does what it's supposed to. Their job is to play the section through a dozen times at home, and after each time give the playthrough a rating out of 10, where 10 represents "Could not have played it any better at the moment!". Instead of being blinded by the brilliance of the occasional 10, tell them to take an *average* from the twelve scores. That score is honestly what shape the piece is in right now.

And then remind them that because they are under a little more pressure in a lesson than they are at home, the average would probably be a little lower still if it were twelve playthroughs in a lesson. And lower still under the glare of performance spotlights. You're not trying to discourage them by doing this—you're helping them to be able to form accurate snapshots of the true state of health of a section.

If they don't think the average is high enough to present in a lesson, then it's a sure sign that they're not done with this bit just yet after all, and that it's time for some more practice.

• If the problem of prematurely declaring a section "cured!" comes about because of inadequate testing of the section on the part of the student, it's time to create some tests for them. The aim is to design some challenges that will require *consistent* demonstrations of mastery over the problem—rather than one-off moments of glory. Challenges such as The Seven Stages of Misery, The Ledger System or the Great Race are perfect for this (if you're wondering what these challenges are, don't worry. There are full descriptions of these practice games and plenty of others in the "Making the piece Reliable" section later in the book.). Any student who passes those tests can be confident that the section won't ambush them in their lesson—as you'll discover later in the book, having to play the passage in a lesson is MUCH easier than winning these games.

• Part of the disappointment that leads a student to want to protest "it sounds better at home" comes from the fact that they had *one shot* at impressing you with this section first time, and they messed it up. Every so often, that will be due to a little nerves on the part of the student. To help them prepare for being able not just to get it right, but to get it right when it really counts, tell them to have a One Shot Only playthrough of the section at the end of *every* practice session. They play it through once only, as if it were the lesson.

Whatever happens, they'll win. Either they'll get right through with no mistakes, which will be a tremendous confidence boost for their next lesson, and a timely congratulations for the good work they have done on the section. Or, they'll mess up somewhere, in which case they'll know EXACTLY which bit is going to need some particular attention tomorrow.

• Once they have been made familiar with some more rigorous tests, have them list for each section the tests that they were able to pass. Add to that then the understanding that unless the section has passed at least a couple of the tough tests, *you don't want to hear it yet*. This is important—by the time you hear the results of their practice, you want to be certain (for their sake!) that the results are worthy of the time they spent. And if that means delaying hearing a piece because you suspect it might be brittle, then so be it.

• In subjecting the section to testing, don't just rely on the games that appear later in this book. One useful challenge to issue is for the student to invent— and successfully complete—a nightmare challenge for the section in question. Can I play it left hand alone, eyes close, at twice the normal speed, while my sister throws tennis balls at me? If I can, then having to play it once, two hands together, eyes open and looking at the music, at the regular tempo, with my sister nowhere in sight is going to feel very, very easy by comparison.

And if I complain after that "It doesn't sound like this at home", it's probably because it just sounded *better* than it does at home.

3.9 Clock-watchers

Defining this practice flaw

Clock-watchers usually only practice for only one reason—to pass the required time so that they can stay out of trouble. Their attention is constantly directed at how far through the practice session they are, rather than what the practice session actually consists of. Giving the endless possibilities for filling practice time with activities that don't actually lead to improvements, clock-watchers will produce patchy results, even though their practice might be regular and plentiful.

How to tell if your student may be practicing this way

When you ask a Clock-watcher how their practice was this week, they will answer with numbers. Clock-watchers usually know exactly how many minutes of practice they did on each day, and will describe a week as being "good" if it was filled with lots of minutes, and "not so good" if there were rather fewer minutes. They're not usually interested in outcomes, and will often have at least one authority figure (you, or one of their parents) who stresses the importance of daily practice of a certain length. This same authority figure probably doesn't talk to them much about what they should be practicing, or how to go about it.

> **Our intentions were good— we insisted on 30 minutes to make sure they wouldn't do 20 minutes.**
>
> **Well, they're not going to do 40 minutes either.**

Why students practice this way, and why it doesn't work

Clockwatchers are a frustrating breed. These are the students who practice with a stopwatch running, and the instant 29:59 becomes 30:00, they will stop. They might be playing the *first* chord of the perfect cadence that ends their piece, but when the clock ticks over, they will down tools instantly, leaving the harmonic question mark sitting on their desk like unfinished paperwork. It's now become a genuine interrupted cadence instead, because the final chord is not going to happen until *tomorrow's* thirty minutes. They pick up their briefcase, punch their time card, put on their hat, and catch the bus home.

Don't go blaming them for this behavior. They are obsessed with the clock because *we have taught them to be.* Who was it that impressed upon them the importance of 30 minutes every day? Our intentions were good—we insisted on 30 minutes to make sure they wouldn't do 20 minutes.

Well, they're not going to do 40 minutes either.

More to the point, with so much attention being paid to how much time they spend practicing, there's no energy left for supervising how effective the practice actually is.

There are other dangers associated with a mindset that says practice should be all about 30 minutes a day:

Danger #1: Very young beginners having their noses skinned by the grindstone

There's a reason that children in Grade 1 at school get less homework than students in Grade 6. In fact most parents would be appalled if this were otherwise. Sadly, parents don't always seem to feel that way for kids who are having music lessons. Six year old pupils are often landed with half an hour a day, just like their ten year old brother. Why? Because that's just what practice *is*. Get on with it.

What can this produce? The glass half full assumption is that by expecting this commitment right from the start, students develop work habits at an early age that stay with them for life. The glass half *empty* concern is that by expecting this commitment right from the start, students learn at an early age that music lessons are mostly about your nose being skinned by the grindstone.

And that can stay with them for the rest of their life too. If we're not careful, a small dose of uncompromising expectations when students are very young can inoculate them against the idea of learning an instrument for the rest of their formative years.

Take it easy—and give their parents permission to take it easy too. Maybe they only do *ten* minutes a day. Maybe they even need to *skip* some days. Comets of retribution are not going to rain down on their house (or on your studio). Their practice will build slowly—remember, you are trying to shape the musician they will *become*, not trying to deliver a complete package straight away.

Danger #2: A fixed amount of practice per day is linear preparation for a curving world.

As teachers we know that there are times where everything happens at once. There will be a dozen exams, workshops and concerts all crammed into the same nailbiting fortnight that your tax return is due, and then your parents come to stay with you for a few days in the middle of it all, while your daughter suddenly has daily play rehearsals that you have to drive her to...and then...

...nothing. Two weeks of regulation lessons. No problems. No dramas. You pace the house, wondering what to do with yourself.

It's the same for most careers. There are insane times, and quiet times.

And you know something? *It's the same for your students.* They have busy times at school, when exams are on and assignments are piling up like tetris blocks. They also have weeks where very little happens (not to mention twelve weeks a year of genuine holidays!)

Their musical demands also fluctuate—the month before an exam has a very different flavour from the time immediately following one. Their practice commitment should *change* to reflect these pressures.

It's a trade-off of course. I am always very sympathetic to my students when school is piling it on, but on the understanding that they become practice machines as soon as things cool off a little. So we work in undulations, with sometimes dizzying vertical gaps between the peaks and troughs. And because I negotiated and cut them some slack when they needed it most, they are more likely to turn around and willingly deliver voluminous practice when *I* need it most.

We work this way, because their *lives* work that way.

Danger #3: It establishes a false picture of dedication

Because the assumption is that dedication equals thirty minutes in each day, parents can see red when their children fall short of this. And the battles begin.

I don't think I need to describe what usually happens next.

However the struggle manifests itself, there are consequences for it having occurred in the first place. Enthusiasm for lessons plummets. The relationship itself between parent and child can deteriorate. The child learns to practice by passing the required amount of time, without caring whether anything gets done.

About the only result that is guaranteed *not* to happen after the argument is the child suddenly seeing the light, and declaring to their parents "You know something? You're *right*...how foolish I have been! From now on, I will be dedicating a full hour every day to practicing! Mum, dad...I'm so grateful you yelled at me...you're the *best!*"...

On the contrary, the single biggest cause of students *quitting* music lessons is because it's all too painful—and it's usually the six days between lessons that are the most painful of all.

The tragedy is, some of these students would have been cheerfully practicing for an hour a day or more in a few years time—*without* watching the clock—if things had been less draconian at the outset. This is even more likely if their parents had invested the same energy praising the positive developments in their child's playing as they did yelling at them for not practicing.

It all comes back to a central truth—twisting someone's arm to make them do what you want might produce *compliance*, but it will *never* produce enthusiasm.

Danger #4: It's about getting the job done, surely?

In students' daily battles with stopwatches, it can be easy to lose sight of why they are practicing in the first place.

It's not just to pass time. And it's certainly not the observance of some arcane ritual—1800 seconds spent in front of the music stand, praying to St. Cecilia, just because our parents did, and their parents before them.

We practice because we have pieces to learn, scales to master, dynamics to polish. We practice so we are ready for our next lesson.

In short, we practice to *get a job done*. And like any other job that needs doing, the notion of how long it takes is not nearly as important as whether or not it gets completed in the first place.

Tips for correcting this practice flaw

• Make sure your students understand that you will be assessing their practice by the *results it produces*, and not by any other criteria. In fact, the ONLY reasons that you are interested in how long they spend is so that:

a) You can tailor their workload to suit the amount of time they have available. If you know the student is able to spend an hour every day, you will give very different practice goals than if the student is in the middle of exams at school, and can only afford twenty minutes every other day.

b) You can help them practice more efficiently. If the student has spent forty minutes every day, but there's no discernible improvement, then it's time for a conversation about HOW they were working. Similarly, if they have got everything done in only ten minutes a day, give them some positive reinforcement about the practice strategies they must have used—and mark down those strategies as being good tools for the future. Not every tool will work for every student, so if you discover a perfect match, jump on it. And then give them more to do next time :)

Aside from that, you really don't care how much time they spend practicing, any more than you would care what color clothes they wear while practicing. It's not the point.

Because the student knows that you are interested in results, not time spent, this becomes their priority too. There's no point in them fussing about thirty minutes every day, because if the jobs haven't been completed, it still won't be good enough—which means that brain-dead-clock-watching practice gets phased out. Why? Because getting the job done will require all-day practice if they are in that mood, and no student is going to volunteer for all-day practice.

The possible downside of them trying to do as little practice as they need to to get the job done... is that they really will try to do as little practice as they need to to get the job done. If they can get everything done in only ten minutes, they will. But even this is actually great news, because to get away with less practice, they will have to practice efficiently. So whenever you tell them that you know a practice strategy that is a great Time Saver, you'll suddenly have their full attention. You can similarly discourage any practice technique you like by labelling it as a time-waster. There is more on this later in the book.

• Have your students keep a practice diary, but instead of recording Time Spent (as would traditionally be the case), encourage them to record "Goals completed!". Not only does it help keep them focussed on the tasks at hand, but they also end each week with a list of accomplishments, rather than a sterile collection of numbers—reminding them that practicing does actually produce results. Just seeing that list grow can help students feel good about their practicing.

3.10 Autopilots

Defining this practice flaw

Students who practice on autopilot are generally just practicing with their fingers—their mind is elsewhere. They'll arrive at the end of a practice session with no recall as to what specific problems were confronted or solved. Unlike drifters, their practice can actually be highly

> **Without autopilot, human beings really could only do one thing at a time—in short, we'd have to walk now, and chew gum later.**

structured, so much so that they don't actually need to be present. They engage the minimum amount of brainpower required to ensure that the pieces don't go completely off the rails, and then use the rest of their processing power to think about more fun things.

How to tell if your student may be practicing this way

Autopilot practicers are often likely to switch into the same mode in lessons too. They will comply with instructions, but will appear not to be fully engaged in what they're doing (at best), or actually will seem completely distracted (at worst). Their playing will be filled with cookie-cutter dynamics and phrasing, rather than any sort of musicianship that responds to the moment. (It's a bit hard to respond to the moment when you're not even *aware* of the moment)

Why students practice this way, and why it doesn't work

Unless your powers of concentration are truly superhuman, there will have been times when you were reading a book or magazine article, and suddenly realized that for the past couple of pages you haven't taken in a single word. The last thing you remembered was a section about a bus breaking down in a deserted wood filled with wolves—and now it seems that suddenly the characters in the book are in the middle of a birthday party (but you haven't got a clue whose), and are wondering why the two sisters at the centre of the story don't seem to be speaking to each other any more. There's not a hint of a wolf in sight.

If you decided at that point that you wanted to make any sense of the story at all, you'd have to go back and re-read a couple of pages to fill yourself in. Like dozing off during a movie, plenty has been happening, but you simply hadn't noticed. (In most 400 page novels, I end up reading a total of 550 pages for this reason.)

The odd thing is that despite the fact you weren't taking in any of the text, you wouldn't have actually stopped reading at any point. Your eyes were still scanning correctly from left to right, and then correctly returning back to the start of the next line at the appropriate time. Every word is actually read...it's just that the reading was happening on autopilot, so none of the information was absorbed. It's almost as though someone were reading it *to* you, while you switched off, just as you might during a boring lecture. All the mechanics of reading proceeded as they should have otherwise.

While realizing that you have been running on autopilot can be disconcerting, the autopilot itself does not always cause disasters. Many times we'll arrive home in the car, and realize that we cannot recall anything from the past five minutes of the trip. We couldn't tell someone whether the traffic had been heavy or light, or how many green lights we caught, because we had been thinking our own thoughts instead of noting down such things. But despite our mind not being completely on the job, we actually stopped at every red light, gave way correctly at intersections, and managed to successfully navigate home. We may not have been actively thinking about what we were doing, but the degree of practice we have had with those skills in the past means that *we didn't have to.* Without autopilot, human beings really could only do one thing at a time—in short, we'd have to walk now, and chew gum later.

Of course, it's entirely possible for autopilot to sabotage practice sessions too. The clock ticks over for 30 minutes, and the student stops practicing...but if someone were to ask them what they actually did in the practice session, they wouldn't have a clue. They weren't really present.

There are several types of students who will tend to have their practice sabotaged by autopilot practicing:

1) Those who rely heavily on sheer repetition to get the job done. Mindless repetition is a great way to have your mind searching for other things to keep busy with.

2) Students who always practice to a formula. Because their practice always

begins with five minutes of scales, two minutes of sight reading and then ten minutes of etudes, a comfortable familiarity descends like chloroform at the start of each practice session. The student realizes that everything is business as usual, and that they don't need to pay that much attention for things to be ok. Their autopilot all but announces to them "It's ok—I can take things from here. Go do something else"

3) Highly creative, dreamy or scatterheaded students (and often all three in one!). Such students often find themselves leaping from thought to thought, and find staying focussed on the extended present a challenge.

As with so many of the other practice flaws, the reason this particular flaw has to be dealt with is because it can mean students spend a lot of time practicing for little measurable gain.

Tips for correcting this practice flaw

• One effective way to combat autopilot is to *startle* it into disengaging. Tell your student to get a kitchen timer and set it to three minutes. Their job is to practice as they normally would, but when the timer goes off it's a reminder to "Focus!". Before the student resets the timer for another three minutes, they need to quickly ask themselves *"what exactly am I trying to achieve at the moment?"*, together with *"What have I been doing over the past three minutes"*. The answer to the second question should support their answer to the first question.

If it doesn't—or worse still, if the answer to either question is "I don't know, I wasn't really paying attention", then the timer that just went off needs to double as a wake-up call. The student can regather their concentration, and start the next three minutes afresh.

Once they find that the timer is not waking them from a period of autopilot, but interrupting focussed work instead, then they can extend the interval to 5 minutes. Then 8 minutes, and so on.

In this way, the timer gradually phases itself out of existence as a tool, and by the time it's gone, the job is done.

• If autopilot is triggered by a sense of sameness in practicing, consider introducing a *random* element into your student's practice. If they are not sure exactly what is going to happen next in their practice session, then it's difficult for them to be lulled into a feeling of "here we go again" (which is one of the sets of Magic Words that will induce autopilot).

So if they have three big goals for the week, broken up into 24 mini-goals (see the chapter on Project Management for more on this), have them write each mini goal on a separate card. They then draw a card at random at the start of their practice session, and work towards whatever goal it outlines.

Once they have completed the goal, they draw another card, and so on—so that each practice session will be made up of 3-4 different challenges, each one unpredictable.

> ...while it might be comfortable and reassuring to ensure all your practice sessions are like Model T's rolling off a production line, it doesn't take into account the fact that the *needs* of your pieces are always changing.

It's tough to nod off when there is a fresh challenge coming your way every ten minutes—particularly when you have no way of knowing in advance what that challenge will be.

• Autopilot usually takes a little while to kick in, meaning that the first few minutes of a student's practice session are the most productive. Seems a pity that they only get to start practicing once each day...

...of course, it doesn't have to be that way. Encourage your autopilot-afflicted student to STOP practicing every few minutes, to stand up, leave the room—and then come back in again to "start" a practice session. Simple tactic for keeping them fresh and focussed. You better explain it to their parents though, or they'll wonder what on earth is going on.

3.11 Pattern Practicers

Defining this practice flaw

Routine is important for any student, but sometimes things can be taken a little too far. A variation on Autopilots, Pattern Practicers create formulas for practice that they stick to rigidly—quite independently of what their task for the week actually is. They'll "learn" new pieces by playing the piece through ten times at 60 bpm while accenting the first beat of each bar. They'll also "fix" tricky bits by playing them ten times at 60 bpm while accenting the first beat of the bar. And if they need to speed up a piece? That's right, ten times for that too, first beat of the bar accented, at 60 bpm.

The actual formula varies from student to student, but once established, they will use it for all practice purposes—memorizing pieces, preparing for recitals, repairing mislearned notes, developing legato in their scales, working out fingering for their new etude, introducing terraced dynamics to their new baroque piece, correcting posture problems when playing loudly, ensuring adequate projection of sound when playing pianissimo...all completely unrelated practice problems that require enormously different solutions, but are given the same one-size-fits-all response.

How to tell if your student may be practicing this way

The first thing to look out for is uneven quality in what they prepare for you each week, despite a steady commitment to practicing. Some tasks will be solid, others will sound like they have not been practiced at all. The difference between this and a student who Polishes Shiny Objects is that the Pattern Practicer actually will have spent the same amount of time on each of these tasks (in fact they will have spent EXACTLY the same amount of time), while the Shiny Object Polisher will completely ignore anything that didn't sound good straight away.

Because the student practices according to a formula, when you ask them how they worked on each section, they will be able to tell you in great detail, unlike Drifters or Clock Watchers. It's when the same details appear for each task that alarm bells should be ringing. As with so many other practice flaws, the student may actually have been working very hard, but have little to show for it.

Why students practice this way, and why it doesn't work

Students like this will probably start, middle and end their practice session exactly the same way each time, with the whole process always taking the same amount of time. The fact that they choose to work this way does not say anything about their capacity for concentration, or their willingness to work hard—in fact many of these students will be highly focussed and motivated. It's just how they prefer to work, and this desire for structure and uniformity is almost certainly not just limited to their music practice.

These are the same students who might prepare for a mathematics test by doing exactly five examples from each of the topics that will be quizzed. This approach does not take into account that some topics are more difficult than others, but it does give the student the warm feeling of being able to say "I *must* be ready for this test...I did five of each example, and three of each probably would have been enough".

The seeds for Pattern Practicing can be sown quite early, and those who fall victim to the technique usually have the best of intentions. Often what happens is that the student discovers a method of practice that produced a great result for them, perhaps a lesson during which praise was lavished on them for a job well done. Keen to ensure that they receive this sort of feedback every time, *they clone the practice method*, and apply it to everything they do from now on.

If the challenges in the subsequent weeks are similar, then the cloned practice technique will work well for them too, reinforcing the behavior.

The problem is that while it might be comfortable and reassuring to ensure all your practice sessions are like Model T's rolling off a production line, it doesn't take into account the fact that the needs of your pieces are always changing—and this particularly becomes the case when the week that spawned the cloned practice method is now five years ago! (What worked so well for "My Funny Donkey" is probably not going to work so well for that new Beethoven Sonata) And it's not just changes in repertoire that cloning ignores—as we'll examine later in the book, the sort of practice you need to do to prepare for a recital is very different from the practice techniques you need to employ to memorize a piece. The "one-size-fits-all" approach of this type of student will occasionally produce good results, but just as frequently will produce bad results—teaching students that practicing is a lottery. And to be fair, if you are going to practice by a never-changing formula, it's a lottery with the odds stacked firmly against you.

Tips for correcting this practice flaw

• For some Pattern Practicers, it's been so long since they worked any other way that they have great trouble picturing any other way of working. Give them a sheet of paper and a pen, and spend a good fifteen minutes brainstorming different ways of practicing. Half tempo, full tempo, one phrase at a time, entire sections at once, with greatly exaggerated dynamics, with your eyes closed, starting at random from anywhere in the piece, visualizing the performance, a set number of times through without an error, ten times in quick succession and noting any problems as you go, separate hands (for pianists), pizz instead of arco throughout (for string players), with a single-minded focus on a particular issue (eg. legato, or fingering), with the lights out, starting from the last bar, then the second last bar, and so on, with inverted dynamics, in different moods (ie. play it "sad", play it "lonely", play it "angry")...

You're making no attempt to distinguish between effective techniques and those that won't deliver—all you're doing is making the point that there are many, many different ways of practicing, and that the world of what is possible between lessons is much bigger than they ever suspected.

Then tell them that this week, the only rule is that *they are not allowed to practice the same way twice*. Ever. And when they are coming up with fresh ways to practice, the crazier the better. (Have they ever practiced in a cupboard, Harry Potter style?) The focus is not so much on efficient practice, as embracing alternatives—and smashing the pattern that they have set.

After a couple of weeks of that, you can take the next step and introduce them to the idea of specific techniques for specific problems (which is what much of the second part of this book is dedicated to). It's not as though they'll never be allowed to use their formula again—it will actually be perfect for a particular type of practice problem—it's just that they can't use it every time. Otherwise it's a square peg in a round, or triangular, or hexagonal, or dot-sized, or slit shaped, or letter "F" cutout hole, depending on what the practice problem is this week.

• Some Pattern Practicers become profoundly uncomfortable with the idea of having to design new practice sessions for themselves. (Part of the reason that some Pattern Practicers work that way in the first place is so they don't have to trouble themselves with structuring their practice) That's ok—you may need to spend a little time designing some for them. Again, emphasize variation, not because it's the best way to work, but because it's a concept the Pattern Practicer desperately need to meet.

3.12 Always from the top

Defining this practice flaw

Asong once suggested that the beginning is a "very good place to start", but that's not always the case when you are trying to practice. Students who are guilty of this practice flaw always practice from the very beginning of each piece, without reference to where in the piece the difficulties may actually lie. Not only does this mean that the beginning is given undue attention, it also often means that the end of the piece is neglected, as there will be many practice sessions where they don't actually get as far as the end. (Particularly if they are reacting to mistakes as they go!)

> **Practicing would be so much more effective if it didn't have to be undertaken by *people*.**
>
> **Our need for positive strokes and reassurance can get in the way of good development sometimes.**

How to tell if your student may be practicing this way

Because the student practices the beginning more than any other part of the piece, and doesn't always get as far as the end, listening to a performance from a student who suffers from "Always from the Top" is listening to a steady slide into anarchy. The opening phrases will be beautifully polished, showing all the precision and flair that only a heavily practiced section can—while the end might be a stumbling sight read disaster, sounding as though it has hardly been touched. Which is exactly right, because it hardly has.

Deeply ingrained inconsistency of quality within a piece can be symptomatic of other practice flaws too (Polishing the Shiny Objects, for example), but if the inconsistency is structured to that each bar is a little less secure than the bar before, then the diagnosis is usually clear. Such a steady deterioration is the calling card of the "Always from the Top" flaw.

Within longer works, "Always from the Top" sufferers won't always start from the very beginning of the work (which would feel like a nonsense in a twenty-five minute work, even to them), but they will still tend always to start from the beginning of major sections, such as a development section. The steady deterioration test then applies within these sections, although it may not hold through the entire piece. (Although with most "Always from the Top" practicers, the section that they will have started from the most will still be the very beginning, meaning that expositions are always in better shape than codas.)

If you are suspicious that you might have an "Always from the Top" practicer, you can confirm this by asking them to pick up from random points within the piece. If the only place they have ever started from is the beginning, they will look at you as though you have asked them to flap their arms and fly around the studio.

Why students practice this way, and why it doesn't work

When we are beginners, the start of a piece is a logical place to return to if anything goes wrong—particularly if the start of the piece is only four bars away from the end. So if I mess up half way through "Middle C Goes Walking", I will be told that it's ok, and encouraged by my teacher to "start again".

After a few lessons, I don't need to be told any more. If I mess up, I'll just start again anyway, and it's exactly the right thing to do. And when I am working at home, I will react to mistakes in exactly the same way.

The problem is that the longer the pieces get, the potentially further away the start of the piece is. All returning to the beginning does is place bars of irrelevant music between you and the problem you are trying to solve. The principal of stopping what you are doing, figuring out what went wrong, backpedaling and trying it again is sound no matter how long the piece is—but there has to be a limit on how far you back pedal.

It's sometimes easiest to explain this problem to the student with an analogy. If you imagine you were an athlete—a steeplechaser—who was having trouble negotiating the water jump. The sensible thing to do would be to go back a little and practice the *jump itself* a few times. It would be a nonsense to practice the water jump by going back to the very beginning of the race every time,

80

thus adding a kilometer of extra running each time that's doesn't actually assist at all with your water-jump difficulties. (I don't think practicing is very similar to steeplechasing in any other regards, so we'll leave this analogy well alone from here on in)

A contributing factor to students always starting from the beginning is that it's the easiest place to start from. Because they have never started from anywhere else, they have trouble starting from anywhere else—and just like the "students who Polish the Shiny Objects", when confronted with a choice between doing something that is easy (starting from the beginning), and doing something that is not (starting from anywhere else in the piece), they go with the easy option.

Taking this link to "students who Polish the Shiny Objects" a step further, when a student messes up while they are playing, they don't feel good about their playing—it's a feeling most people are fairly keen to avoid. One of the fastest ways to distract yourself from the pain and doubt of making a mistake is to play a section where you know you'll sound good. Since you have always started from the beginning, the beginning becomes the sanctuary you turn to when your playing is not going so well, and in so doing becomes even stronger, and therefore even more likely to be the section you turn to next time...and so on.

Practicing would be so much more effective if it didn't have to be undertaken by *people*. Our need for positive strokes and reassurance can get in the way of good development sometimes.

Tips for correcting this practice flaw

• Divide the piece up into zones, with each zone only being a few phrases in length—maybe 3-4 zones on each page of music. Once the student is clear on where each zone starts, there are two things they need to do:

1) They need to practice so that they are able to start easily from the beginning of any zone. To test this, you should be able to point to the start of any Zone at random, and they should be able to pick up from there without any hesitation. They can prepare for this at home by numbering the Zones, and then pulling numbers out of a hat to determine where they start—until they can do this comfortably, they know that they won't be ready for their next lesson.

2) Once they can do this, a slight modification needs to be made to the way they already work. If they get into trouble while they are playing, they still need to react by backtracking—but instead of going right back to the start of the piece, they are only allowed to head back as far as the beginning of the Zone that contained the error.

Working this way allows them to continue to work the way they are used to (they still get to go back after a mistake), but ensures that the journey is not too long. This technique will also work equally well for pieces that are one hundred pages long as it does for single page pieces.

• When you assign new pieces, instead of asking to hear "the first two pages next lesson", start by asking to hear "the *last* two pages". Just as movies don't have to be shot in the order that the scenes finally appear, there is no rule that says that pieces have to be learned from the beginning. The fact that we tend to ask for the beginning first only helps reinforce the preference students have for starting there when they practice.

• A more extreme version of the same tactic is to have students learn pieces BACKWARDS, sort of like a Dutch Auction. The idea is that they practice until they can comfortably deliver the last bar of the piece. Then they practice until they can comfortably deliver the last two bars. Then the last three bars—and so on.

This method is really only a once-off to help them understand that there are viable alternatives to always starting from the beginning—it certainly shouldn't become the standard way they practice. (Otherwise all you do is replace the problem of the *beginning* being unduly dominant in their practice with the *end* of their piece being overpracticed.)

> The problem only arises when exactly the same sections are used every time...
>
> ...and when the student fails to treat the "bridge" between two sections as being a section in its own right.

82

3.13 Bad Bricklayers

Defining this practice flaw

Bad Bricklayers are students whose practice might otherwise be in excellent shape, but who choose to work by dividing their piece in the same sections every time. So individually, section A, B & C will sound excellent—but the student has never practiced the transition from the end of A to the beginning of B, resulting in a performance that sounds disjointed and blocky at best, and riddled with section-end-gaps at worst.

How to tell if your student may be practicing this way

This is one of the easiest practice flaws to diagnose. If it's not already marked on the score, have the student define the boundaries of the sections that they practice in, and then listen to them play the piece through. If the sections themselves sound fine, but the joins between sections are marked by hesitations, inaccuracies or tempo changes, the student is almost certainly a Bad Bricklayer.

If your student is not aware having divided the piece into sections, or protests that they don't practice that way, ask them to pick up from several points at random in the piece. Tell them that their job is to start from as close to the pickup point as they can, but that if the pickup point falls at an awkward time for them, they are welcome to choose another pickup point a little further away.

If the student has places near the pickup point that they are able to start from easily and comfortably, then chances are that these locations mark the start of sections that they (perhaps unconsciously) use to practice with at home. And if the joins between those sections are much rougher than the sections themselves, then whether they are aware of it or not, the student is a Bad Bricklayer.

Why students practice this way, and why it doesn't work

Breaking down bigger jobs into smaller units is a core skill for anyone

83

who practices, the absence of which leads to the "Gluttons" practice flaw. As a result, teachers will often insist that students practice in sections, and the students really can't be blamed for complying.

Even if we are not dividing pieces up for our students, the score itself tends to break things into units—units that would then seem to make logical practice chunks. Movements are clearly marked, major sections within movements will often have double bar lines or repeats, phrases are clearly marked, and students who are sensitive to the rhetorical structure of phrases will develop an intuitive feel for how they resolve into periods. Even students who have no natural ability to feel when the piece *logically* divides into sections will note that this part of the piece is on page 11, while that part is on page 12—and there are more than a few students who use pages in the score as their section divisions.

Not only can we not avoid the use of sections in practice, we should be actively encouraging it. The problem only arises when exactly the same sections are used every time, and when the student fails to treat the "bridge" between two sections as being a section in its own right. Without this bridge having been rehearsed, there will always be an awkward moment of orientation at the crossover from the end of one section to the beginning of the next. Being a Bad Bricklayer is not the sort of crippling practice flaw that many of the others outlined here can be, but it does shatter both any feeling of unity in a piece, and any atmosphere the student had managed to create.

Tips for correcting this practice flaw

• Introduce the student to the concept of "bridges", and then clearly mark those bridges in the score. Typically the bridges will run from four bars BEFORE the end of one section, to four bars AFTER the beginning of the next. It becomes the equivalent of a brick laid across the join between the two bricks below.

Then tell them that for a whole week, the only sections they are to work with are the bridges themselves.

• One simple method for overcoming the bridging problems that come with Bad Bricklaying is for the student to work with a metronome as they play the piece right through—not to keep them in time, but to help identify any moments where orienting themselves meant that they fell behind the metronome beat.

This achieves two things:

a) It provides a tangible way of students identifying which sections needed extra time (and therefore extra practice) for such orientation, together with

b) A tidy way for students to measure when the bridging is strong enough to no longer be a problem. Once they pass the metronome test, they're well on the way to eliminating the most obvious evidence of a Bad Bricklaying problem.

3.14 Ignoring the map

Defining this practice flaw

These students may practice quite hard, but do so without referring to the score, or to any notes you may have made last lesson. As a result, they fail to target many of the problems that have already been identified, while adding new problems through careless errors that could easily be prevented by checking the source.

> Like a game of *Chinese Whispers*, each version of the piece mutates a little more, as reality and memory diverge.

How to tell if your student may be practicing this way

Students who Ignore the Map are almost always strong memorizers, and will also usually ignore the score during lessons unless prompted to do otherwise. A simple way to check whether a student practices without referring to anything is to write a nonsense instruction on the score (eg. *Yodel like a bicycle when you play this bit*), and then see whether they ask you about it at the next lesson. Or to make sure they will remember: "*Say the word "octopus" at the start of next lesson, and I'll give you a chocolate*".

Another tactic is to (secretly) open their book and stick pages together with double-sided sticky tape, so that they cannot actually see the first page of the piece. Or in extreme cases, you could simply forget to give them their book at the end of the lesson, and see how far into the week it is before they even notice.

You're not doing these things so that you can "catch" the student and give them a hard time, but it is a powerful way of being able to prove to them what is really going on. Until they accept that they practice without referring to the score, it can be difficult to move forwards on a cure, because they can simply counter assert (and believe it) that they DID look at their book, it's just they can't exactly remember when...

Why students practice this way, and why it doesn't work

This practice flaw is a classic collision between students who prefer to work from memory, and the need for regularly checking the score. The best way to understand the cause of the problem is to look at it from their point of view.

If you are a student who plays well from memory, *having to check the score while you work is going to slow you down.* Partly because it interrupts the flow of your preferred working method, but mostly because a lot of memorizers are not particularly comfortable reading in the first place.

This means that as a memorizer, agreeing to check the score regularly is not simply a commitment to look at the music once in a while—it's an undertaking to regularly bring otherwise productive sessions to a crashing halt. (At least that's how it can feel to the student) Not only that, if your reading really is struggling, taking this time to check the music *might not actually tell you anything in any case*, making it pain for very little gain. At its worst, all it does is reinforce the student's preconception that reading is an inefficient method of practicing—slower, and less reliable than simply getting on with what they already do best.

Many memorizers will try to head off this unpleasant assault on the way they work by protesting that they don't *need* to check the music—that because they memorize so well, by definition, they'll remember what was there. No checking required.

The problem is that even with excellent memory skills—assuming they reliably memorize 99% of what they learn—every so often the laws of probability dictate that a weird note is likely to creep in. A flat where a natural should go. A quarter note instead of a half note. A fifth repetition of a bar that actually only repeats four times. To be fair, in the course of a week that's not going to make a huge difference, with only a handful of errors likely to emerge.

But as with all evolution, the longer you stretch the time frame, the more drastic the results. If that same student were to practice for a *month* without consulting the music—or worse yet, for the entire summer holidays—a couple of little mistakes can become a dozen well-practiced ogres, and you're going to have to schedule some serious time to fix problems that didn't need to occur in the first place. Like a game of Chinese Whispers, each version of the piece mutates a little more, as reality and memory diverge.

A similar problem emerges for those students who fail to check your notes from last lesson. It may well be that they remember three out of four of all the points you make—but some lessons can see a *lot* of points made, meaning that from sixteen corrections, they will have forgotten four. And every point overlooked is a point you'll need to revisit the next time you see them, robbing you of time that you could have used to give fresh feedback. Sometimes when lessons seem to go over the same old thing, it's really not the fault of the teacher.

Tips for correcting this practice flaw

• For students who honestly never look at the music, it's worth setting up a week during which they *always* have to look at the music, just to get them used to the idea that working with the music is possible. That's not going to happen through a simple request—you're going to have to make it worth their while.

Create a new rule with the student's parents—for this week only, 15 minutes of practicing *with* the music is now officially worth 30 minutes of practicing *without* the music. To earn the free practice time each day, there are two things the student needs to do:

1) To have the music open in front of them at all times at the piece they are currently working on.

2) Whenever parents walk past at random and ask "exactly where are you up to now?", the student should be able to point without hesitating at their location in the score. And they need to be right.

87

Reinforce this with a similar scheme in the preceding lesson—for one lesson only, they have to play with their eyes glued to the music throughout, and need to stop and point at their actual location whenever you ask. And they know you're going to ask a lot. You're not trying to encourage them to always play this way, as that thought would absolutely horrify most memorizers. You just want them leaving with a sense that it's not only possible to read music as you play, but that doing so can actually make a positive difference.

• Once the week has passed, you can let the student know that they are off the hook, and not condemned to having to stare at the music for the rest of their lives (you can remind them that apart from anything else, you actually really like and admire the way they can play so comfortably from memory, and that you don't want to take that away). What you are proposing though is a compromise. They can revert to doing *most* of their practice without the music, just as long as every so often they stop to check. Let them know that you occasionally write some strange things just to test whether or not they are looking.

To help remind them to check the notes every so often, have them roll a dice before each new practice task they attempt. If the result is between one and five, then they are welcome to work on the section entirely from memory. If they roll a six though, they need to play the section through with Eyes on the Score. The six effectively tells them "Use the music already!", but comes across more nicely than if you have actually had to make the same request of them.

• There are plenty of little practice diaries out there that require the student's parent to sign off on how much practice the student actually did. Instead of that signature, it's time to chase one that's much more interesting. The student's.

They won't be signing off on how much practice they've done, but every day they need to read quickly the notes you made from last lesson, and then sign at the bottom to say they have. The signature needs to be witnessed by the parents.

And just to provide the possibility of a reward at the end of all of this, let them know that next lesson you will be giving them a blank sheet of paper and a pencil. If they can write down from memory every point that was recorded about last lesson, there's an edible reward waiting for them at the end of the lesson. Or a sticker. Or whatever.

The irony here is that they will earn the reward courtesy of their ability to memorize—a skill which was never actually in doubt. But for them to ensure that they memorize *accurately* (because if it's not accurate, then no banana), they'll take a little time checking what was actually on the list.

In that way, they learn that reliable memorization is about a *partnership* between memory skills, and occasional checking of the source. It's not a bad lesson for students who Ignore the Map to learn, and they'll learn it without you having to explain a thing.

3.15 Red Light Runners

Defining this practice flaw

Again, these students might practice quite hard, but seem oblivious to any errors they may make, or difficulties they may encounter. They'll motor straight on through such red lights in their

> Most often, students who don't stop for red lights are students who genuinely don't *notice* the things they ought to be stopping for.

pieces, continuing their practice session as though the problems had never occurred in the first place. When asked how their practice session went, they'll say "Great!", no matter what calamities may actually have taken place. The saying that follows such students may well be "ignorance is bliss", but it doesn't help their playing any, and results in a lot of wasted practice time.

How to tell if your student may be practicing this way

Students who don't stop for red lights are usually identified by their assessments of the week that was. The telling questions are *"What did you have trouble with this week?"*, or *"Which three passages were you most likely to mess up when you were practicing this week?"*. Most red-light-runners simply won't have a clue—not because they're generally clueless, but because they simply weren't paying that sort of attention when they were practicing. Moving forwards took priority over assessing progress, and it's not surprising that they can't recall which parts of the ride were bumpy.

They may also exhibit poor self-critical skills in lessons, looking blankly at you when you implore "didn't you notice *anything* about your playing of that passage that you would like to change?"

Why students practice this way, and why it doesn't work

This is one of the most complex practice flaws, as there are many different causes that can lead to the red light running.

Some students fail to stop for red lights for the same reason that many students Polish Shiny Objects—in other words, they are all too well aware of the problems in the piece, but choose denial over repair. Stopping for an error would mean that practice time will be devoted to not sounding so good, and to confronting weaknesses in their own playing, rather than strengths. So they hit the accelerator instead of the brake.

Other students may well be prepared to work on bits they don't like, but get too caught up in the flow of the piece, and are reluctant to interrupt proceedings just to fix an icky bit that they can always fix up later. Problem is, they don't fix it up later.

But most often, students who don't stop are students who genuinely don't *notice* the things they ought to be stopping for. Sometimes this can point to a technical weakness in the area of the error—so for example, if a student could not figure out how to read a syncopated rhythm if their life depended on it, it's not entirely surprising if they cruise straight past rhythmic errors when they practice. On other occasions, it can be that they simply have not developed their critical faculties well enough yet to be able to extract specific problems from the bedlam of the competing issues that go into each performance. Intonation, dynamics, articulation, posture, correct notes, rhythmic precision, pedalling, phrasing, balance and projection all combine into one giant issue, and it becomes impossible for the student to create useful feedback on any of them, because all the potential problems seem to be yelling at them at once.

Tips for correcting this practice flaw

• It's time to break out some Practice Hats. To help the student direct their attention to potential trouble spots, make a list of all the different issues you would like them to be listening for. The length of this list will vary depending on how advanced the student is—but let's imagine that our student is a beginner, and has been told to watch out for four things this week:

- Fingering
- The E flat that's actually in the key signature, but that they always leave out
- Ensuring the piece does not gradually get faster
- Ensuring that the dynamics match those in the music

Taken together, that may well be overwhelming for the student, and in trying to fix everything, they may well fix nothing. So instead, have them imagine that they have four hats, and that each hat has a label on it:

- Fingering
- E Flat!
- Steady Tempo
- Dynamics Patrol

The student chooses one hat to put on. (In fact, for younger students, it's worth actually making some paper hats with the appropriate labels). While they are wearing that hat, they become completely obsessed with the issue that the hat describes. So if they are wearing a "Fingering" hat, they will be on the lookout for incorrect fingerings while they are playing.
They keep the hat on for ten minutes, during which time they will notice plenty of fingering errors that may well have passed them by otherwise—not because they are suddenly more able to spot them, *but because they were actually looking for them in the first place.*

Once the ten minutes has passed, they swap to a different hat. In this way, they are operating in a framework which actually encourages them not only to be suspicious that there may be errors in their piece, but has them looking out for the issues you identified as being important in the lesson.

• The various government departments responsible for the upkeep of our roads will periodically come out with a list of "black spots"—sections of road that have been demonstrated to be dangerous and needing attention.

Instead of telling a student to come back next week with their piece fixed, tell them that their job for the week is simply *to create a list of Black Spots in their piece.* So in other words, their practice won't be about making changes to their playing—instead it will be about identifying where those changes need to be made. You can sit down with them at the next lesson and discuss their list with them, and then make plans for how to deal with each problem.

This approach is the perfect antidote for red light runners, as they will know that the ONLY thing that will impress you this week will be the production of that list. So they had better go build one, and that means keeping their eyes wide open for errors.

• Implement a ban on them working on more than four measures at once, and then set a minimum time limit of five minutes for those measures. This will ensure that the student is forced to confront the same passage many, many times in a short space of time.

This won't make any difference to those students who are genuinely *unable* to spot problems in the first place (they'll just miss the problem 50 times in a row!), but will make life very difficult for those who are *unwilling* to. They might be able to turn a blind eye to an error the first time, but on every subsequent pass, the mistake will yell at them a little louder. There's only so long you can remain in denial when the evidence of the problem loops past you every fifteen seconds.

So what's next?

Before we start to look how to match practice *techniques* to specific practice *tasks*, there's one more practice flaw we still have to understand.

And this one's so big, it gets a chapter all to itself.

Why Students Don't Practice

"Toil is man's allotment; toil of brain, or toil of hands, or a grief that's more than either, the grief and sin of idleness."

Herman Melville (1819–1891)

The Practice Revolution: Chapter 4

• Time Management Skills • Reading Problems • Lack of Parental Help • Parental Interference • A Week with Wings • Impossible Workloads • Not Clear on what they are Hoping to Achieve • Discovering that Practice Doesn't Work •

4. Why Students Don't Practice

4.1 Introduction

While the focus so far has been on overcoming practice flaws, there's one major practice flaw we haven't covered yet. Sometimes students will be unprepared for lessons because they simply haven't practiced *at all.*

Teachers are divided along ideological lines as to how to handle this. Some will bear in like a wronged and vengeful SWAT team on the non-practicing student, easing off only when the student's bottom lip is trembling nicely, and there is a general understanding in the room that if the student *ever* comes to a lesson unprepared again, that they had better write a will first. While some students do need an occasional kick in the backside, this approach does nothing to develop a feeling of rapport between teacher and student, instead replacing it with a 19th Century "School-marm" atmosphere of compliance through terror.

Other teachers (and I have been guilty of this at times), are so keen to preserve the atmosphere of trust and warmth in the studio that the reaction can be altogether too gentle. Such non-productive weeks are greeted with quiet encouragements to please try to turn things around in the future. If it's not too inconvenient. There are no fangs, no venom—and often, no change. Granted, at least the student is not terrified of you, but they're probably not practicing either.

The problem has been that for too long, teachers have focused on trying to establish which of the two approaches is better. This debate is actually giving undue attention to *two candidates that shouldn't be in the race in the first place.* The saber tooth tiger teacher will occasionally produce compliance, but never enthusiasm, and will often irreparably damage the child's view of music lessons. And the kitty cat tactic often produces nothing at all, leaving the teacher looking weak and wishy-washy.

At their core, both types of cat fail because each of them targets symptoms, not the cause. When students don't practice, there is *always* a cause. And until you understand the cause, no amount of admonishing, encouraging, cajoling, threatening, pleading or rewarding is going to produce long term change.

To make matters even more complex, these causes are not always self-evident, despite the fact that we think we know what's going on. For most teachers the cause seems easy to identify—a student who doesn't practice is not motivated. That's the cause. No motivation.

So we deal with that by effectively either yelling at the child to "be motivated" or gently suggest to them to "be motivated", depending on what type of cat we feel like today. It doesn't matter how we couch this message to "be motivated", whether it's a request or an order—the message itself is nonsense.

People don't become motivated because they are asked to, any more than people can become long-sighted just because they're told to. Motivation, or lack thereof, is a *symptom*. It's caused by other things. Target those causes, and the motivation will follow.

This chapter is dedicated to looking at causes—an examination of the most common reasons that students are not motivated to practice, and how to turn them around.

4.2 Time Management skills

It can be very easy to confuse students who *can't be bothered* to find time to practice with those who simply *don't have the skills* to find time. And a lecture from you that is appropriate for the former type of student can be devastating for the latter.

It's no co-incidence that books on time management have sold millions of copies, while corporations throughout the world spend fortunes on time management gurus and their seminars. But even those who already have excellent time management skills will be the first to admit that they were not *born* with them. Such skills have to be developed, as most of the principles run counter to human intuition.

Here's the newsflash: it's not just busy executives who need help with time management. Your music students do not come pre-equipped with time management skills either. Which means that some weeks—no matter how motivated they are feeling about their music lessons—they simply won't get *around* to practicing. Their week will have other plans for them.

The problem is that when we hear excuses as flimsy as "I had to work on a school project", we immediately picture the student lying in front of the TV all week, only getting up when their PSP needs fresh batteries. They're lazy, nothing surer, and the lecture is half delivered simply by the withering look we give them as soon as their plea for understanding is over.

But before we surrender to such assumptions, let's walk a mile in the shoes of the student who came to you blaming their lack of practice on a school project. The following outline is quite detailed, but as teachers, we sometimes forget just how effectively a seemingly minor commitment can hijack practice, and just how great the feeling of panic and helplessness can be. The aim is not to validate the excuse, but to understand how weeks like this do not necessarily reflect at all badly on the student's dedication to music lessons.

In fact, weeks like this have nothing whatsoever to do with how well music lessons are going. You still have to talk to your student about a better way of doing things, but the issue of motivation can be left well alone, because it's not the problem.

4.2.1 A walk in the shoes of a Time Management challenged student: The Moon Project

At first glance, the project in the scenario below doesn't sound much like a practice-killer. In fact, if all we knew about it was the stated task itself, it would be easy for us to be annoyed with the student for allowing such a trifle to disrupt a whole week of practice. I was—until I found out a little more about what it meant for the student involved. Needless to say, I won't be using real names ☺

The question on the front page of their project is "Observe the moon on seven different clear nights in this month, and draw its shape on each night". Not so bad, and a generous thirty days to complete it all—at least there *were* thirty days to go when the assignment was first given. Problem is, that's three weeks ago now, meaning that there are only *six* nights left this month, ensuring that the whole assignment will have to be completed in a panic this week.

To make matters worse, on Wednesday your student realizes for the first time that there were *more* instructions printed on the reverse side...oh no...they also have to build a telescope...their pulse rate goes up to 150 bpm as they read this...and then hits 200 when they read one more instruction about a two page report on the Apollo XI Mission, or a short film review of Apollo 13. (Their choice)

For some reason, even though they were your best student last lesson, they're not thinking about practicing too much now. The world seems to be collapsing in on them in an Escherian collage of blurred deadlines, crescent moons and leaking hourglasses, with sand now pouring all over the remains of what was their week. Somewhere in those remains were supposed to be practice sessions.

Their family wants to help, so Dad jumps in the car with them to go to their local video store—"Yes, we have copies of Apollo 13, but they're all out right now...it's strange, nobody hired it for six months and then suddenly WHAM this week, everyone wants it". (Does anyone else in their class have music lessons with you?)

Pulse rate hits 205. Ok, so maybe we forget that and do the Apollo XI report instead. Back home, and time for some research. Now where are our encyclopaedias? Abacus, Apertures, Apples, ah...here were are, Apollo...hang on, doesn't say anything about moon missions, just some god I never heard of before...what year was this encyclopaedia printed? Dad! Mom! 1963! You are KIDDING right? How am I supposed to get into college with resources like this? Five-thirty now—I should be practicing, but I'll have to do it later..."

Uh huh. Later.

Ok, so some practicing goes to accommodate the emergency. What now? Where do they look up Apollo mission info?... Internet maybe? Great, upstairs, hope there's nobody using the computer... there is, but they'll fix that... *"Lucy, get off the computer NOW, I need to look up something. Don't tell me "In a minute", this is an EMERGENCY?...what? when's yours due? Yeah, Chemistry Final, right. Tomorrow huh. You're just making that up so I don't get a turn, you're always hogging the computer and I never get a go, and now I'm going to get an F in my school project and it's all your fault and you don't even care what my report says... Daaaad! Lucy won't let me do my moon research!...*

Wailing and gnashing of teeth. We've gone beyond simply delaying practicing now. The whole idea of practice has been obliterated from the student's mind by Forces Greater than Themselves. In fact, as I write this, it's pretty much passed from my mind too.

Doesn't matter though. By the time Lucy takes a break, the ISP has gone down anyway. "We regret any inconvenience caused...please try again later". There may well be thirty million websites with information about the Apollo Mission, but this household won't be connecting with any of them in the immediate future.

Back in the car again. The student is yelling at anyone within earshot, and panic has clearly set in. This time to the local library, both to borrow a book on the Apollo Mission, AND to use their internet connection. Forty minute wait to get access to a computer, then they're in. Finally. Ok...now, hang on, which Apollo was it. Ten? Seven? Eleven? Twelve? It's ok, it's just on the sheet...what do you mean "what sheet?", I thought *you* had it? Oh no...

...you get the idea. I could relate immediately to the scenario because I was a child like that. I teach plenty of them too, and so do you.

Throughout every second of this madness, your student was actually still a dedicated music student—just with much more urgent and terrible things on their mind. Trust me, they would much rather be practicing than doing this project.

But for them to satisfy our daydreams and announce "FORGET my project...I have PRACTICE to do!" would not be the utterance of a dedicated music student, but the pronouncement of a fanatic, or someone in deep denial. School deadlines can loom very, very large.

They will still be a dedicated music student tomorrow too, when they have to use up their practice time writing up their first draft of the Apollo XI article. And the day after when they discover—to their horror—another website that contradicts most of the information they already had, but is sanctioned by NASA.

And the day after that, when the school teacher reminds them that although 500 words was the *minimum*, that those who really want to do well should really be thinking of 800. 1000 if they want to excel. You could not conspire to destroy practice this week more effectively.

You see, your student is not just a dedicated music student. You would hope that they are also a dedicated *school* student. And sometimes these scatter-headed but dedicated students can be the most dangerous kind of person to be taking music lessons—hopelessly disorganized, and with the time management skills of a herd of camels, but genuine in their desire to excel. Which means now that they *have* to turn 500 into 1000 words...no problem, they just have to spend some extra time tonight and tomorrow...

The week used in the illustration above might seem like an extreme and isolated example, but any parent will tell you it's not. This week was the great science project. In two week's time there might be a school camp to prepare for, go on, and then recover from. Two weeks after that, and cousins might come to stay for an extended weekend to co-incide with grandpa's eightieth birthday. Poor time management skills will guarantee that life's everyday events become frequent and impossible to ignore emergencies.

None of these things actually is severe enough to prevent adequate practice—in the hands of someone with even rudimentary organization skills. But for the majority of students who have no TM skills whatsoever, they are practice killers, and there are plenty more where they came from.

There was a sign at the student help center at Indiana University that said "Lack of planning on *your* part does not constitute an emergency on *my* part". It's true, but lack of planning on your student's part at the very least constitutes a reason for discussions about planning. It's not "none of your business"—if a student decides to do no regular revision at school at all for a whole year because they "can always cram later", it's not just their marks their messing with. When their world ends for a month while they panic cram before their finals, their practice will end too for the same month, and that's very much your business.

So when they come to you with the Project that made practice impossible, don't talk about how they could have handled their practice better. Ask instead how they could have handled their *project* better.

Of course, there are ways you could have helped to head all of this off before it even began.

Tips for dealing with this problem

Ok, so you've identified a couple of students who seem to be exhibiting all the classic signs of having Time Management problems. It's obviously an issue which goes well beyond the scope of music lessons—and therefore your expertise—so how can you help usefully without being seen as interfering?

First thing is to assess the extent to which their time management adversely affects their music lessons—this is to give you permission to become involved. It's *not* unreasonable for your response to this whole issue to be in proportion to the degree of impact the problem has on your job. If your student is frequently coming to lessons with little or no practice because their week tossed them about like a small dingy in the North Atlantic, then it's entirely appropriate to spend some time talking with them—and their parents— about the problem.

Find out what the other pressures are—both regular and unpredictable. Who are the homework givers? What sorts of patterns are there in this homework? Is assessment based on the completion of small weekly tasks, or does it depend instead on one REALLY big annual project, and two mid-term quizzes? You need to know about these things now, not once they are already causing problems.

In fact, is there a big annual project underway at the moment? How far is the student into it? Can you be of any help? (Hey! We don't just know about music after all—maybe we have a book on the subject we could lend). If they were given the assignment details a month ago, and haven't started it yet, which day this week would they like to choose to kick it all off? (That's one of those "You don't get to go home today until you've answered this" questions, and make sure their parents hear the answer!). And before you squirm, remember, it *is* your business. If the student fails to plan for this assignment, you could easily lose them for a couple of weeks while they do it in a panic.

If the problem is particularly well entrenched, it might be worth taking the initiative and offering to convene a coalition of Adults Who Have To Give Jason Deadlines. Sort of like a support group, but for him, rather than for each other (most of the time anyway!). You, his school teacher, his parents and his soccer coach, swapping occasional phone calls that just quickly bring each other up to speed on what's coming up for Jason, and how he's coping with it. That way, you can tell Jason that you heard from their School Teacher that their most recent project was the best yet, while their soccer coach can praise the music practice Jason has been doing recently. Jason won't mind the extra positive attention—and in fact will probably love it that you know when he does something good at school.

Which means that when you want to try to influence how early he starts his work at school, he won't resent it.

You can even give him occasional "scoops":

"Hey Jason, you don't even know about it yet, but Mrs. Henderson mentioned to me that next term's project is going to be on Egypt. Nobody else knows either —I certainly wasn't supposed to tell you—but you might want to start borrowing all the cool Egypt books from the school library before the other kids find out and get them all. She said it's a three month project, but I'm hoping you can get it in a few weeks early so that it's not hanging over you while you're trying to polish things for the end-of-year-concert."

(This liaising with Jason's teacher, quite apart from giving you both a better understanding of Jason, is highly likely to have that teacher singing your praises to anyone who will listen...there are much, much worse ways of building student numbers than having local school teachers who think you're fabulous. But that of course is studio promotion...which is another book entirely, check out www.practicespot.com for details.)

The second thing is to create a single chart which allows Jason to record all his deadlines. He brings that chart to music lessons. He takes it to school to record homework and project details. He reviews it with his parents on a regular basis—it tells him what's coming up, when it's due, and gives him enough space to make notes about where he's up to on the whole adventure.

That chart will also allow all the Adults Who Have To Give Jason Deadlines a glimpse at the big picture—ensuring that they don't unwittingly create situations where all his deadlines seem to converge on a single date.

But the final thing is the most important. Students don't normally stop going to school for a few days, simply to create time to finish a project. Why not? Because school is regarded as being a non-negotiable. You have to steal time in emergencies, but you can't steal time from *that*.

Well, guess what. The practice time that you had carefully scheduled as part of his week is not negotiable either. It's not a "practice now—as long as there are no more pressing demands on my time" arrangement. It's a "practice now, no matter what" arrangement. In other words, Jason is more than welcome to steal time to complete the project...but he can only steal it from his *discretionary* time. And there's nothing discretionary about the time he has earmarked as "practice time".

None of these steps is designed to suddenly have Jason as a Time Management expert. But they will put in place some important basic changes:

1) His various Deadline Givers will know about each other, and will also know about other existing deadlines which affect Jason.

2) Jason is being sent the important signal that those various Deadline Givers in his life are actually on his side, and are very, very interested in what he does. It reminds him that there is help all around him, and handling all of this does not have to be a struggle he undertakes alone.

3) It will help you to better tailor Jason's workload to meet the ebb and flow of his other demands. If his cyclic pressures at school really can be charted

by a giant sine wave, then you should probably construct his practice demands to be the inverse of that wave, so that your peaks coincide with the school's troughs.

4) While it provides support for Jason, nowhere does it give him permission to continue this inefficient behavior. In fact it's sending him the message that a week of no-practice-because-of-my-project was an emergency he probably sowed the seeds for quite some time ago—and that procrastination of such projects has consequences that go well beyond the project itself. He knows that from now on his parents won't be the only ones taking an interest in why his latest project remains unstarted after three weeks.

5) It tells him that the trade-off he made this week is *not* a valid one. He cannot react to time crises by stealing time from practicing. He has to go get the time from somewhere else.

6) And most importantly, it reminds you that Jason is not an uninterested music student. He's simply a disorganized school student. So stop giving him a hard time about "being motivated", and help him to be organised instead.

4.3 Reading Problems

Despite occasional evidence to the contrary, music students really are rational creatures. And like most rational creatures, they will often employ a quick cost-benefit analysis before committing to spend substantial time doing something.

It's not as if students spend an hour making detailed lists of pros and cons for every little decision they have to make—these weigh-ups happen in a flash…but they do happen. And if the result of any of these weigh-ups is that the *cost* seems disproportionately high for the *benefit gained*, then the activity under consideration is not likely to take place.

Whether they are actually aware of it or not, students perform similar cost-benefit analyses when deciding whether to practice. Simply put, practicing uses up a lot of time, and if their reasons for *not* practicing outweigh the benefits they perceive from the process, then practicing won't take place. Given this, any single element that can tilt the outcome of such an analysis becomes a key factor in determining whether or not they practice at all.

And of all these elements, the student's ability to read music is one of the most powerful—because it has the capacity to cripple the benefit side of the equation.

Look at it from their point of view. Because students with reading difficulties lack the equipment for being able read notes immediately, every note they see has attached to it a laborious (and often inaccurate) process of working out what the pitch actually is. After ten such notes, they probably can't remember what the first one was supposed to be. Not a very rewarding experience. Never mind rhythm, or interpretation or any subtleties. The inability to read the notes becomes the bottleneck, and everything else becomes impossible before they even get a chance to begin. There's no flow, there's no context. There's certainly no music.

Worse than that, it reduces practice sessions to being note reading exercises—pitched typing drills for dyslexics. So if these students try to dodge practicing, you have to remember that the practice that these students try to avoid is very different from the practice that good readers embrace.

It's easy enough to illustrate this through the contrasting cost-benefit analysis of two different students as they consider practicing—one a strong reader, the other not.

Student A, who reads well, will be confronted with the following summary:

Cost: *I lose half an hour of otherwise prime free time*

Benefit: *By the end of that half hour, I should be able to play through the first page of my new piece—well on the way to my goal for the week. I will feel good about that, and more relaxed about being ready for next lesson.*

Student B, who has limited reading skills, has the following analysis in the same situation:

Cost: *I lose half an hour of otherwise prime free time*

Benefit: *I might be able to stumble through the first line.*

The cost is the same for both students, but it's clear that Student A stands to gain a lot from their thirty minutes, while Student B cannot guarantee making much progress at all. In fact, we can probably add to Student B's *cost* the fact that they are likely to spend the half hour feeling inadequate, helpless and frustrated while they drown in notes they can't decipher. Any person who wants to avoid feeling like that would avoid the situation that brings on such feelings—which means avoiding practice.

So on the surface, if Student A practices one week, and Student B does not, it's easy for us to conclude that Student A is more dedicated. But it's not a fair comparison—Student A is motivated to practice because they can imagine deriving a big and measurable benefit from it. There's no sacrifice involved here. Faced with the same unpalatable cost-benefit analysis that Student B had to confront, Student A would probably have elected not to practice too.

Tips for dealing with this problem

• To ensure that practice does not shut down just because their reading is weak, give them plenty of weekly tasks that *don't* involve reading. Speeding a piece up. Creating a dynamic plan for a piece. Memorizing a piece (although most non-readers usually have this one covered automatically). Scales and arpeggios. There are plenty of tasks that don't involve reading, so that it does not become a bottleneck of any sort.

It means you'll need to wait much longer than you normally would before retiring pieces—but pieces that your student already knows are pieces that they can practice whether they read well or not.

• With that having been said, there should still be a large component of their weekly practice that involves careful reading (otherwise their reading won't improve), but the works for this should be commensurate with their *reading* ability, not commensurate with the their technical and musical ability. This is something that as teachers, we often get wrong.

In other words, the pieces they are polishing at the moment may well be from Book 5, but their reading pieces will be from the equivalent of Book 1. To make sure they don't feel as though this is a regressive step, let them know exactly what you are doing—these pieces are for READING practice only. You certainly don't want them thinking that it's your idea of their recital pieces from now on.

If you don't believe they could make tangible progress through a new score in a fifteen minute read-only practice session, then the piece is too hard to read—even if it's insultingly easy to play.

• Long term though, if you really want to help Student B, it's pointless lecturing them about being more dedicated, or merely reshaping the content of their practice. We have to tilt the cost-benefit analysis in favour of practicing—in other words, spending less time asking them to practice, and more time teaching them to read.

To help them embrace your reading program, sympathize with them about how hard it must be to learn new pieces when reading them is so difficult. Let them know how easy the reading students have things (they can play their pieces straight away with NO practice in some cases).

Then tell them you can help them be a student like that, meaning that they will need to do a *fraction* of the practice they currently do to learn new pieces. Again, whenever this promise comes up—and it comes up often in this book, because it's the core of the Practice Revolution—you'll have their full attention.

When they ask how much time they should spend working on this, you can remind them that *every minute* they spend working on their reading now will end up saving them an *hour* of practice in the future. They will effectively be purchasing future free time when they practice their reading.

So when they practice harder this week, it might therefore be more out of a desire not to have to practice harder in the future, rather than their love of music. But they'll still practice harder.

4.4 Lack of parental help

If I send my six year old to tidy her room, she will sometimes just stand in the middle of the room and do nothing.

It's not a protest. It's not that she is dodging the work. It's simply because she sometimes can be overwhelmed by what seems to her the sheer enormity of the task at hand. Confronted by mess on all sides, she simply doesn't know where to start, and so she doesn't start anywhere.

All I need to do to tip the scales and get the result we're both after is to come in and make a few suggestions for her. How about you start by putting the books back on the bookshelf. That's it, good girl, looks better already. Now how about you put that jigsaw puzzle away, and while you're at that shelf, you might want to get that old apple and put it in the bin...

Obviously this doesn't just apply to room-tidying. Younger students in particular really should be getting plenty of help when they practice at home—it amazes me that parents who still need to help their children tie shoelaces think that the same child can learn new pieces of music by themselves. If you have a younger child in the studio who doesn't seem to be practicing, gently find out whether they are getting any help at home or not. Believe it or not, some parents feel like they need to wait for permission of some sort to involve themselves with their child's music lesson preparation. You need not only just give such permission, you actively have to *insist* that help is at hand.

Lack of parental help can manifest itself in another even more dangerous fashion. Households can be tremendously busy places, and no matter how important *you* may regard practice as being, unless the parents also regard practice as a priority, it simply won't happen. Some parents resent having to make the regular effort to ensure that practicing stays on their kids to-do list. As a result, when I interview prospective students, I always check to see if parents are prepared to be involved in the whole process—and if they're not, I often find that my timetable is unfortunately full at the moment. (I regard parental involvement in the practice process as being so important that I have dedicated an entire chapter to it later in this book)

Tips for dealing with this problem

• Have a handout available for parents, detailing ways in which they can help their kids as they practice. Most parents are very keen to help, but simply don't know where to start. This should be available from the interview onwards (which is when they will be at their most enthusiastic), meaning that the first few weeks will be as much about training the parents as they will about training the kids. (For those teachers who don't have the resources or time to create such a handout, you can download and print one for yourself from the Practice Revolution website at www.practicespot.com)

• When you give practice instructions at the end of the lesson, don't just tell the student—tell the parent too. You should also ask the parent how this week went at the start of each lesson. Apart from being a simple way to find out whether they actually were involved at all or not, if you keep parents in the loop in the studio, they are much more likely to want to stay involved at home.

• Create a section of the student's notebook which is specifically reserved for the parent to leave candid notes about practice sessions. Not only does the very existence of such a section create a framework for greater parental involvement, the feedback itself will be invaluable when giving practice instructions for the week ahead.

• Teachers with their own PracticeSpot studio website (there's more on this in Chapter 14) can do a similar thing, since parents can see exactly what is going on at lessons simply by visiting their child's webpage. As well as being able to look up practice instructions for the week, parents can send the teacher quick updates during the week about the progress of practice, and particularly about any problems or frustrations they might be experiencing. You don't necessarily need to respond until the lesson itself, but by the time the lesson arrives, you can quickly pull up a list of all such messages, and know exactly how the week went even before the lesson begins.

4.5 Parental interference

Despite the fact that parents have the potential to make an enormous positive difference to their child's practice, sometimes it just doesn't work out. It's not necessarily anybody's fault—it can simply be a reflection of the current dynamics between parent and child. (Any parent trying to deal with teenage children will know exactly what I mean) At this point, the parent's continuing "help" can actually ensure that practicing is so stressful that the student will actively avoid it, even if they are quite serious about the music lessons themselves.

The classic indicators of parents who should NOT be involved in practice are:

1) Overly critical and pushy parents who turn practicing into a parade of failings on the student's part, where nothing the child does is ever good enough. Remember, as trained teachers, we understand models of teaching based on positive reinforcement—there are a lot of parents who don't, and think that the best way to teach is to pick on the kid until the mistake is gone. These parents should be nowhere near their kids while practicing is taking place. They should probably keep away from their kids while homework is happening too.

2) Parents who actively reject your practice advice, and who, for example, are telling their kids to practice fast, when you need them to practice slowly. These parents often have a musical background of their own, and their brand of "help" is particularly destructive. If your values really collide with theirs, they should handle it by finding a compatible teacher, not by overruling your calls.

3) Parents who have decided that the best way to get their child to practice is to nag them until they are unconscious, perhaps so they can drag them into the practice room. While reminders are certainly important, you don't want nagging like this, and you certainly don't want the nagger following their victim into the practice room to "help" them by trying to nag their mistakes away too. This approach can make the entire institution of music lessons smell bad to the student, and they are probably better off not practicing at all.

4) Parents who are helping, but in a half-hearted, eye-on-the-clock fashion. Not only do music students learn from such parents that near enough is good enough (so that the parent can get on with whatever it is that they'd rather be doing), they can also sense the part of their parents that is not interested in what's going on. It's hard to be excited about practicing when your greatest role models approach it with all the enthusiasm of a trip to the dentist.

5) Parents who are having other difficulties in the relationship with the student. If exchanges between (usually teenage) student and parent are becoming heated and are often ending in tears, then you don't want practicing to be caught in that crossfire. In the "Us versus Them" world that can sometimes dominate teenagers' world view, you don't want practicing—and music lessons in general—being viewed as part of the Establishment, and therefore to be resisted. Like most teenagers, if I was in the process of putting on a red shirt, and I heard my mother call out "You should put on your red shirt before we go out today", I would have taken it *off*. I'm still not sure why. I certainly would not have been particularly interested in her views as to whether or not my new etude was gradually speeding up as I play.

Tips for dealing with this problem

• This can be a tough one to deal with, as there are not many parents who are prepared to admit that their particular brand of "help" actually hinders. Not only that, even the most negative of parents will usually have their child's best interests at heart, and will not take too kindly to an outsider to the family telling them how to handle their own kids.

The easiest way to deal with the potential conflict is to sidestep it completely.

If you are worried about an antagonistic reaction from the parents, you don't even need to flag the issue as a problem in the first place. Instead *bill it as an opportunity and a positive*—tell the parents that the past few lessons have been so good that student has been showing signs of being ready to work *independently* at home! That you feel the student's concentration and application are such that you want to try a fortnight with them getting NO help at home, just to see if they can cope. Of course, this will be difficult without all the excellent help that the parents usually give, but let's just see if it's possible...

And then give the appropriate positive feedback at the end of trial to ensure the practice continues. (If you were right about parental interference being the problem, you won't have to make up this positive feedback!)

• If the parents are a little more amenable to suggestions, you might want to work with them to try to change some of the existing practice models, rather than removing the parent's presence from the process entirely. If you have several students who are in the same position, it might be worth scheduling an information evening for parents who need to help their kids with practice. Not only can this help modify their approach to being a practice-helper, they will also appreciate the time and professionalism shown for you to put on such an evening in the first place. A practice-saver and PR coup all at the same time.

4.6 A week with wings

Most music teachers are painfully aware of how fast seven days can go by. What they sometimes forget is that the same seven days can hurtle by for students and their families too.

The students leave the lesson on Wednesday, full of good intentions. And then, quite suddenly, it's Wednesday again. They're still full of good intentions, and in fact have been all week. But they are nevertheless reduced to having to do a panic practice session half an hour before the lesson, and come in heads bowed, hoping the teacher does not remember everything they were supposed to have completed.

It's not really the student's fault. Kids today are very busy—as well as music lessons, they probably have sport, another musical instrument, chess clubs, martial arts, bands, choirs, after-school care…some of the older ones may even have a job of some sort. And that's not allowing for homework, family life or Nintendo.

Tips for dealing with this problem

Here's what you need to remember:

Anything that is not actually scheduled may not actually happen.

Not because the student is lazy, but because their waking hours will quite easily be filled without that precaution. So if you want practicing to form part of their day, you have to *make* it part of their day.

Spend half of one lesson really getting to understand the student's weekly commitments. And then create a time each day that belongs to practicing. Make sure they understand exactly when this time is, and that it cannot be exchanged for anything else. Even if the child suddenly gets a lot of homework, their music practice time is off limits to anything except practicing.

Their part of the bargain is to stick to the timetable. Your part of the bargain is that if they agree to stick to it, you'll give them one day in the week off. It's worth it.

It's the same reason that people are much more likely to exercise regularly if they have a gym class that starts at a specific regular time, than if they can just turn up whenever.

The problem is that "whenever" can always be tomorrow. You just need to cement it as a non-negotiable part of today.

4.7 Impossible workload

The easiest way to have a student abandoning all thoughts of practice is for them to feel that the task for the week ahead is impossible. If working hard this week still won't help them be ready for their next lesson, then the student could achieve the same outcome—and have more fun with their time—by not practicing at all.

Again, it goes back to a basic cost-benefit analysis. The perceived benefit for practicing is simply not there, while the cost is only too evident. While the student's analysis looks like that, you're really going to have to be at your persuasive best to get them to do any practice at all.

This problem doesn't just arise when you genuinely set too much work—all that has to happen is for the student to *believe* that it's too much work. As soon as that feeling of being overwhelmed kicks in, many students will react by avoiding the practice altogether. However noble the sentiments surrounding "to try and fail is better than not to have tried at all", when your free time is on the line, the idea of trying and failing doesn't sound too attractive.

It's a common problem, but it's not hard to fix.

Tips for dealing with this problem

• Independently of how much work there actually is, be careful not to present the work for the week as a single enormous goal. Even if there is a lot to get through, list it as a series of smaller, achievable stepping stones. So you wouldn't ask your student to learn the first two pages of a new piece, but you may well set four mini-goals of half a page each. Or if they need it, eight micro-mini-goals of a quarter of a page each.

The outcome is the same, but bite-sized instructions (even if there are more of them) will sound more achievable to nervous students.

• Your choice of language in setting tasks can set assumptions about the likelihood of success in completing that task. Use "when", not "if". So you wouldn't tell a student *"If you can learn both pages this week, we'll be in a good position to speed it up next lesson"*—instead, you'd tell them *"When you come back next lesson with both pages learned, we'll be in great shape to speed them up"*.

Using "if" not only gives the student an out from having to do it, it also tells them that a part of you is picturing the possibility that they won't get through all of this…at which point, they have to wonder why. It's a short step from there to think that perhaps your "if" is a hesitation reflecting the possibility that the job *might be too hard*. Don't allow for such possibilities, and the implied can-do assumptions that flow are contagious.

• Once the work for the week has been presented as a series of smaller tasks, ensure that some of those early tasks are actually very easy to complete—so that they can get on the scoreboard quickly. Nothing will encourage them to do more practice more effectively than the feeling that the practice they have already done is producing results.

• Sometimes mini-goals that sound small are actually harder to complete than you might think. To be certain that you are not genuinely setting an impossible workload, have the student attempt one of the tasks *in front of you* at the lesson. This will give you feedback on how long the task might take them, together with how difficult they might find it. If they are struggling with the sample task at the lesson, you can count on things being much, much harder for them at home.

4.8 Not clear on what they are hoping to achieve

If the only reason students practice is because they know they are *supposed* to, sooner or later they won't. In such a scenario, the principal reward has simply become avoiding punishment, and you'll quickly discover what professional motivators around the world already know—motivating through fear of consequences produces compliance, but never enthusiasm. If you want someone to be excited about what they're doing, there has to be a positive consequence for doing it, and an even better reward for doing it well.

Despite the need for rewards, there are no cash bonuses or free gifts for students who practice. Instead, one of the most powerful rewards is something that money could never buy—the simple feeling of having made progress. Because music lessons depend on regular progress, evidence of improvement and achievement are vital feedback for any student, and are central to them feeling good about what they are doing. If you want to make a student smile, make a fuss over something they can do this week that they *couldn't* do last week—the twin positives of having made the breakthrough in the first place, and then having your teacher praise you for it are powerful motivators for more work.

It's not enough, however, for these breakthroughs to be evident only with the benefit of hindsight—there has to be the promise of progress *before* the activity begins. A teaser. Remember, you want the student *heading into* the practice week with enthusiasm, not simply looking back on it with affection. The student has to believe *in advance* that if they practice intelligently this week, improvements will appear in their playing, and they'll need to know which ones. That they'll be able to play the new Sonatina from memory. They'll have learned four brand new scales. They will have doubled the speed of their etude. They will have mastered that tricky bowing in the passage on page 4.

Students who are clear on their goals like this are much more likely to chase them.

The flip side is that if you have a student who is at all muddled about what they are aiming to achieve this week, then they probably won't be practicing too hard in the first place. Not because they're suddenly bad students, but because the carrot has been taken from the end of their stick. With the promise of good things coming from their practice now missing, the only reason they have left for practicing is appeasement, and that won't be good enough to have them sacrificing their free time to serenade their music stands.

As the teacher you're in a great position though—each week you have the opportunity to clearly define a fresh set of benefits for your student if they practice. You can tell your students "If you work intelligently this week, here are five things you'll be able to do by next lesson that you currently cannot do now.", and then you describe them in detail. Without any other rewards on offer at all, the student will now be able to see something that is essential to motivation—that their practicing makes a *difference*.

4.9 Discovering that practice doesn't work...

This is one of the deadliest of all the practice obstacles, and to make matters worse, as teachers, we often contribute directly to the unfolding disaster. Here's how it works.

The student comes into the lesson smiling and confident, effervescing about what a great week of practice they had. But despite the air of optimism, within a few measures it becomes clear that nothing has changed since last lesson. There are still flats where sharps should go, they're holding notes through rests, misreading rhythms, making up fingering, ignoring dynamics...the works. Hearing the disaster, we invite the student to try it one more time (maybe they just needed to warm up).

Nope. And it's usually shortly after that *second* collapse that we launch into the lecture about how they really should turn up to lessons prepared. In fact, based on the available evidence, it's hard to imagine that they have done any work at all.

It's when the tears start, and the student protests that they did practice and that it didn't sound like this at home, that the truth dawns. They *had* worked hard this week. It's just that *how* they worked didn't *work*.

Nothing is more demotivating than learning that your efforts have been in vain. If students endure a few weeks in a row where their practicing simply does not deliver for them, none of us should be surprised if they start to grow suspicious of practicing itself. In other words, if you cannot help that student practice more effectively, it won't be long before they don't practice at all—and it has nothing to do with them being a lazy student at heart.

It's similar to people who are dieting. If they lose faith in the ability of the diet to deliver the results they are hoping for, the diet is doomed—the sacrifice suddenly seems pointless. Once confidence has been lost in the process, the process will be abandoned.

In this way, a student with ineffective practice techniques presents a grave emergency. It's not just that if you cannot help them practice better, they'll stop practicing. *If you cannot help them practice better, you'll eventually lose them.*

The exciting thing though is that the reverse is also true.

If you can empower a student by teaching them how to practice more effectively than ever before, teaching them how to get more done in one practice session than they used to achieve a dozen, then practicing is going to look like a much more attractive proposition. Students who were previously not practicing will start to, and students who used to do a little are more likely to do a lot—not because you have found some magic words, but simply because they now can see how the time spent will help them improve.

The next part of the book is dedicated to helping you achieve exactly that, helping your students find exactly the right practice tool for the job at hand, so that they can get the job done quickly and well, and get on with things that are more fun.

Using the Right Tools for the Right Job

"If the axe is not sharp, it doesn't matter how hard the wood is."

Chinese proverb.

The Practice Revolution: Chapter 5
- The *Body Designers* lesson
- Three steps to choosing the right tools

5. Using the Right Tools

5.1 The *Body Designers* lesson

Let's imagine a career change for a moment. Instead of being a music teacher, you now run your very own gym. Truly. It's called "Body Designers", and it's doing very nicely.

Music stands, metronomes and treble clefs have been replaced with treadmills, weight benches and sports drinks. Your clientele is also a little different, but at its core, things haven't changed that much since your music teaching days. People are coming through your doors trying to get better at something, and you're going to show them how.

Some of your clients will want to supplement their gym sessions by working out at home a little too—after all, it was you who told them that they can *accelerate* the impact their exercise is having if they do more of it. So they'll come to you with the question "What should I do this week?".

Until you know a little more about their goals, you cannot answer that question. In fact, you *shouldn't* answer the question—the wrong type of exercise might not just be a waste of time, it might actually be harmful for them. Unfortunately, when you ask most clients what they are hoping to achieve from their exercise, the answer you get is usually fluffy and vague:

"To get fit?"

At which point you'll need to push them for some more specific information. There are literally hundreds of different at-home exercise programs you could recommend, but they need to be chosen carefully according to their specific needs. Once they have been forced to think about their reply a little more, you'll get some information you can work with. The goals you'll hear will be as varied as the clients themselves:

"To get rid of my 'spare tyre' "
"To help rehabilitate from my recent heart attack"
"To improve my upper body strength"

"It's a reclaim-my-body-shape-after-childbirth thing"
"To increase my aerobic fitness levels"
"Because I love the post-exercise buzz"
"To meet people at the gym"
"To set an example for my kids"
"So I can fit into that dress I want in time for my sister's wedding"
"To prepare for my first ever marathon in February next year"
"To develop leg strength and flexibility, to supplement my martial arts training"
"It's a quality time thing with my wife"

Now as the gym owner, you have to be careful. You can't give out a one-size-fits-all solution, because obviously the needs of your heart attack recovery patron will be very different from those of the person preparing for the marathon. In fact each of the scenarios above have unique solutions. But if the answer you got was never any more precise than "To get fit", then they can't blame you if the program you design for them doesn't really produce the results they were actually hoping for.

So what does this have to do with practicing?

The parallels are not too subtle. Each week, your music students will ask "So how should I practice this week?" (and you should be telling them even if they don't ask!). It's tempting to leap in with a solution for them, but until you know exactly what the goals are for this week, you shouldn't even think about designing the program.

Why? Because practice techniques are not one-size-fits-all any more than exercise programs are. There is a huge variety of different practice techniques, each designed for a specific job. And like any other tool, if you use them for purposes other than those for which they were intended, the work becomes inefficient at best, and a total calamity at worst.

Picture your student out in the garden, with instructions to dig half a dozen holes to plant trees in. That's not such a bad job if the tool they are given is a shovel. It's a whole lot more difficult if the tool given is a spoon.

And if the tool given was a toothbrush, or a paperclip, then the job may not be possible at all.

This book will provide dozens of different practice tools. Some will be perfect for speeding pieces up. Others are designed specifically for building confidence in the few days immediately before a performance. But the speeding-up tools won't help with confidence building before performance, nor will the vice-versa arrangement work. You'll end up with a student who becomes disillusioned with practice—they spent the time, but it didn't work.

Nobody could blame such a student for not wanting to practice in the future.

As the teacher, *your role is to match tools to the task*. Your student is counting on you, and if you get it wrong, you can turn their practice into a complete waste of time. On the other hand, if you find the perfect tool, they'll get more done in ten minutes than they might have otherwise in an hour.

In other words, if you are able to advise your student well about which practice tool to use—and they follow your advice—they will need to do *less practice* to be ready for next lesson than otherwise would have been the case.

I don't think there is a student on the planet who would not be interested in that.

5.2 Three steps to choosing the right tools

With the idea of matching tools to tasks in mind, let's just review the practice instruction-giving process so far. This process is probably not enormously different from what you do currently, but it does contain a couple of important extra steps.

First of all, you need to **define the goal** for the student for the week ahead—work out exactly what they should be able to do by next lesson that they cannot do now. Perhaps it's to be able to play through the next page of their piece without the gaps that currently plague it. Or to have memorized their etude. Or to have got on top of that tricky bit on page fourteen.

This step is the part that teachers have traditionally got right—we usually tell our students what their practice this week should *produce*. This doesn't tell students how to assess their progress, nor does it give any information about *how* to practice, but it does ensure that their eyes are on the goalposts.

To help your student pursue the goal with greater enthusiasm, you could also help them feel as though it was their idea—give them some **ownership** over the plan.

Having clearly defined the goal, you then need to turn that goal into a **quantifiable challenge**, so that the student has some objective way of determining when they have completed it. For example, to prove they have "got on top" of that tricky bit on page fourteen they might have to play it through three times in a row with a metronome at 120 bpm—with no mistakes. Because they can self-administer such tests at any time, they will always know whether they are ready for their next lesson or not, rather than discovering at the lesson itself that their version of "ready" was not quite as rigorous as yours.

This means that so far, the student has a clear understanding of two things:

1) Here's what I am supposed to have done by next lesson
2) Here's a way I can measure whether I've done it or not

Remember, step 2 is not a practice method. It doesn't help the student *achieve* their weekly goal—it simply measures whether or not that goal has been reached yet. A useful analogy is to regard it as being the testing stick that you use to work out whether a cake is properly cooked or not. While that stick is an essential tool to ensure that you don't declare a cake ready before it actually is, it doesn't help at all in getting the cake ready in the first place. And if the student does not pass their test for the goal, it's back to the practice room, just as surely as the cake would go back into the oven. After they've done some more work on the section, they can retest.

All of this means that there's one important piece of information the student still needs—and it's the instruction that teachers often forget to give:

3) Here's exactly HOW I'm supposed to practice to reach my goal in the first place.

Your student won't just want any old method of practice. They want the practice technique that is BEST suited to reaching their goal quickly. After all, it's their time we're talking about, and there's no point in trying to work towards a memorization goal with a practice technique designed to make semiquavers more even.

In the next section of the book, each of the common practice goals is given its own chapter, and then each chapter is filled with practice techniques that specifically target that goal. So if the goal for a student is to prepare for an imminent performance, look up the chapter on "Preparing for Performance"

In the course of your own teaching, you'll discover some goals that aren't covered in this list. You'll also discover plenty of effective practice techniques of your own. That's fine—although the list provides a huge range of practice techniques, the main point is the *structure*. You'll eventually build your own collection of practice techniques, together with your own conclusions as to which types of practice goals each practice type is designed to help with.

As long as you are recommending the right tool for the right problem, it doesn't really matter where you got your own list from. This book is just an enormous head start.

NOTE: One easy way to give your students ready access to hundreds of new practice options is to ask their parents to get the **student edition** of this book. *Practiceopedia* is a fully illustrated 376 page color guide to practicing, and is an A-Z of practice techniques, tricks, tips and traps that has been written especially for students and parents.

They can look up whatever is bugging them in the index—say "Speeding pieces up", and they'll be shown to dozens of different ideas to try. Each entry is then cross referenced to other related techniques...you'll recognize some of those techniques from this book, but many were put together especially for *Practiceopedia*.

Previews and the book itself are available from **www.practiceopedia.com**

Learning the New Piece

"He had the deed half done, who has made a beginning"

Horace, from the Epistles

The Practice Revolution: Chapter 6

• Defining the task • Reframing • The Level System • Nightmares First • The Tabletop Challenge • The Power of Recordings • Scouting • Shooting the Movie •

6. Learning the New Piece

6.1 Defining the task

The writer's terror of blank sheets of paper is nothing beside the music student's fear of pages that are full. For many students, having to learn a new piece is the single most daunting step in the practice process—the symbols are abstract, the conversion is painstaking, and progress is not guaranteed. As a result, many of them will actively avoid tasks like this altogether, either by practicing pieces they already know, or by simply not practicing at all. Either way, that new piece is not going to get learned.

The problem is that if the student falls at this first hurdle, the race is over before the student has any concept of how well they actually could have run. As teachers, we are entirely dependent on the student having a certain level of familiarity with any piece before we can give them any detailed help with it—meaning that if they turn up to the lesson without having looked at their new piece at all, we'll feel inclined to send them straight home again.

Tempting though it is to apply the label, it's not always that the students are simply lazy. Instead, it's often that our students just didn't have a clue where to start when they tried to tackle their new piece by themselves.

To be fair, it's not as though we're silly enough to send them home with no help whatsoever. In fact we'll usually give them a guided tour of the piece, and perhaps even play it for them. But that so often is the essence of the problem— the introduction we give is to the *piece itself*, not the *process* for learning it. Tasks as complicated as learning new pieces should come with instructions, and it's time that we started giving some.

This chapter exists to help you provide your students with a plan for tackling new pieces—systems they can use and reuse with *any* new piece, removing the fear from the process, and replacing it with a feeling of control. Students don't need to worry about the enormity of the task of learning the entire work, or fret about how they will ever assimilate all those accidentals on page three. Instead of such worries, all they need to do is ask themselves a simple question:

What is the next step in the process?

These processes are not designed to produce performance-ready works, subtleties of interpretation or solutions to technical problems, but will quickly provide a level of knowledge and fluency in a new piece, so that you can spend less time coaching notes, and more time working on issues that genuinely need the help.

6.2 Reframing

Before we look too hard at processes for learning new pieces, there's a vital piece of groundwork that you need to lay before a student starts the whole adventure.

Sometimes the process of learning new pieces is sabotaged before it begins, simply because the student allows a spirit of doom to hang over the whole exercise. That bit's HARD, because it has too many sharps. And that bit's TRICKY, because I can't figure out the rhythm straight away. And that bit's DIFFICULT because those notes are higher than I'm comfortable with. This bit over here is a NIGHTMARE, because there are lots of chords to learn, and I hate learning chords.

Hard. Tricky. Difficult. Nightmare. In so far as they refer to those specific passages, these assessments may even have a grain of truth. But the problem is that such words tend to persist in the student's mind long after the reasons for thinking such thoughts have been forgotten, creating an atmosphere of defeat which will also infect even the easiest passages in the piece. The failure here has not been one of motivation or practice habits—it's in the fact that the student was allowed to form adhesive and negative preconceptions about the task ahead.

I'm not going to suggest the student tries to negate the power of preconceptions. Far from it—we're going to be using preconceptions as one of their biggest allies. It's just that they need a *different* set of preconceptions, and you're going to need to spend a little time helping them build them. Like any coach, it's worth your while talking down how big and strong this week's opponents really are, while talking up the attributes of the player in front of you.

So what if, instead of "hard", "tricky", "difficult" and "nightmare", the student's assumptions were "easy", "effortless", "obvious" and "no problem"? It goes to the heart of one of the most valuable pieces of advice you can give any student:

Whether you think you can, or you think you can't, you're right.

Before the student does anything at all with their new piece, we have to reframe the whole thing so that they are filled both with self-belief, and with faith in the achievability of the task in front of them.

6.2.1 *Proving* that the piece is easy

It's not going to be enough for you to simply to put on an air-hostess smile and encourage your students to "think of the piece as being easy!". If students hear sentiments like that, they will feel that you're just trying to pour sugar into medicine, and will suddenly wonder what it is about the piece that needed sugar like that in the first place. For the student to truly regard the new piece as being approachable, they need to see genuine evidence that it actually is. Your first task is to help the student become aware of this evidence *before* they start their new piece, so that they discover that they are learning a piece that is riddled with Easy Bits.

The good news is that *all* pieces are riddled with Easy Bits, no matter how tough they may appear at first glance—students just need to know what to look for. You'll have plenty of suggestions of your own, but some of the most common elements to look out for are listed on the next few pages:

Repeating section discounts

Students really get value for money with these. They only learn one measure of music, but might immediately be able to play twelve measures as a result, because the section repeats. By being aware of these, students might slash what seemed to be a four page job to a two-and-a-half page exercise.

You can also include in this category sections that are *almost* repeats—recapitulations, repeating rhythms, sequences, motifs—anything that they can learn once now, and reapply later.

Go through the piece, find all examples of this, and highlight them for the student.

Key signature delights

Students can sometimes be so transfixed by the difficulties in the piece as a whole that they might be staring at their favorite key signature and not even notice. Help them to notice—it's a small tick, but it's the combined weight of small ticks that is going to win this battle.

Go through the piece, find all examples of this, and highlight them for the student.

Pattern Magic

Scales, arpeggios, chromatics—passages like these won't require "learning" once they have been spotted (assuming the student has a reasonable command of their technical work). Every one of these features that the student uncovers is one passage less that they have to worry about.

Go through the piece, find all examples of this, and highlight them for the student.

I've seen that before

This allows students to call on their experience with pieces that they have already mastered, by finding sections in their new piece that remind them of pieces that they have already played (and coped with!) It's hard to be quite so afraid of an enemy that you have already defeated once.

Go through the piece, find all examples of this, and highlight them for the student.

Playing to my strengths

Every student will have specific technical challenges that they cope with particularly well—it might be playing staccato, holding long notes without running out of breath, extended passages of *piano*, jumps or trills. Point out such sections, and let them know how much you are looking forward to them showing off their best in a passage that was obviously designed just for them.

Go through the piece, find all examples of this, and highlight them for the student.

Nothing Much Happening

Some sections of the piece will look easy…because they *are* actually easy. If there are eight consecutive bars with nothing but whole notes, the student can add that to their growing list of Reasons This Piece is Not So Tough After All.

Go through the piece, find all examples of this, and highlight them for the student.

Quarter notes in disguise

Even if the notes themselves are looking dangerous, if they are meant to be delivered as a steady stream of triplets, then there's actually one less thing to worry about hidden in here. No matter how fast the notes are actually intended to go, if the passage consists of the same note *value* being repeated over and over, it's exactly the same is if the student had to learn the passage using quarter notes. This is a great technique for disarming a lot of etudes (many of which tend to be endless streams of sixteenth notes!), and for helping pages not look so "black" to the student.

Go through the piece, find all examples of this, and highlight them for the student.

Student's own quirky preferences

Not all of the things that strike students as easy will make sense to you, but you should run with them anyway. Some students might not like using their fourth finger, so show them the passages that don't require any use of fourth finger whatsoever. Others love to play loud, and are happier still if they can play even louder. Twelve bars of ff might not appeal to you, but if it rings your student's bell, list it as one of the Great Things about this new piece.

Go through the piece, find all examples of this, and highlight them for the student.

And you add your own

Because you know your students better than anyone, you'll have your own list of elements that the students will regard as easy - even if the student may not immediately have spotted those elements for themselves.

Go through the piece, find all examples of this, and highlight them for the student.

Here's the exciting thing though:

By the time you have gone through and highlighted each instance of each of these elements, *there really won't be much of the piece that is not touched by at least one of them.* Your pencil marks highlighting Easy Bits will be everywhere, and the student now has reasons for regarding just about every measure in the piece as being easy to learn in some way.

This reframing technique won't learn the piece for them. But it does put them in exactly the right state of mind to make the most of the techniques we'll look at next.

6.3 The Level System

The Level system converts the otherwise monolithic task of learning a new piece into dozens of small and friendly steps. When your student practices using this method, instead of fretting about the size of the job, or dithering about what to do next, they simply need to ask themselves three questions:

1) Which step in the process am I up to?

2) How will I know when I have completed this step?

3) What step comes after this one?

The Level System answers these questions for them, laying out the whole practice process like a blueprint. They don't need to work out a plan of attack—it's all been done in advance. That way they can spend less time worrying about whether they are doing the right thing, and more time practicing. They just need to take one small step at a time, and they'll get to their target.

6.3.1 Preparing for The Level System—Divide and Conquer

Splitting up a large task into small stages is not just smoke and mirrors—it's an essential step for anyone with a big job to complete. Before the Level system can begin, the student needs to forget about targeting the piece as a whole, and instead divide it up into sections. *Small* sections.

To help the student regard these sections as unique and complete entities in their own right (and so you can easily refer to them in the future), they should give each section a name. So their new Minuet, which started life as one big two-page task, might now have been transformed into *eight* short pieces:

Location of the section	Section Label
Page 1, Lines 1-2	"Elephant"
Page 1, Lines 3-4	"Monkey"
Page1, Lines 5-6	"Leopard"
Page 1, Lines 7-8	"Kangaroo"
Page 2, Lines 1-2	"Swordfish"
Page 2, Lines 3-4	"Hyena"
Page 2, Lines 5-6	"Ostrich"
Page 2, Lines 7-8	"Deer"

One of the first questions you will be asked is "how big should the sections be?". The answer depends on what is going to give your student the greatest encouragement:

• If they create *lots of tiny sections*, as you'll see shortly, each step will be easier to complete, but there will be more of them to get through.

• If they create *fewer but longer sections*, then there won't be quite so many steps, but they'll therefore need to be ready for less frequent and tougher-to-get milestones.

If in doubt, tell them to err on the side of keeping the sections small—the two lines per section given in the illustration above is often about right. Remember, the name of this game is regular and frequent triumphs.

Once the piece has been divided up, and those sections labeled, it's time to introduce your students to the extra ingredient that really makes this process shine. It's time to meet the Levels that give this system its name.

6.3.2 Meet the Levels

The "Levels" provide a simple way for students to *measure progress* as they learn each of the sections that they have now created. Traditionally there have only been two possible states for a new passage—the section is either "Learned" or "Not Learned yet". Which to the student can sound a lot like "Passed" or "Failed!".

The Level System allows you to define *many* more specific degrees of readiness, so that students can progress from "No idea" to "fluent" in a series of measurable and discrete steps.

In other words, instead of expecting your students to leap the river, the Level system provides stepping stones. This means that even if they are not there yet, they feel like they are at least *somewhere.* And they can also see how they are a couple of steps further on than last time they checked.

Because there are so many more steps involved, the student is given more regular feedback of having reached a milestone, and is never too far away from their next one—both crucial elements in keeping them motivated. Students can easily see their own progress for themselves as they work their way up the Levels ladder.

Levels are given numbers, to reflect the fact that they represent progressive degrees of competence. Once a section has attained that Level 1 proficiency, the student works towards taking it to Level 2, and there are usually somewhere between six and ten levels for any new section of a piece. So in this way, Levels not only allow the student to see how they are progressing—*they also provide a clear structure for what to work on next.*

So what are all these levels? That's the beauty of the system—as the teacher, you can actually define your own, both to suit the student, and to reflect your own preferences in working with new repertoire. Each level needs to demand a greater degree of proficiency than the level before, and the first level should always be easy to attain, but aside from those cautions, the actual content of your Levels is up to you.

Just to help you picture some possibilities, I've outlined a couple of sample Level sets on the next two pages. Yours may well end up differing considerably, but notice how easy the first step is, and the gradual ramp up in requirements as the student heads towards the top levels.

Sample Level Set 1:

Level Number	Requirement for the section to attain this level
1	Can *follow along the score* while listening to the recording without getting lost
2	Can *tap through the rhythm* of the section while counting out loud.
3	Can *play through the notes* slowly with no errors. Gaps are allowed while the student checks ahead for the next note.
4	Can play through slowly while *counting out loud*
5	As for level 3, but *with a metronome going*, thus not allowing the student to stop and think if they get stuck.
6	Can *play through from memory*—can stop and think if need be.
7	Can play through from *memory with the metronome* going
8	Can play through with the metronome, from memory, at *three-quarters of the recommended tempo*

So if at the lesson, the student tells you that *Elephant is up to Level 4*, then you know they can play those two lines through slowly while they count out loud. You also know that they have also completed the first three levels too (otherwise they wouldn't have qualified to be tackling Level 4 in the first place!)

Once they have demonstrated Level 4 for you, you can then encourage them to make things slightly harder by tackling level 5, and introducing a metronome into the picture. And once that's done, Level 6 only looks a fraction more difficult...and so on.

In this way, the entire section slides gradually from "No idea" through to a state in which they can play through with a metronome, from memory, at three-quarters of the recommended tempo - which would be thoroughly well enough learned for you to be able to work with it at the next lesson.

With 8 different sections of the piece, and 8 levels to get through, the student now has split the single daunting job of learning the piece into 64 little and easily attainable jobs. That's 64 little pats on the back they get along the

way, and each new Level only feels a fraction more difficult than the one before
- and therefore always within reach.

An alternative set of levels, for a piano student this time:

Sample Level Set 2:

Level Number	Requirement for the section to attain this level
1	Can play through the left hand slowly
2	Can play through the right hand slowly
3	Can play through the left hand from memory
4	Can play through the right hand from memory
5	Can play through the left hand with a metronome
6	Can play through the right hand with a metronome
7	Can play through both hands together slowly
8	Can play through both hands together from memory
9	Can play through both hands together with a metronome

The most important benefit of the Level system is that the student starts to
feel measurable progress *even when the section is almost brand new.* They don't
have to wait until they've "learned it" (whatever that means) until the first pat
on the back arrives. For the piano student using the first set of Levels outlined
above, all they would have to do to take a section to Level 1 is to play it very
slowly through once with the Left Hand alone—giving them a new Level, and
the taste of success that comes with it, almost straight away.

It's a very short step from there to have them looking hungrily at Level
2…and so on.

6.3.3 Recording the Completed Levels

Despite the highly organized framework of the Level System, students actually have a great deal of freedom as to the order of proceedings. While they do have to tackle the Levels themselves in order (so they can't do Level 8 in a section before they have done Level 7 in the same section), they have complete discretion when choosing which *section* they will work on.

The only rule is that once they have completed a Level, the next time they choose to practice that section, they need to be working on attaining the *next* level. So once they've finished Level 1 for "Alligator", the next time they are practicing "Alligator", they are attempting Level 2, ensuring that they are always moving forwards. There's no provision for Shiny Object Polishing in the Level System. (See Practice Flaws chapter).

To help them keep track of where they are up to, as they complete a new

Level for a section, they should *record the number of the Level next to the section name*—partly so they know where to start from next time, but also so that you can see at the next lesson how things have progressed:

Students should expect to attain several new levels in each practice session. If they can't, then it's usually a sign that the sections were too long in the first place.

6.3.4 The Level System at the Lesson

Instead of asking "So how did you go with your new piece this week?" and hearing vague and useless replies such as "Really well" or "Not so good" or "Yeah, it was ok I guess", your student can tell you exactly how many new Levels they prepared.

You will also be able to see at a glance how much progress they have made, together with any trouble spots, simply by checking the Level numbers that have been recorded next to each section. If everything is at Level 8, except for one section in the middle that's only on Level 3, then the agenda for the lesson pretty much sets itself.

6.4 Nightmares first

The Level System provides enormous freedom as to where to start in the piece - but that doesn't mean that the decision for what to work on next should be arbitrary. There are some important tactical considerations that can make a tremendous difference to the effectiveness of the whole process.

Some students begin the process of learning their new piece well enough, only to run out of steam as they hit the first difficult sections in the piece. Faced with the feeling that the more they do, the harder things are getting, they choose not to go any further.

There's nothing you can do to eliminate those difficult sections from the piece, but you can change the psychology of the process by converting the perceived *uphill battle* into a d*ownhill coast.*

When your student first meets the piece, have them divide the piece up into sections exactly as they would if they were beginning the Level System. Then have them *rank* those sections in order from scariest to least scary. The only science they need to apply to this process is their own gut instincts, because in the end, that's what would have counted anyway. So if they think a section is scary simply because it has a lot of flats in it, so be it. Up to the top of the list it goes.

When they actually start learning the piece, instead of simply starting at the beginning of the piece, tell them to start with the section at the top of that "scary" list—with the promise that once they take care of that section, everything will seem easier by comparison afterwards. In fact, by working their way steadily down the list, the more they do, the easier things get.

It's going to be much less likely that the student will get the "mid-piece-blues" and get stuck, when all that remains are sections that are *easier* than the one they have already successfully completed.

6.4.1 ...or for some students, in reverse

The psychological shift in Nightmares First is not going to work for all students, and may not be appropriate for all pieces. If you have a student who tends to assume that things are impossible at the first sign of resistance, it can sometimes be better to use the Nightmares list in *reverse*, to help them sneak up on the difficulties contained in the toughest section.

The logic is that once they have successfully completed the first section (which this time would be the easiest section), you can point out to them that the next section is only a fraction more difficult than the one they have just shown they can do so well. In other words, they are learning to cope by *gradually* raising the bar, and in this way sneak up on the difficulties contained in the toughest section.

It also means that by the time they are confronting that final tough section of the piece, they already have most of the piece behind them, and the end is in plain view. When they are this close to the finish line, it's much easier to encourage them to give it their all for a final push.

6.5 Tabletop Challenge

This technique is not intended to be an alternative to the level system so much as a supplementary method of processing new notes.

You hear stories from time to time about concert artists who can take the score for a new concerto on a plane with them, read it through like a book, and then be able to play the work once they land. Well, maybe. I'm not sure whether such stories are designed to make them look good, or the rest of us feel bad, but they do provide the basis for alternative models for learning new pieces.

Just like our apocryphal aviating concert artist, when a student practices using the Tabletop Challenge, they are practicing *without* using their instrument. All they have to work with is the score itself. They don't need to be an international concert artist with a reputation for a prodigious memory to do this—any student can use the tabletop challenge, *if the section they are working on is small enough.* In this way, it makes the perfect partner for the Level System approach.

To kick things off, the student might begin simply by looking at the first two measures. They start by analyzing the pitches of the notes, asking themselves dozens of questions, like a toddler wanting to know how something works. Do the notes head up, down, or stay the same? What accidentals come into play? Do the notes move by step or jump, and if by jump, then how big are those jumps? Is there a pattern of any sort? Can I hear the notes in my head? What fingering would I use for those notes? Where are the rests? How long are the rests? What dynamics are indicated? What are the articulation markings?

Once such questions have been asked and answered, then the student needs to go through the motions of "playing" the section on an imaginary instrument. They hold their imaginary violin, or play their imaginary piano, placing their fingers where they should go to play the notes themselves. The idea is that if someone were to substitute a *real* violin, then the finger movements they have been rehearsing with the left hand, together with the imaginary bowing they were rehearsing with their right, would result in the passage actually being played.

The final step in the process is the moment of truth. Closing the score, they go and get their instrument, and try to play the passage *from memory.* They then open the score, play it through slowly once more, and compare the two performances. If there are any discrepancies, then they put their instrument away, and return to the tabletop with the score to gain a more accurate understanding of the passage. And if there weren't, then they can congratulate themselves—the section has graduated, and they can move on to another short passage.

It's not always practical to learn an entire piece in this fashion, and this technique is really designed to be used in conjunction with more hands-on methods, such as the Level System. The analogy I would use is that if the Level System is the concrete for the foundations of a new piece, then the TableTop method is the steel that reinforces the concrete. The foundations could never be *entirely* steel, but the very presence of the steel will strengthen the entire structure.

6.6 The power of recordings

It's something that Suzuki teachers have understood for decades, and that the rest of us might well learn from:

Knowing thoroughly what your new piece *sounds* like makes it much easier to learn.

Some teachers are reluctant to involve recordings in the learning process because they fear that their students will never learn to read, or will be unduly influenced by the interpretation on the disc. The important thing to understand at the outset is that the aim is for the recording simply to be *part of the team—* it's not designed to replace the score, any more than it's designed to replace your own advice. No matter how developed your student's aural skills, they will still need to use the music to absorb details of dynamics, articulation, rests, pedaling, fingering, position shifts and phrasing.

But that having been said, a recording is such a powerful asset that forbidding your students from using them simply handicaps the learning process for them.

Not only that, if you remove recordings from the loop, then reading for students will forever be primarily an abstract visual exercise. It's not. It's a means of disseminating information, *and the information itself is the point.* If I wanted my student to learn a new piece, and I knew that putting the score under their pillow at night would help them learn that piece, I'd tell them to put the score under their pillow. Just as if I knew for a fact that drinking orange juice helps them learn pieces faster, I'd have a citrus squeezer in my studio.

In the same way, because I know that using a recording can help them learn the piece faster, I think CDs make great birthday presents for my students.

The point is, *whatever helps, they should use.* This is not some history exam that they are cheating on. We're trying to make the process simple and productive for them—not telling them that because the cure may have side effects, the entire process has to remain crippled in some way.

Before we take a look at how your student can use recordings in the practice room, it's worth understanding just what all the fuss is about.

6.6.1 How recordings can transform your students' practice

1) First and foremost, recordings help students *self-correct,* meaning that

they won't come to you with the F sharp where the F natural should have been, because they would have been able to hear for themselves that something was wrong. Every time they pick up something like this, you have saved valuable lesson time, and can get on with showing them things that they genuinely couldn't have figured out without help.

2) Recordings provide an *alternative source* when the reading challenge seems insurmountable—providing students with a means of continuing the fight, even when they have lost a particular battle.

A classic example of this can be heavily syncopated rhythms, which present in such an unfriendly fashion on paper, but are normally easy enough to copy once you know what they sound like. As the teacher, you'll still need to work on your student's ability to read such rhythms for themselves, but the way to do that is NOT to send them home with a piece filled with syncopations and expect them to figure it out by counting somehow. If you throw them in the deep end like that, all they will be learning is that such rhythms are too hard, and they'll avoid them altogether.

Instead, armed with the recording, they can internalize what the rhythm *sounds* like, and then can make the connection in reverse: "Aha! So the rhythm that goes dum-dah-ah-da dum-dah-ah-da looks like *that*—I always wondered what that pattern on paper would actually sound like"—and the next time they see that rhythm, they will know what to do with it.

So, far from hindering a student's reading, intelligent use of recordings can actually help it.

3) Recordings provide inspiration and encouragement by reminding the student *just how good this piece will eventually sound.* Sometimes when the student is knee deep in accidentals and the piece is crawling along while they figure things out, the concept of what all this work was for in the first place can get lost. We can become so absorbed by the drudgery of the construction task, that we forget to be inspired by the promise of the beauty of the finished product. Listening regularly to the recording of their new piece will not only help keep your student's eyes on the goal—it can actually put stars in their eyes in the first place.

4) Recordings can also provide food for thought for interpretation—particularly if the student listens to more than one version. The aim is not to copy, but for the student to understand what it is about the approach they are listening to that they like, and what they would perhaps do differently. That way, the student's first impression of the piece is not just of a succession of abstract notes, *but of a living performance.* If you want your student delivering their piece with passion and conviction, it doesn't hurt to have them listening to someone delivering the piece with passion and conviction.

6.6.2 Using recordings to help students learn new pieces

The most powerful way for recordings to work their magic is for the student to be completely immersed in them. It should be on while they do their homework, while they read at night, in the car, during dinner—whenever they can. The aim is for their pieces to feel like something they have known forever, so that even if the recording doesn't help them work out what to play, they'll know immediately if they are playing something that isn't right.

They still would use the music to work out the notes, but would use their aural knowledge of the piece to check the results of that reading. Along the way they'll pick up missed accidentals, incorrect octaves, wrong notes—and a whole load of other minor irritations that you would have to have dealt with in lessons otherwise.

The recording will prove even more useful if they can follow along the score while they listen. By far the easiest way to render comprehensible even the most confusing of passages is for the student to be able to hear what they are looking at. Triplets can tend to remain as abstract concepts, no matter how eloquently we may explain them—but once the passage has actually been *listened* to, the student knows that triplets are the bit that goes "Dum-dah-dah Dum-dah-dah".

They'll also be able to hear that page three is not a mass of semiquavers—by bringing out the second semiquaver in each group, *you can actually hear the melody!* They would have discovered this anyway after you had pointed it out in a lesson, but the recording allowed them to make this discovery for themselves, transforming how they think of that section before they even begin.

For slower works, the student can actually *play along* with the recording once they are familiar with the notes. Quite independent of the benefits to their practice, it can be enormously motivating to be playing along with an expert—and to be producing the same notes they are. (Which means you must be getting it right)

6.6.3 Making your own recordings

Recordings are usually easy enough to come by for advanced students, but are more difficult for intermediate and beginners because the repertoire is not typically concert material, and so is not recorded in the first place. "Six Prancing Ponies" might be a great teaching piece for your new clarinet students, but it's not going to be released by Sony any time soon.

In the absence of existing recordings, there's only one thing to do—you have to build your own. It's not as scary as it sounds.

Remember, you're not trying to win a Grammy with the result. You're just providing a tool for your student to use during the week—almost like a portable music teacher that can demonstrate the piece for them on demand. So while recording it into an old tape recorder will have plenty of hiss and do rotten things to your tone, the end result will provide the student with everything they need.

But it doesn't have to be an old tape recorder. Even the basic soundcards that come with most new computers now, together with a $5 microphone will allow you to make clean digital recordings that will leave the tape recording for dead. Save the result as a sound file, and either burn it to a CD, or email it to your student. (If you have no idea what I'm talking about, ask a local computer store to show you how—it's actually very easy now!)

Alternatively, if you have a MIDI keyboard and some basic sequencing software, you can quickly record problem passages for your students. If the only way they are going to get that rhythm right is to be able to hear it a *lot*, you can quickly record it for them as a MIDI file, put it on a floppy disk, and they can play it back on their own computer at home whenever they need to. You can even set it to *loop*, so that they hear the rhythm over and over again, giving them something they can play along with. It's like having you there with them—and the whole recording process, from the keyboard being turned on to the disk being ready usually gives you plenty of change from five minutes.

Music technology provides a huge range of exciting benefits to students as they practice, but that's the subject of another book entirely. (Again, stay tuned!)

6.7 Scouting

This technique is a slightly more forgiving variation on the TableTop Technique, and allows your student to conduct a thorough reconnaissance mission before doing battle with their new piece. The aim is for the student to develop a clear sketch in their own mind of the entire piece, so that when they start to learn it, every feature strikes them as familiar. Instead of wrestling with alien and unfriendly notes, they already have some idea what to expect, removing much of the fear from the process.

Students don't need their instrument to scout. All they need is the score, and a pencil—scouting, like the "sketch" technique for memorizing pieces outlined later in this book, can take place on a bus, in a train, at the kitchen table…wherever.

So what do they look for when they scout? The process is similar to the scan that takes place before attempting to sightread something, but is more thorough. The plan is for them to focus on these items one at a time, discover *all* instances of that item—helping them to perceive the piece as being a collection of readily explained patterns. You'll recommend your own features to scout for, but the following pages outline some typical targets:

> ### Initial key signature
>
> We've all had students who have learned their new piece beautifully—but for the fact that the key signature asked for three flats, and they used one sharp instead (because their last piece was in G Major).
>
> The student can save themselves a lot of time by getting this right from the start. They should also be aware of the fact that five sharps can look a *lot* like six if they just read quickly—as soon as the key signature looks complex, they need to take a moment and actually count the sharps or flats to be sure.

Key signature changes

Again, just because the composer took the time and effort to switch from A Major to Bb minor doesn't mean that your student spotted it. If your student finds all instances of key signature changes now, they won't be surprised by them later.

Time signature

Students are often asked to count in before they start playing—I am constantly amazed by students who will start counting "One two three *four*, one to three *four*" for their new waltz, and then want me to write to the composer complaining that the rhythm in this piece doesn't make any sense.

Time signature changes

Some twentieth century pieces seem to think that a time signature reaches a use-by date once it is four measures old. Students should get to know these changes before they actually try to play the measures themselves.

Initial Tempo

Before the presence of thirty-second notes prompts your student to declare the piece as "unplayable", they might want to take note of the fact that the piece is marked "Grave ma non troppo".

Tempo Changes

Again, it's easy for students to lock in values for an entire piece, and thus miss departures from the norm. If things suddenly speed up on page two, the student should know about it before they get their heart set on an inappropriate tempo.

Structure of the piece

Is the piece in Sonata form? A Rondo? A Theme and Variations? A Fugue? A Canon? Knowing this won't tell your student which notes to play (nor will it make them interesting to talk to at parties), but it will help them form expectations about what might be coming up next when they eventually tackle the piece.

So instead of looking in horror at a section filled with accidentals—almost as though it's a blight upon an otherwise tidy piece—they will know that it's just a development section, and that while the accidentals look scary, the section itself is likely to be built out of repeating and therefore predictable motifs. In other words, it's going to be much easier to learn than they first thought.

Easily labeled components

That's an *e minor scale*. Here's an *Alberti bass*. Over there are a series of *broken chords*. And hiding on page two is a *chromatic scale*. Instead of having to deal with masses of unrelated notes, the student is looking for patterns that they already know how to play—or at the very least can easily work out. (Even if F# minor scale is not in their technical bag of tricks yet, they know what a minor scale is supposed to sound like, so will find working out that passage much easier than otherwise would be the case)

We looked at a similar technique in the "Reframing" section of this chapter, the difference here being that the student is not just labelling their favorite scales and technical elements.

Distinguishing features of the piece

If they had to release a description of this piece for a "Wanted!" poster, what would you say about it? Melody contains lots of repeating notes. Spends a lot of time going backwards and forwards between tonic and dominant. Faster sections are always marked pp. Accidentals are almost always sharps, with the occasional double sharp. First part of piece is slow and reflective, second section is virtuosic and scherzo-like.

The more points your student can list, the better they will understand the piece. And remember, *they are still yet to play the very first note*. The scout analogy is a good one, in that scouts don't take part in the battle itself, but their work in advance makes the battle winnable. Whatever method your student ends up embracing for learning notes, they really should have *met* those notes first.

6.8 Shooting the movie

Independently of whether or not students elect to use the Level System, they should at least be aware of the flexibility offered by this next technique.

Not all students like to approach things in a linear fashion, and not all pieces lend themselves to such an approach in the first place. When movies are being shot, they are rarely shot in the sequence in which the final movie will appear— similarly, there is no rule that says that students have to learn their new piece by starting at the beginning and working through until they get to the end.

Suggest to your students that instead of their job being to prepare the first two pages of their piece, that their task instead is to choose *any twenty short passages from the piece*, and prepare those instead. These passages can be scattered throughout the piece wherever they like.

This provides two important advantages for the student. First of all, in a similar fashion to the Level System, they now have lots of small tasks to complete, instead of one major one. Instead of the question at the lesson being "Did you learn the two pages" and their answer having to be "No" if they are anywhere short of that mark, you can ask instead "How many passages did you prepare?". Their answer to this question does not contain the implied failure that having to answer "no" does—instead it helps focus on what they actually *have* done.

Secondly, it give the student the feeling of control over *how* they progress. You're effectively telling them "I trust you to work out which parts of the piece you want to do". If any of the sections becomes overwhelmingly difficult, instead of simply stopping their practice altogether because the section felt like a prerequisite to what comes next (as so often happens when students work sequentially), they can simply switch to something else. It helps them choose practice that is going to be productive for them.

6.8.1 Hit and Run

The Shooting the Movie technique often works best if used simply as a prelude to a more structured approach, rather than a technique for learning the entire piece. Given free choice over which twenty passages to learn, most students will select the twenty passages that they think are the easiest to play. This means that while in the first week of Shooting the Movie, the results tend to be quite spectacular in terms of ground gained, each following week sees a law of diminishing returns, as the practice tasks are progressively distilled until only the truly tough ones remain—almost like Nightmares First in reverse.

The plan is to use the fact that the first week was spectacular to boost confidence levels for the task ahead. Apart from anything else, the piece now has peppered throughout it passages that the student already knows, meaning that once they do work sequentially, *they are never more than a few measures away from something they can already play*, giving them the illusion of having to do less work.

And like so many of these Learning New Pieces practice techniques, it's the perception that counts most.

Making the Piece Reliable

My work is a game, a very serious game.

M.C. Escher

The Practice Revolution: Chapter 7

• Defining the Task • Pressure Through Games • The impact of Games on Practicing • The Limitation of Pressure Games • The Seven Stages of Misery • The Great Race • Tic-Tac-Toe • The Ledger System • The Lap • Card Games • The Twenty Minute Consequence • Hangman • Tweaking the Challenges for Games

7. Making the Piece Reliable

7.1 Defining the task

This stage becomes active as soon as the student has learned their piece well enough that they are *no longer surprised by information in the score*—in other words, once their new piece has been through the boot camp of techniques recommended in the "Learning New Pieces" chapter.

At this point, their piece is by no means performance ready, with plenty of work yet to be done with dynamics, phrasing and other interpretation issues, but at least they're not being flummoxed by unfamiliar passages. In fact, most of the time they probably play it quite fluently.

Most of the time—and that's the issue at the center of this chapter. Every so often, their piece will still collapse in a tangle of smouldering sixteenth notes, prompting protests of "It sounded better at home!".

When students make this complaint, they're actually admitting to more than they'd like. They're effectively telling you "I can play this bit, but only sometimes—and probably not under pressure".

It doesn't matter how well your students have played their piece at selected glorious moments in their past. It's now how well they can play the piece *when it really counts.* At the concert. In the workshop. Or even simply getting it right for the lesson.

7.1.1 Embracing the fear

Traditionally the solution for maximizing reliability has been to try to *minimize the pressure* that students feel at performances. The audience won't eat you. The sun will still rise tomorrow even if you make a mistake. Don't worry about it, I'm sure it will be all right on the night. That sort of thing.

Problem is, it doesn't work. Feeling nervous to some extent is inevitable for anyone who cares about the outcome of a particular situation, and no amount of flowery rhetoric from the teacher is going to change that. (Was there EVER a concert that you weren't nervous for as a student?)

So instead of trying to eliminate the notion of pressure from our student's consciousness, we should be trying to get them *used* to operating effectively in the face of it. And there's only one way to do that.

Introduce it into the practice room.

Because just like scales, new pieces or difficult runs, *having to play under pressure can be practiced*, and will improve noticeably with attention. The next time the student has to perform, and is feeling a little nervous, playing while nervous will be familiar territory for them. They'll know exactly how the piece will respond when the temparature is hot, because it's been in the furnace many times at home already.

In fact, compared to some of the techniques that this section of the book has in store for them, the performance itself should seem positively *easy*.

The aim of this chapter is to provide practice methods that will allow your students to put their pieces under genuine pressure in the practice room, and to discover any passages which might be brittle—before the performance uncovers those sections anyway.

7.2 Pressure through games

Part of the reason that practice rooms can seem so delightfully pressure-free is that there are *no consequences for errors*. If students mess something up, they can simply try it again—*if* they even noticed the mistake in the first place.

This is not a luxury they have at the lesson, hence the complaint that "it didn't sound like this at home!" when the mistakes are produced and noticed. The reality is that it actually *did* sound like this at home much of the time—it's just that the student wasn't paying attention.

It's time to create some consequences for errors at home too. Not to punish the student, but to increase their awareness of what really happens as they practice. Because if they practice mistakes, they'll perform mistakes, and ignorance is only bliss until the day of the concert.

In talking about "consequences", I'm not proposing that the student be locked in a cupboard every time they play a wrong note. However, the reality is that they *will* practice with greater focus if there is a prescribed reaction of some sort to errors. The presence of consequences for errors won't eliminate mistakes that are caused by the student genuinely not understanding a passage, or those that are a reflection of technical shortcomings. But it will eliminate errors caused by lack of concentration. And that is a *lot* of errors.

The point is that as soon as automatic responses to errors are introduced to the practice process, students approach their work much more carefully—which then has profound implications for their ability to deliver pieces reliably.

7.2.1 Games as a vehicle for defining consequences

The practice techniques that follow are all dressed up as games the student can play, not because they're trying to disguise practicing as "fun" (although a lot of them can be!), but because by their very nature, *games provide consequences for the actions of the player.*

In other words, the student will not only have a framework for noticing mistakes in the first place, the game will also provide a reason for the student to *care* whether or not the mistake took place. If they make a mistake, there's a penalty, if they don't there's a reward.

So if they want to win, they need to play not only accurately, but accurately *consistently.* The same holds true for the performance itself—it's just that the penalties and rewards are different.

Quite apart from introducing some quality assurance into the practice process, games also provide a clear set of *rules*, so that the student's practice session *runs itself,* without them having to constantly wonder about what they should be doing next.

And most importantly, games can be *won*. Most of the games outlined in this chapter are tough to win, and the moment of victory can be a tremendous confidence boost. If anyone were to ask them on performance day "So—you think you're ready for this?", the student could provide a long list of evidence demonstrating that they are, simply by listing all the games they have played—and won—while practicing.

7.3 The impact of games on practicing

Most of these games share a common theme: Your practice session is over as soon as the game has been won. But it's not over *until* the game has been won.

In other words, if as a student, you want to maximize your free time, then the game *has* to go well for you—all of which gets them thinking about what they can do to ensure the game does go well. After playing a few games, they will discover that *how* they practice has a huge bearing on the outcome of the game. By modifying their behavior, and being smart about how they play, the games are over much sooner.

It just so happens that most of these behavior modifications are ideas that as their teacher, you would be applauding anyway:

The games go better if I practice slower

It won't take your student too long to discover a link between playing too fast and making game-prolonging errors. So paradoxically, the fastest way for them to get through each game is to play *slowly*.

The games go better if I don't try to tackle too much at

Students who normally practice by trying to deal with the piece as a whole will quickly discover that smaller sections are much more co-operative. In short, every extra phrase they add to the section they are working on increases the odds that something will go wrong during the game.

The games go better if I'm careful with fingering

Particularly for piano students. Pupils who like to improvise their own fingering will discover that games can go on forever. So they learn to stick consistently with one fingering that works.

The games go better if I truly understand the passage in my head *before* I try to play it with my fingers

Games all but eliminate the practice technique of "fishing" for the correct notes with your fingers. Most of the rules are stacked heavily against trial and error approaches to practicing, forcing students to use their brains a little more when they work, rather than waiting for their fingers to stumble on the answers.

The games go better if I find out what *causes* stubborn mistakes

If all the student does is simply try the same section over and over again, they will often get bitten by the same mistakes time and time again. They'll discover that the best way to stop an error from giving them a hard time is to find out what makes it tick in the first place. It might be an unworkable fingering, or a clef change, or a missed accidental—but until they can label it, the problem is likely to recur. It comes back to a simple maxim:

"If you keep doing what you've been doing, you'll keep getting what you've been getting".

If the student doesn't like what they've been getting, they need to make intelligent changes, or risk history repeating itself.

The games go better if I frame things positively

Some of these games are tougher than others, and students need to maintain a "can-do!" assumption, otherwise their own thinking will defeat them. Students will soon learn that there is a close relationship between how they think a playthrough attempt will go, and how it actually goes—a lesson they need to understand long before they try the piece on stage .

7.4 The limitation of pressure games

Like all the practice techniques outlined in the Practice Revolution, pressure games are designed with a specific problem in mind. They excel in creating a practice framework that encourages *concentration* from the student, while also helping the student identify sections that are brittle under pressure. Similarly, they also allow students to "tick" sections that are lesson or performance ready.

However, while these reliability games produce *evidence* of mastery, they are not necessarily designed to be instruments for the *development* of such mastery—despite the fact that sometimes the combination of intense focus and repetition built into most games is enough to turn stubborn sections around.

But once passages start regularly failing the various games, and have therefore been identified as being "unreliable", they need to be subjected to other practice techniques. Precisely what those practice techniques need to be will depend on what was *causing* the unreliability in the first place.

So if the unreliability is present because the student simply doesn't know the notes well enough, they should be using techniques from the previous chapter on "Learning the New Piece". If the unreliability is because of a *technical difficulty* inherent in the passage itself, they should use techniques either from the "Speeding the Piece Up" chapter, or the chapter on "Taming Tricky Bits". And if the problem was to do with insecure memory, then the chapter on Memorization will provide the techniques that the student needs.

The best way to imagine these pressure games therefore is as *diagnostic tools* and instruments of focus, rather than cures in their own right. With those warnings aside, it's time to meet the games themselves.

7.5 The Seven Stages of Misery

This is a heck of a game to introduce first, but if a student ever wants to prove to themself that they know a particular passage, all they need to do is subject it to this aptly named piece of psychological warfare.

You need to choose carefully which students you recommend The Seven Stages of Misery to in the first place, otherwise you can end up with tears—I probably only use it with around a third of my own studio. It's unforgiving, inflexible, and completely intolerant of *any* insecurities that there may be in the passage.

But that caution aside, there is something very solid about passages that have passed through the forge of this game, making it a technique that all students should have in their practice bag of tricks. They can pull it out when they're feeling brave enough.

Enough with the hype—here's how to build it.

7.5.1 How this game works

This game looks innocent enough. The student needs to quickly build a simple board with eight squares, labelled as "Stage 1", "Stage 2", "Stage 3", "Stage 4", "Stage 5", "Stage 6", "Stage 7" and "Home!". They don't need to spend hours constructing it—students can simply fold a piece of paper in half three times to create the squares they need.

The aim of the game is for the student to move their token from "Stage 1" to "Home!". The game, and their practice session, is over as soon as they have done that, but is not over *until* they have. Of all the practice games, The Seven Stages of Misery is particularly merciless both with students who are not concentrating, and those that are "fishing" for the correct notes with their fingers.

The student kicks things off by placing their token on "Stage 1", and choosing a passage in their piece to test. They then play through the target passage. One of two things will happen—either they will play it through without errors, or there will be one or more mistakes.

If there were no mistakes at all, they advance the token to "Stage 2", at which point they attempt the section again. If there are no mistakes again, they move forwards once more.

If anything went wrong though, no matter how small, they go *back* one square. (The only exception to this is the starting square—if they make a mistake while they are on that square, they simply stay where they are)

They continue moving forwards and backwards in this fashion until eventually—and sometimes it really is eventually—they end up on the "Home" square. Game over, and congratulations. Sounds simple enough.

It's not. The Seven Stages of Misery is aptly named, because after a while, it starts to mess with the student's head.

7.5.2 The "Almost Home" syndrome

Because of the advancement requirement of *no* errors, sometimes it can take students quite a while to end up at the second last stage. It's at this point that they will discover that not all squares are equal. Now that they are so close to their goal, they will realize that if they can just get this next playthrough right, the game is over, and they can go and do something more fun. Having realized this, the next playthrough takes on added significance, and the student becomes a little nervous, often producing a little error. Back to Stage 6.

The student will often now be a little annoyed at being pushed back when they were so close to their goal, and may be impatient enough to attempt the next playthrough a little faster. Not surprisingly, this leads to another little error. Stage 5.

Now they're really mad—after all, they had to work hard to get to stage 7—and they play faster still. Oops. Back to Stage 4…and so on…

It might have taken them thirty-five minutes to get from Stage 1 to Stage 7, but it's taken them thirty-five *seconds* to go right back to where they started. And they're not done until they win, so they pick themselves up, dust themselves off, and continue. Or they run screaming from the room (see my warnings earlier in this section).

The Seven Stages of Misery makes a powerful distinction between those sections that students can *sometimes* get right, and sections they can reliably call upon when the stakes are high, so that students know which parts of their piece are still brittle under pressure. Once students have played this game a few times, it's astonishing how nervous they can actually become once they reach the final couple of stages, but they'll discover no matter how nervous they are, sections that they truly know well end up traveling "Home!" without too much fuss.

In this way, The Seven Stages of Misery *always delivers the perfect amount of practice on each section.* If the students knows the section very well, then the game takes very little time to complete—but that section really didn't need that much practice anyway. On the other hand, a demanding section can take a long time to bring all the way home—which again is entirely commensurate with how much practice that section actually needed.

The true benefit of the Seven Stages of Misery? The realization that if you know a section well enough, *being nervous is not enough to undo it.* It all goes back to the core target of helping students *accept* nerves as a normal part of performance, and knowing that their pieces have been toughened to survive in their presence.

7.5.3 The need for occasional "Time Out" calls

Sometimes the student will start to take a battering as the same section trips them up over and over again. When this happens, instead of simply charging into the fray again, they can call a Time Out, and spend some time analyzing the difficulty without that work having a bearing on their progress in the game.

They can effectively suspend the game while they sort out the problem.

Bear in mind though that this suspension works in both directions. While they no longer are moved backwards in the event of an error, they also no longer move forwards if they get things right. The game remains genuinely in stasis until they declare "Time On" again, at which point the normal rules apply. The resumption of the Seven Stages of Misery effectively becomes a declaration of "Ok—I think I've got it now".

Chapter 10 is dedicated to equipping students with tactics for dealing with particularly tricky passages should they encounter stubborn problems. Like all practice tools, the Seven Stages of Misery is designed to help with a specific problem: in this case, subjecting the student to pressure as they play. It does *not* provide them with any further information or assistance if the added focus alone does not repair the fault.

7.6 The Great Race

No matter how powerful it may be as a reliability indicator, The Seven Stages of Misery is not for everyone. (The name alone is enough to put off some students!)

The Great Race is not only a more gentle alternative, but is unique among the pressure games because it will also reveal a thing or two about the student's *confidence* levels.

Like most of the other pressure games, it is designed to help bring consistency to sections that the student currently gets right some of the time, but not all of the time, and will separate errors that are caused by lack of concentration from those that genuinely need further help.

The game is a contest between the student and another person (although the opponent can be imaginary), and the aim is to be the first to get to 30 points. As with many of these practice games, the student's practice session is over as soon as they win the game, but it's not until they have won. In other words, they have a strong incentive to practice *carefully*.

7.6.1 How this game works:

The student chooses the section to work with, rolls the dice, and the game is underway. Whatever the dice says is the number of points *both* contestants are playing for.

The student plays the chosen section through once only, and if there are no mistakes at all, the student earns the number of points the dice show. Congratulations to them.

But if there is the tiniest little mistake, their *opponent* gets those points.

So if your student rolls a four, and everything goes well when they perform the section, the score will be 4-0 in their favour. They now need 26 more points to win. They then roll the dice again, play the section again, allocate those points based on how that next playthrough went…and keep going in this fashion until someone gets to 30.

Sounds straightforward. It's not though. The dice in this game are particularly strange, and it provides a twist to the tale that will tell your student a lot more than how reliable the section is.

How? The dice are *imaginary*, and will automatically roll *whatever number the student chooses*—guaranteed—and that's where this game gets really interesting.

7.6.2 The imaginary dice as a confidence barometer

Because the student can nominate the value of the next playthrough, they are effectively *voting* on how confident they are of success. Before they choose to roll a 12, they need to be very sure that everything will go well, because they know that their *opponent* will end up with the 12 points otherwise. As a result, if they are feeling unsure of outcomes, they're likely to "roll" a low number.

In this way, it's not just whether or not the student wins or loses is the game—*it's how they went about it.* If their victory came because of a series of rolled 2's and 3's, then they know that their confidence is still low enough that it's worth revisiting this passage again at some future point.

Independently of how well they may actually know a section, if their *perception* is that the section is still a little unreliable, then that perception can become a reality in the performance itself. So the Great Race is not just a game you want to win. You really need to win it in style.

159

7.6.3 Variations on The Great Race

* **Steadily increasing pressure.** Rather than allowing the student to choose the value of the roll, this variation *gradually increases the stakes*, and there is no fixed target total. Instead the first attempt at the passage is worth 1 point, the second 2, the third 3 and so on—until the twelfth round has been completed, at which point the scores are added up. Because the third round is worth as much as the first two put together, the student will be under extra pressure to deliver that playthrough properly, and that pressure continues to grow as the game progresses. (In fact, the final playthrough will be worth more than the first *four* playthroughs put together, meaning that the student's heart should be beating just a little faster when that time comes!)

* **Use *real* dice:** Again, this has the effect of making some playthroughs more important than others. If the student rolls a total of 11, they know that they have to pull out all stops to ensure that this playthrough goes well—otherwise they risk taking a big step towards losing (and therefore extending) the game. In this way, they learn to deal with situations in which care is required, skills that they can reapply in the performance itself.

7.7 Tic-Tac-Toe

Younger students in particular like this practice game because it's familiar, it's quick, it's gentler than the likes of the Seven Stages of Misery—and as you'll see in a second, it's possible to *cheat*.

This version of tic-tac-toe has no concept of taking turns, which means that unlike the game on which its based, most of these tic-tac-toe contests end with a victory for *someone*. Because of the absence of draws, the feedback is clear— either the student will win, and can move on to something else, or they won't, in which case the section being targeted by the game still needs some more practice.

In this way, the game is not so much about repairing a piece, as a Quality Assurance test on something that they think already *has* been repaired. A tic-tac-toe victory is a little checkmark they can put that says "if my lesson were today, this part of my piece would be ready".

160

7.7.1 How this game works:

The first step is for the student to go and find someone to be their opponent. It's not compulsory to actually have an opponent, but the whole exercise is a ot more fun if there is someone to beat.) They draw up the board, put it near he music stand, and choose the target passage from their piece.

The student plays through the target passage, once only. If they manage his with no mistakes, it's their turn to make a move on the board. If they mess up at all, it's their *opponent's* turn.

Once the move has been made, the student then refocuses, and attempts he section again. As for last time, whose tic-tac-toe turn it is will be decided not by alternation, but by whether or not the playthrough was successful or not. The game continues in this fashion until someone wins.

What happens next is dependent on the outcome of the game.

7.7.2 If the student *wins* the game:

The target section is probably ready for showing off to their teacher next lesson, or is ready for tougher challenges, such as the Seven Stages of Misery, or the Ledger System (see later in this chapter). The parent can make a fuss about being pummelled in the game, and about how strong that section now is...

...and then invite their child to play another game tomorrow, but this time with the section on the *next* page. They can turn it into a grudge match, promising revenge for today's defeat. They can even promise spoils for the victor—perhaps the winner of the game gets a bar of chocolate, or has their bed made by the loser for a week. The point is, they are hyping the event as though it is a World Heavyweight rematch.

There are very few kids who will be able to resist that challenge, and they'll practice to ensure victory.

7.7.3 If the student *loses* the game:

A loss does not indicate that the child cannot cope with this section, or that they have failed somehow. Remember, it's possible to be certain about every note in the passage *except one*, and still lose a tic-tac-toe challenge. But a loss does indicate that there is still work to be done before this section is ready to present at the lesson.

First thing the parent should do with the child is spend a couple of minutes identifying exactly which part of the passage was letting them down. Was it a note that they were misreading? Or a rhythm they hadn't figured out properly yet? Was it a difficult jump that they perhaps could prepare better for?

The logic behind this approach is that you don't want the child feeling like the whole piece failed just because of one moment of uncertainty. They can be proud of 95% of what they played.

Now they need to go and teach the other 5% a lesson, and then meet back here in fifteen minutes for a rematch. Then we'll see if those mistakes are still so tough.

7.7.4 If it's a *draw*

Because of the twisted rules you are using, draws are really not going to happen too often, but if a draw results, there is still work to be done. Again, analyze and isolate the trouble spots, and schedule a rematch. Their tic-tac-toe mission is only complete with any section once they have actually *won* the game.

7.8 The Ledger System

This pressure game is going to take a little imagination on the part of the student, and is designed specifically to help the student visualize just how much of their practice time can be *wasted* time. The results can be dramatic, and most students find their very first encounter with The Ledger System quite disturbing.

All they need to do is to imagine that every time they practice, someone teleports in and sits next to them, watching everything they do. This is not just any teleporting person though. This is a *music teacher*, invisible, armed with a piece of paper and a pencil, and taking notes furiously.

Each time the student plays their chosen passage, this invisible music teacher *simply records whether they played it correctly or not*. They get a tick if it was right, a cross if they messed up at all. Simple enough so far.

When the student has finished repeating the section, this teacher then looks at their tallies and makes a very important calculation—one that the student needs to be aware of too. They are not interested in how many ticks or crosses there are altogether. They are interested in the *difference* between the two.

The idea is that if the student plays the section once correctly, and once incorrectly, *the two cancel each other out*. To that invisible music teacher, it would be the same as if the student had not played it at all. So if the student works really hard, and plays the section four thousand times—two thousand times correctly, and two thousand times incorrectly, this teacher is not going to be any more impressed than if it had *never been attempted in the first place*.

Sounds a little draconian, but this teacher has a good reason for being so tough.

You need to explain to your student that if their *practice* is a muddle between correct and incorrect attempts, things could similarly go either way when they are actually *performing*. If they are lucky, they will get it right. If the gods are not smiling on them, they will get it wrong. It's very much like tossing a coin, and is not the way recital results should be decided.

While the numbers don't really bear closer scrutiny, it's useful for you to argue that if your student has played the section 100 times incorrectly, and 300 times correctly, they could reasonably expect to have a *one in four chance of messing up on stage*. (One quarter of the versions they have of the piece in their head are wrong, after all!) If your student doesn't like those odds, then they need to stack the deck with more correct playthroughs.

Because you cannot actually teleport or become invisible, your student will have to keep their own records. They play the section through, record the result with a tick or a cross. They repeat a dozen times. Then they stop for a moment and look at the scores. If they had to perform this tonight, according to those scores, what are the chances that they will get it right? (Which is why they do it 12 times—12 has such a lot of factors that it is easy for them to work out their odds).

Do they like what they see? Could they really be relaxed on stage with only a three in four chance of getting the section right? (You'd hope not, because there's no way you or their parents could be relaxed in the audience with a roulette wheel like that)

7.8.1 Setting a target—winning the Ledger System Game

As well as simply being used to make a point about consistency (or lack

163

thereof!) in a student's practice, The Ledger System can also serve as a structured game in its own right.

Instead of playing the section twelve times, the student simply repeats it until they have got it right six times *more* than they have got it wrong. As soon as they have done this, they can stop practicing. But until they've done this, they can't.

There are many ways your student can achieve this result. They could do it *six times* **correctly** and *no times* **incorrectly**, for a total of six attempts. Or they could do it *one million and six times* **correctly**, and *one million times* **incorrectly**, for a total of two million and six attempts…the Ledger System is equally happy with both outcomes. If they don't want to be there until their next birthday, they had better concentrate.

Which is exactly why the Ledger System works. It provides an atmosphere in which students are more likely to concentrate on getting things right every time, because unless they love practicing for hours every day, it's in their interests to do so. And unlike the Seven Stages of Misery, there are no protections built in for errors you make the very first time—as soon as the student starts playing nonsense, the "crosses" score goes up, meaning that they have to play it once correctly just to erase that cross, and than another time correctly to end up in front.

In other words, every careless mistake generates *three times more work* than if the student had been careful. Any student who is interested in dividing their work by three will therefore also be interested in practicing with diligence—which is exactly what you would want in the first place.

7.9 The Lap

Whereas the games to date have been intended for working on *sections* of pieces, this game is designed for students who are ready to start testing the piece as a whole for reliability. Most of the pressure games have zero-error requirements for success, something that may not be feasible when dealing with such a large mass of notes. The Lap helps *ease* students into error minimization, and leaves them aware of the location and nature of potential trouble spots, without such immediate and draconian penalties for lapses.

7.9.1 How this game works:

The student starts by choosing any measure in their piece at random. The aim of the game is to play through slowly from that point to the end of the piece, and then again from the beginning of the piece until they get back to where they started—thus completing a "lap" of the piece.

In the course of doing that, they may make some errors, but this is one of the few pressure games where there is no automatic penalty. The point of the game is to complete a lap of the entire piece without exceeding their *quota* of errors. Once victory has been achieved, the quota goes down by one for the next time they play the game. So if they were allowed five errors, and completed the lap with fewer than five, then the next lap with this piece will see a quota of four. This continues until eventually the quota is zero—which is the quota the student would be aiming for in the performance anyway.

7.9.2 Reacting to the errors

As soon as each lap is completed, and while the location and nature of each error is still fresh in the student's mind, they need to revisit those passages and make some repairs. To be certain that the repairs have taken, they should probably subject those problem passages to pressure tests designed for smaller sections (such as Seven Stages of Misery, or The Great Race) before attempting another lap.

7.9.3 Variations on this game

Poison mistakes: When students employ this variation, there are no quotas, but instead *a prohibition on making the same mistake twice.* It's a simple modification, but has a profound impact on the student's awareness of mistakes that might otherwise creep in under the radar if their concentration relaxes.

The game begins in the normal fashion, as they play through the lap, marking and repairing mistakes once the lap is complete. The actual number of errors is not crucial, but their exact location is more important than ever before.

When they attempt the next lap, the student is still entitled to make errors without penalty, *but they are not allowed to make any of the mistakes that surfaced in the first playthrough.*

The penalty if they do? Any section that lets them down a second time like this is subjected to a special version of the Great Race (cf 7.6), but to a total of 100 points (!). In other words, if a mistake has the temerity to rear its head a second time, it's going to be responsible for creating a great deal more practice before the student can move on to other things.

This game is cumulative—so that by the third playthrough, they are forbidden from making any of the errors that appeared in either the first *or* second playthroughs. The logic is that by eliminating existing mistakes, after a while, the student will simply run out of errors.

7.10 Card Games

Every home has a deck of cards somewhere, and they add to the process something that can be missing from the day to day drudgery of repetitive practice—the *random* element. Students playing with cards can never be quite sure what the practice session has in store for them, and for some students, that can make the difference between wanting to practice and not.

Once students have been introduced to a couple of card games, they will almost certainly end up inventing some of their own. So be it—have them teach you the rules, and then use their creation with other students if it sounds good. The most exciting thing about targeted practice techniques in general, and pressure games in particular, is that you and your students will frequently come up with your own.

Outlined below are a couple of simple games, just to get your students thinking about what's possible.

7.10.1 The Towers of Mozart

Ok, so the name is not one of my best, but the game is easy enough for students to use. They'll quickly discover that if their concentration is anything less than one-hundred percent, that the game can get out of hand though.

The student starts by dealing four cards face up onto a pile. The aim of the game is for them to create a *second* pile of cards that adds up to more than this first pile. As soon as they have done that, they have won the game.

For the purposes of this game, cards count as face value, J-Q-K count for 10 points each, Ace counts as 20.

So if the hand is J-10-4-A, the total of the pile is 44.

The student then turns up one card from the deck. This is the card they are hoping to add to the second pile, which means that they're probably hoping for a nice big card.

To determine whether or not they get to add the card, they play their chosen passage once through. If there are no mistakes, they can add the card to the second pile, and they are that much closer to winning the game. If there are mistakes though, it's not just that the card goes back into the deck and better luck next time...

...instead, that card now goes onto the *first* pile. In other words, their target has just got bigger.

The student then turns up another card, plays the section again, and continues in this fashion until the second pile adds up to more than the first, or until they run out of cards—whichever happens first. And if they run out of cards first, that's simply an invitation to have another game, with the scores carrying over from the previous one.

This game can become very nasty, very quickly for students who are daydreaming while they practice. They'll find that their initial target of 36 has suddenly ballooned out to 120, meaning that they are looking at plenty of extra work. If the score blows out like this when they *are* concentrating, then the section was so obviously unreliable anyway that it almost certainly needed the extra attention.

7.10.2 The Towers of Haydn

Similar to the Towers of Mozart, but a little tougher. This time it's not just that the second pile has to *exceed* the first pile—the second pile has to eliminate all the cards in the first pile by providing cards (or combinations) of cards that are *perfect matches for them.*

So for example, a 10 in the second pile could get rid of a 10 in the first pile. A 7 and a 3 in the second pile could also combine to get rid of a 10 in the first pile. Similarly a 10 in the *second* pile could eliminate a 7 and a 3 in the first pile.

Such combinations mean that a 1,3 & 4 could also get rid of a 6 and a 2, since they both add up to 8. The student can find any adding combinations they like—but the match has to be exact. That means that if the student has only a 3 left on the first pile, and earns a 5 for the second, that won't help them.

As for the first game, successful playthroughs mean that the turned up card gets added to the second pile in the event of a clean playthrough, or the first pile in the event of an error.

This game differs from the Towers of Mozart in two ways. First of all, it creates particular cards *that the student becomes hungry for.* They'll discover that they badly need a 6 to finish the game, and when it arrives, the pressure is right on for that playthrough.

And secondly, sometimes it can take a while for the cards to co-operate. Even if the student is playing the passage well, they might be getting useless cards which can be added to the second pile, but don't seem to be able to combine usefully with any other cards to cancel out anything in the first pile. The end result? Because the game takes longer to win, the section gets more attention than it might otherwise, making the Towers of Haydn ideal for sections that you would like to see have a little extra work.

7.11 The Twenty-Minute Consequence

This is the simplest of all the pressure games, and provides the most honest assessment of how a passage is likely to respond when the student only has *one* shot at getting it right—which is what they have to be able to confront in the performance anyway.

The game is played only at the very end of a student's practice session, preferably at a time when the thought of having to do any further practice that day fills them with horror. If the student has a must-see TV show that is about to start, then better still.

The idea is that the student calls in a family member, and then needs to perform the target section or piece *once* only. If anything goes wrong, no matter how small, *the student is up for another twenty minutes of practice*, then and there. Like an on the spot fine. Most students find that they actually get quite nervous in such a situation, which is exactly what you would be hoping for. Remember, the aim of these pressure games is not to stop a student from feeling nervous in a performance, but for them to know that they can cope *even if they are,* because they have experienced it before.

The twenty minute consequence cannot happen more than once in a day (if it were repeated at the end of the twenty minute penalty, then there is a possibility that the student could get trapped in a loop of never ending practice), but it should happen regularly, and is an effective way for the student to assess the effectiveness of their practice for the day—even if all it does is target a single passage.

7.12 Hangman

Hangman is another game that works because it's familiar for the student, but this time also helping to involve parents in the practice process.

The parent thinks of a word, writes down one space for each letter—just as they would for conventional hangman. The student's aim is to guess the word before their chances run out. The student chooses a section of their piece to test, and the game is afoot.

There are two rules unique to this version of hangman. One makes life much easier for the student. The other definitely does not. Whether they are on the receiving end of the nice rule or the nasty rule will depend on how their playthrough attempt goes. And that in turn will depend on their focus.

So what's the nice rule? If the student plays through the chosen section with no mistakes at all, they can point to *any* space in the mystery word, and their parent will have to TELL them what the letter is. No guessing. Just show me the answer. And if that letter should happen to appear elsewhere in the word, those other instances should be filled in too.

If, however, the student messes up their playthrough attempt, they have to guess a letter, just like regular hangman. But unlike regular hangman, *they only get four chances altogether* in the event that they guess badly. So if you were actually drawing the condemned figure, you would only be allowed to add arms, legs, head and feet. After that the word is automatically uncovered, and they lose.

That's all there is to it—the game proceeds one turn at a time, until either the word is discovered, or the student uses up four chances.

But there's actually more to this than meets the eye. The parent has control over the number of repetitions a section gets—and can set that number discretely without having to resort to "I think you should play this ten times please" (Any numbers more than three always sound enormous to students, and are best not said in the first place) The logic is that if the section in the piece contains difficulties for the student, parents can make sure the hangman word is a long one. Since the student is not allowed to guess the word at any stage (they have to "discover" the word by actually uncovering each letter—even if the word currently says UMBRELL_), a longer word will mean more repetitions of the section.

Similarly, if the child has chosen a section that they already know well, the teacher will probably choose a word like "SIT" or "EPEE" (Repeated common etters are great if you want to get through a game quickly!)

7.12.1 Variations on Hangman

1. Reverse Hangman. Students who tire of guessing can actually *set* words themselves—words which their parents need to uncover.

The game proceeds as outlined above, except that the consequences for a correct or incorrect playthrough are *reversed*. So if the student sails through the section with no problems, their parent will be required to guess a letter (only four chances for them too, in case they guess badly).

Any errors though, and their parent can compel them to uncover any letter they point to (together with all other instances of that letter in the word!). Hangman becomes very easy, very quickly for the guesser if they are being told the answers. If the student wants to keep their word a secret, they have to concentrate hard while they play their passage.

2. Clues instead of letters. This time, instead of a correct playthrough yielding an uncovered letter, it will result in a *clue* being given about the word. The student is welcome to guess once at the end of each clue. Parents who recognize that the current section needs plenty of playthroughs should not feel bad about giving cryptic or esoteric clues! (Otherwise the game might be over before it has served its true purpose)

3. Music words only. There are plenty to choose from, and not only would the piece be improving, but so would the child's general knowledge. Musical terms, composers, genres, instruments—anything musical is fair game. Can be combined with 1) and 2)

7.13 Tweaking the challenges for the games

With such an emphasis placed upon reliable delivery in these games, (and therefore upon no errors), the student needs to be intelligent when choosing passages to run through each game. If they find they are constantly losing games, it might not be a function of their concentration or command of the section so much as the fact that the section itself might be inappropriately defined.

Similarly, if the student is winning every game with ease, then it's time they chose challenges that are a little more demanding. The ideal challenge is one that they know they will have to be at their best to attain—but that they *will* attain it if they are at their best.

There are several things they can do to tweak the difficulty of the challenges:

1) **Change the length of the section.** The easiest way to make a game tougher is to choose a longer passage. To take this to an extreme—nobody is going to win the Seven Stages of Misery with an entire concerto. But by the time they are easily winning it with the opening two phrases, it's time to extend that to half a dozen phrases.

2) **Play the section from memory:** The Great Race can be challenging at the best of times, but if it stops commanding respect from a particular passage, then it's time to give the section a Great Race again, but this time from memory. (For more help with memorizing music, see the next chapter)

3) **Deliver the section while playing with a metronome:** Most of these games demand such caution that students will often find themselves tiptoeing through them, with plenty of pauses thrown in too. Having to

stay with the metronome will force them to deliver notes ready or not... and sometimes they'll discover that they weren't ready after all.

4) Require several consecutive playthroughs for a positive result: Instead of the student just needing to deliver the section cleanly just once, they would have to play it twice or three times in a row with no errors. This type of extension is really designed for either shorter sections, or critical passages in the piece.

5) Multiply the penalties: If the student is playing tic-tac-toe, and has enjoyed easy victories, change the rules so that an error results in *two* turns for their opponent, instead of just one. Each of the games can easily have their penalties augmented in this fashion.

6) Create time limits for a victory: And a draw counts as a loss. This has the effect of forcing the student to play faster, and minimize gaps—while still maintaining the need for accuracy.

By the time each passage in the piece has survived The Seven Stages of Misery, The Great Race, Tic-Tac-Toe, The Ledger System, Hangman, The Towers of Mozart, The Twenty Minute Consequence—together with whatever games you dream up for yourself—a mere performance is not going to worry the student.

When asked "What if you get nervous?", they'll shrug and say "I've been nervous with this piece plenty of times in the past when I've practiced it, and it's never been a problem"

The irony here? The very fact that the student can assert such a thing so confidently means that they are *less likely to be nervous in the performance in the first place.*

You can quietly give yourself a high-five...and your less-nervous student will never know the real reason they are feeling so relaxed at their next concert.

Memorizing it

"Memory is the greatest of artists,
and effaces from your mind what is unnecessary"

Maurice Baring

The Practice Revolution: Chapter 8

• Defining the Task • The Theory Accelerant •
Lessons from Platform Games • The Scribe
• The Sketch • The Migrating Book • The
Steamroller • A Parade of Small Pieces •

8. Memorizing it

8.1 Defining the task

There are differing views as to whose fault it is that musicians are required to play from memory, although traditionally the blame seems to rest with Franz Liszt. Whatever the initial cause, it's now an expectation from many audiences, panels and adjudicators, and students need to be comfortable delivering music without the score in front of them. Even aside from such expectations, there are a lot of students who simply play with greater freedom and expression if they are not also involved in the translation of notes.

The mechanics of memorization go well beyond the scope of this book, but before leaping into recommending practice techniques to deal with the issue, it's important to bear in mind that different students memorize in different ways.

Some students memorize according to *visual patterns*, others are heavily dependent on being able to *hear* what comes next. Other students rely almost entirely on *muscle memory*, letting their hands pull them from note to note, while others still have quite an abstract *theoretical approach* to the whole process, remembering notes as a mixture of scale fragments, cadences or common broken chords. And every so often, there are students who have *photographic memories*, and who can almost see the score in front of them—to the extent that they could point to a location on the invisible page where bar 7 should appear.

To complicate matters, most students are *not aware of which method they use*. They just remember things—or they don't—and are never entirely sure why.

The techniques that follow in this chapter are therefore designed to provide memorization techniques that will suit a broad range of learning styles. By sampling widely, students will not only approach memorization in a comprehensive fashion—they'll also discover which techniques work most effectively for them, saving them practice time in the future.

8.2 The theory accelerant

Music theory often seems like an unavoidable and largely irrelevant punishment to music students, but it can play a powerful role in making memorizing easier. For all its limitations, one thing music theory does very well is to take a seemingly unrelated group of notes, and label them with a single meaningful description—turning what would otherwise be many different things to remember into one easily digestible unit.

So instead of trying to struggle with the apparently random distribution of sharps in a passage containing seven notes, a student could simply recall that the excerpt is in fact an F# major scale, but going from G# to G#—a G# Dorian scale. The bar that follows might be the second tetrachord of a d harmonic minor scale. And over there, that's not five completely random notes—that's actually the start of a G flat Major arpeggio, root position.

As a student, those *three* pieces of information will cover the entire passage, whereas previously they would have had to process *twenty* separate notes. Faced with having to remember fewer things, the student has a much better chance of remembering—or at least reconstructing—the original section.

For students who are terrified of memory lapses, it's very reassuring to know that even if they forget the notes, *they now have a fighting chance of working them out anyway.* Chunking like this has always been an essential tool for anyone assimilating large amounts of information, and it just may be that those cadence exercises your student suffers through may yet come in handy if things unexpectedly turned ugly at the end of that Schubert sonata.

Obviously this technique is only going to work for the students with a solid theory background—three consecutive notes can look a lot like a second inversion e flat minor broken chord to a theory-trained student, but will simply look like a Bb, Eb and Gb to everyone else, no matter how long they spend staring at it.

8.2.1 How does the student use this technique?

When the student practices with this technique, they won't need their instrument. Since they will be creating theory-based descriptions of the selected passages, they could probably complete their practice at the kitchen table. In fact, similar to the TableTop Challenge outlined in the chapter on

"Learning the New Piece", it's an ideal way for students to be able to get some useful practice done on buses or trains

The challenge is for them to be able to *describe* every passage of their piece in terms of theory. Some sections will be immediately self evident. *G major scale, two octaves*—allowing 15 separate notes to be chunked into a single easy-to-remember piece of information. Others descriptions will have to be weird and wonderful, and really would have taken some creative (and tenuous) logic to cook up—but like nonsense mnemonics, it's the wacky theory descriptions that are most likely to stick in the student's mind.

From the teacher's point of view, having the student analyze their piece in this way provides a number of benefits.

First of all, it provides a much more tidy vehicle for *prompting* during lessons. In the event of the student forgetting where they are up to, instead of having to push-start them by calling out individual notes, you can simply remind them "whole tone scale, starting on E".

Secondly, it's a great way of not only developing their theory in a drill-book-free environment, it also helps students start to *understand what the theory is for in the first place.* While this might not suddenly produce enthusiasm for the subject, it should at least create a healthy respect. New theory concepts won't seem like pointless mandatory exercises any more—they could well end up saving the student valuable practice time in the future. (Scales and arpeggios can also become attractive in a similar way!)

With the view that they are buying free time *later*, spending the time *now* doesn't seem quite so painful.

8.3 Lessons from platform games

If you've never played with a Nintendo, X-Box or Playstation before, you might be a little confused by all of this. Read it carefully anyway, because I promise you, when you introduce this particular practice technique to your students, they'll know *exactly* what you mean, and will be all ears while you describe it.

Why? Because courtesy of their games consoles, they have already been practicing this way for years—it's just that they haven't applied it to music yet.

8.3.1 How Games Consoles teach students to memorize

In amongst all the shoot-em up, martial arts and driving games, there is a genre known as "platform games"—they are runaway best-sellers for kids of all ages, and are largely responsible for the success of games consoles in the first place.

Basically, the idea is that you control a little character on the screen, and need to steer them safely to their destination as they undertake a long journey. But this journey is not a hike in the meadows. The creators of the game have placed all sorts of tricks, traps and obstacles between you and your eventual goal. Pits to jump over. Gates that close if you tread in the wrong place. Sleeping lions that will wake up if you forget to tiptoe. Doors to choose between—some of which lead to safety, others to crypts filled with angry skeletons.

Do yourself a big favour. Beg, borrow or steal access to a games console, and then watch the child who owns the game play for a while. Prepare to be amazed. This child might not be able to play a G Major scale reliably, but in this game they'll make their character leap from log to log across the river, deftly avoiding crocodiles, and remembering to duck at the right time for the bird which suddenly swoops down. They'll have to make an extra big jump at the end, because the final log submerges without warning, and then they have to remember to pull their parachute chord while they are in the middle of that jump, because the river suddenly turns into a waterfall, and it's now a long way down...

It will look as though they have superhuman reflexes. They don't. They were able to do all these things, not because they reacted in an eyeblink to the threats as they emerged, *but because they have played the game many, many times before, and have learned what to do.* In fact, if you watch closely, you will notice that much of the time they actually anticipate what's coming up, because they *remember* what comes next. They'll say "ok, here we go" and move their character to the left of the screen, seemingly for no reason, while you watch, confused as to why they would react so oddly in the absence of any threats. Then suddenly WHOOSH!—a stampede of wild elephants obliterates everything on the *right* of the screen. A London city bus would not have survived the collision.

It's not ESP. They've practiced this, and they're now very good at it. Not only that, but obviously the way they have been practicing this *works*, and works very well. This means that the question has to be asked:

What would happen if, instead of memorizing the locations of waterfalls and trapdoors, they applied exactly the same practice method to memorizing their music?

Before we try to answer that question, let's just spend a moment or two analyzing how the practice system for Platform Games actually works. Because as you'll see, the fact that it works is no accident.

8.3.2 The platform game practice mechanics revealed

Platform games might as well have been programmed by music teachers— the structure is a wish list for memorization practice techniques.

1) Students are forced to repeat particular sections until they get them right. If the student forgets to jump over the sleeping turtle, and treads on it instead, they get sent back to the start of the section. What the game's really saying to you is "That's not it...try again". The student learns from their mistake, modifies their behavior—and after a while remembers that the turtle is there. The same principle can be used to prevent students from being surprised by key signature changes in a piece.

2) Despite the use of the device of *repetition* to help the player build their skills, the game is not automatically impressed just because the player repeats things. In fact, it doesn't care how many times the repeat took place, but instead *patiently waits until the objective is met*. Students who play platform games learn that outcomes should be the focus if they want to progress, and music students who want to avoid wasting time when practicing should have the same priority.

3) If the player loses concentration, they will almost certainly make an error that will cause the attempt to be unsuccessful. Students who play platform games quickly learn that lapses in concentration can lead to a *lot* of wasted play throughs—and therefore actually learn to concentrate hard.
4) The game does not allow the player to try to process too much information at once. When it sends you back to the beginning of a section, that's usually not so far from where you are now. In other words, if your quest is to

memorize page three of your piece, it will start you each time *on* page three, so that you are targeting your practice towards the problem itself. Students who play platform games learn that big tasks are best handled in stages.

5) Platform Games are carefully graduated so that things start off easy, and then gradually become more difficult as the player becomes more skilful. In this way, a player who once had trouble jumping over a single barrel will eventually find themselves coping with dozens at a time with ease. The lesson for our musician who plays such games? Things that feel impossible now can feel very, very simple in time—and that practicing is the difference.

6) The game never, *ever* gives in to the student. Even if the student has had one hundred attempts at a particular problem, the game will not see that they are frustrated and let them have their prize out of pity. Until the student completes the specific challenge for moving on to the next level of the game, no movement takes place.

Despite this, most students end up finishing the games eventually anyway. The lesson they learn? Persist. So when you tell them that a six part fugue *can* be memorized, as long as you are ready to stick at it through some fairly frustrating practice sessions, you know that they are already made of the right stuff to cope with a challenge like that. In fact compared to some of the games, memorizing a six part fugue is very easy.

7) The player can apply lessons learned *early* in the game to similar situations *later* in the game. This ends up saving them a lot of practice time later on. Music students can similarly kill several birds with one well-practiced stone, if they are smart about spotting how what they have just worked so hard on can be applied to other sections of the piece—with the work now already having been done.

8) Despite my constant reminders for a focus on *objectives*, the platform games have turned into entertainment the idea that arriving is not the fun part—it's the journey that counts. And to take this even further, with platform games, the journey is built entirely from one thing:

Practice.

Who would have thought that such a concept would have turned into a best-selling leisure product for kids? It's time to take advantage of this in our own studios.

8.3.3 Turning their memorization practice into a platform game

So how does it all work in the practice room?

The metaphor of the platform game as a journey is a useful one, and translates well as we look at memorizing pieces of music. The piece becomes a landscape to be traversed, filled with unique dangers that exist to thwart would-be travellers.

Just like the platform game, the aim of our player is to be able to travel from the beginning to the end without stumbling, but in the place of sleeping lions and dark pits, we have unexpected rhythm changes, or treacherous fingering passages to trap the unwary.

The journey in platform games is broken up into many stages, so that the player can tackle just a few problems at a time. Similarly, we would need to break up the piece of music into sections before the game begins, meaning that the piece now has *geography* as well as *obstacles*. Section A might be the slow introduction, Section B the dance-like first subject, Section C a development-like section, Section D a return of the slow introduction, but in a different key...and so on. The student only needs to worry about coping with the section they are currently in, so that they do not become overwhelmed by the memorization demands of the piece as a whole.

To lend the whole process a feeling of platform-game authenticity, you need to name *everything* so that it all feels like part of the scenario. The sections of the piece are not just A,B and C now. They have become the Jungle of Death, the Tomb of Tokamen, and the River of the Serpent Gods.

Having mapped out the piece as a journey, and having defined sections of the piece as stages in the journey, it's time for the great memorization game to begin. And it's really not a complicated process.

The student starts at the beginning of the section that has been labelled "The Jungle of Death" —otherwise known as the first two lines of the piece.

Their mini-goal is to be able to play through all this section from memory, with no mistakes. When they attempt this, one of two things will happen. Either they will get right through, or they won't.

If they do, then they congratulate themselves, and move on to the next section. It looks like this section didn't really need the help anyway. (Platform games will give the player a triumphant "Stage One Completed!" message once the stage has been successfully negotiated, and kids seeing that message will often pump their fists in the air with triumph—normally because they had to work hard and endure plenty of setbacks to get there.)

If they *don't* get right through the section, then they need to pinpoint exactly *where* their playthrough broke down, and they need to realize that the breakdown only occurred because a moment occurred in which they couldn't answer the question "so what comes next?". Before they go back to the beginning of the section and try again, they need to make sure that they have answered that question, and have played it through a dozen times or so.

In so doing, they will have *defined* what the obstacle was, have *mapped out* a way of getting around it, and *rehearsed* the solution—exactly as they would have for the platform game. The thought process is very much "Blast! Ok, give me a second, let me figure out what I should have done, and then let me try it a few times."

To help them remember the possibility of that error in the future, they should *label* it. Not with a literal description, but with the name of an obstacle that is appropriate to the scenario. So the mistake in this case was not *"forgetting that the D jumps up an octave"*...it was Khala the Tiger, who is ravenously hungry. (In fact he has been able to eat nothing but lettuce for the past three weeks. What sort of mood would you be in if you were Khala?)

Now that the mistake has a name, the student's awareness of it will have been heightened, increasing the chances that they won't fall victim to it again. It's such a simple thing, but it makes an enormous difference.

Having labelled the mistake, and constructed and rehearsed a solution to prevent it from happening again, they then return to the beginning of the section and try once more. They still might not get right through to the end, but hopefully, they will have pushed a little further before the next breakdown occurs.

In other words, they should certainly aim to get past Khala the Tiger (they remembered to jump up an octave to play the D—great!), but may fall victim to the Quicksand of Doom (B flat, not B natural in bar 37). Again, once there is a breakdown of any sort, they react by analyzing the mistake, and then answering for themselves very clearly *"what comes next?"*. They label the error, rehearse the solution, and attempt the section again. The student continues in this fashion until the section has been successfully completed.

If they do, then they can congratulate themselves, record the triumph and move on to the next section. Even when they don't, because the mistakes all have labels, they can have a series of mini victories over various obstacles—even though they may have fallen at the final Creeping Vines of Suffocation.

8.3.4 Once they have won the game...

They play it again, but this time, they extend the size of the sections. Eventually, they may well aim to be able to get through the entire piece in one go. And yes, there are plenty of students who can do that with platform games, although like our music student, they will only do that once they have beaten it conventionally in sections a number of times.

8.4 The Scribe

This is an idea you shouldn't recommend to your students until you've grabbed some manuscript paper, and tried it for yourself. That way, when your students complain to you about how difficult this technique is, you'll understand what they mean, and can nod sympathetically before telling them to get on with it anyway.

This technique should only be used by students who already feel that they have thoroughly memorized their piece, and are now resisting suggestions that there's still work to be done. The Scribe has been created specifically to quickly (and mercilessly) bring any memory weaknesses to the surface, while helping the student understand just how brittle our knowledge of "memorized" pieces can be.

It's not designed to discourage, although the results it produces can be brutal. It's actually designed to encourage students to continue to develop their understanding of the piece past the point where they have played it through from memory for the very first time.

They'll need a pencil, an eraser and some manuscript paper, and at least ten minutes during which they can work without interruption.

Their task? To *write out* the first eight bars of their piece.

That's all, and no peeking at the score. If they do know it as well from memory as they claim, then they should have no problem doing this—and to make things even friendlier, they can correct any little mistakes they might make (which is a luxury they don't have when performing!). They are also allowed to stop and think between notes as much as they need to, and are even allowed to play their instrument if it seems helpful to them. Sounds like everything is stacked in their favour.

Then all you need to do is sit back, and watch the Titanic sink.

Most of these sessions come to a crashing halt before the student even begins. Why? Because the first thing the student needs to put in is the time signature, and most students discover to their horror that they haven't a clue what it actually is. Even if they count, and then establish that the time feels twoish (simply because counting to three just didn't work)—is that going to be 2/4, 4/4, 6/8 or 2/2? In which case, are those opening notes eighth notes, sixteenth notes or just fast quarter notes?

And just what was the marked tempo? Allegro? Andante con moto? If they were to use their transcription to set a metronome, how many beats per minute would be appropriate?

Having been humbled by such fundamental and transparent gaps in their knowledge—without so much as a note having been written yet—most students will be fairly keen to redeem themselves at that point by proving to you that they can write out the notes themselves. After all, they are able to play this piece through from memory a dozen times in a row without forgetting any of those. But it's not going to be as straightforward as they think—even if they are jogging their memory by playing the piece through on their instrument.

The problem for them is that in order to write notes out, they will have to stop periodically (simply because you can't write and play at the same time!). This has the effect of interrupting the continuity of the phrases, and shattering any possible utilization of muscle memory, ensuring that students who rely primarily on muscle memory are doomed at that point. And even students who rely more on visual or aural memory will find that at the very least, they experience some nagging doubts. Which note should that scale passage get up to before the scale turns around and comes back down? Were there one or two Cs in that chord in bar 5? Just how many times did that ostinato figure repeat before switching back to the main melody? In that highly chromatic passage, was the second last note a C or a C flat? And was it a quarter note, or an eighth note with a rest? Which bar does the big crescendo on page one actually start in? What dynamic level was indicated at the start of that crescendo? Which notes in the passage, if any, were marked as being staccato?

If questions like this are asked, then what you are hearing is a collection of issues *about which the student has doubts*. It's better to confront the existence of such uncertainties now, rather than in the performance. (Which is why you obviously NEVER run this exercise a couple of days before a concert!)

So how do students use this while practicing? While the student will need you there for the very first introduction to The Scribe technique, thereafter it's something that they can try at home whenever they like. They would use it for three reasons:

1) If they are ready to declare a passage "memorized!", and want to test whether that claim is actually premature.

2) They can use it as a *drug of last resort* for sections that are resisting all other efforts to memorize. Because the demands of the scribe are so rigorous, and because it requires that dozens of questions about the passage be asked and answered, it can provide a powerful leap forward in the student's understanding of an otherwise recalcitrant section.

3) They also use it as a *diagnostic* for otherwise well memorized pieces, to identify where the brittle sections are likely to be. Almost like a stress test of an aircraft component—the Scribe will show cracks at an early enough stage for the student to be able to do something about them.

8.5 The Sketch

Many of the traditional memorization practice techniques are based on assimilating the notes in a sequential fashion. Memorize bar one, and then when you've done that, then memorize bar two. All finished? Good, then it's time for bar three, with bar four to follow that. Only one hundred and twenty three bars to go, and you will have covered the whole piece.

The problem is that some students don't like to deal with forests one tree at a time like that. Instead of trying to wrestle with the details straight away, they will remember things much more effectively if they can start with a rough sketch of the whole work first.

As a result, they should be operating with a completely different set of dimensions— instead of working from the beginning to the end, they should work from the *outside in*.

How does this technique work? It's similar to a process many artists use when constructing pictures. Artists don't produce landscapes by painting one object at a time in high detail—they'll begin by capturing the scene as a whole with a series of vague shapes, curves and lines. It won't be possible to tell exactly what the picture is yet, but the framework for the higher definition to come has been established.

After that initial shape-sketch, each subsequent pass will see more and more detail added, until we eventually see the finished product. That gentle curve becomes a hill, becomes a hill covered in trees, becomes a hill covered in *pine* trees, becomes a hill covered in pine trees in the snow with a track disappearing into it and a full moon overhead, while villagers stand at the threshold, fearful of going in.

Your music student can easily work in the same way. Instead of fussing over the finer details, they would simply be creating a rough description of the piece as a whole.

The opening is made up of plenty of scales, always going up, but never down. Center is slower and altogether less busy, and is in a new key signature (f minor), but with plenty of accidentals, mostly flats. Final section is similar to the beginning, but scales are in triplets this time.

It's not enough information to reconstruct individual moments in the piece, but it does give the student a global picture of what to expect when they're playing it. If nothing else, the student can immediately see that this particular piece seems to form a loose ABA pattern, and also provides plenty of fresh reasons for the student to spend some time on their scales.

Once the rough sketch has been created by the student, it's time for them to choose one of the sections mentioned in the sketch and flesh out some details. So they're going to look at the big curve shape, and see how that is in fact a hill—a closer examination of the first scales section reveals that the scales are all actually based around Ab Major, it's just that the *starting* note changes each time. Like a common broken chord, the first scale starts on Ab,

185

second on C, third on Eb, and the final scale on Ab again. Each scale has the same rhythm, and relies on an anacrusis each time to get things started. And the higher the scales run, the louder the dynamics, resulting in a crescendo throughout the section.

Having filled in the sketch to that level of detail, the student can take things even further. It's time to zoom in and create a three-dimensional view of each passage in the section, starting with the very opening scale passage. They can look at fingering patterns, changes in register, total range covered and phrasing, articulation, rests, rubato—so that the student not only memorizes the section in detail, but will now be aware of finer points in the score that may have been missed otherwise.

This final detailed sketch provides two very important benefits for our memorizing student. First of all, it now contains enough detail that the student should be able to reconstruct the whole passage if they needed to—not through muscle or aural memory, but through a firm understanding of its *components*. And secondly, the student will have a clearer picture of how every part fits into and supports the greater whole, making it easier for their performance to convey a sense of unity.

8.6 The Migrating Book

Not all memorization techniques are complicated systems. The Migrating Book is a technique simple enough for all students to try, and provides a gentle introduction to coping without the score in front of you. It's particularly useful for students who don't think they will ever be able to play from memory—The Migrating Book technique doesn't ever actually require them to play without the music. It just makes it progressively more inconvenient for them to do so.

The idea is that they begin the practice session with their music on the stand in front of them, as they normally would. After each playthrough though, the book will be moved slightly, so that it becomes more and more difficult for the student to see. After the first attempt, the music would remain on the stand, but might be somewhat off-center. The playthrough after that, and the desk of the music-stand might be laid flat, so that the music is facing the ceiling—still viewable, but a little awkward.

186

Following that, the student might lower the stand to knee height, forcing them to bend over to see notes. Then it's on the floor beside them. Then on the floor *behind* them. Then on a table on the far side of the room.

The student is welcome to check the music whenever they need to, but because it becomes quite a nuisance to do so, they will tend to hold off a little longer than they otherwise might have before checking . By the time the book is another room, the only reason a student would check is if they were absolutely, hopelessly stuck—whereas in the past, they might have resorted to the music whenever they felt the tiniest bit insecure.

The best analogy is that it's very much like trainer wheels on a bike. They gradually get raised higher and higher, therefore providing less and less assistance, gently teaching the student not to rely on them as they ride, but without giving the student the awful feeling of there suddenly being nothing between them and the pavement.

This technique by itself will not necessarily deliver an entire piece from memory, nor does it teach the student how to memorize. However, it will help the student differentiate between those sections where they would simply *like* to use the music, and those sections where they genuinely *need* to. Having made that distinction, they can target their practice much more effectively towards the sections that actually need the help.

8.7 The Steamroller

The Steamroller provides a more traditional methodical approach to memorizing, and is best suited either to students who thrive in highly structured environments, or those who have had difficulty memorizing in the past. The method is slow and unglamorous, but it's also relentless and thorough, and provides regular evidence of progress to the student—which is particularly important for those who don't think they are capable of making any.

The logic behind The Steamroller is probably best illustrated with an example that lies *outside* music lessons. Let's imagine that your task was to memorize the symbols of the periodic table. No matter how discouraged you may be feeling about the enormity of the task, it would be a simple enough matter to memorize *one* element. Here it is: "H"—hydrogen. You might write it out a few times (I know, I know, you already know what "H" means, but we're assuming here that you've never seen it before). Then you might say it to yourself, or stick it into a song:

"H is for Hy-dro-gen. Dum dee dum de dah"

Then pace the room, wave your arms and tell your furniture that "H is Hydrogen", while you imagine a giant cylinder of Hydrogen with a bold "H" emblazoned like Superman's "S".

Once you've rehearsed it so much that you could not imagine how H could ever possibly have been for "Horse", it's time to test yourself. Get your pencil, take a deep breath, start your watch (you only have thirty minutes!) and start your Periodic Table quiz. Here goes, and the answers are on the next page once you're done.

Q1. What element has the symbol "H"?
Q2. Of the periodic table elements, which one is identified by the letter "H"?
Q3. When looking at a periodic table, what element does "H" make you think of?
Q4. There is an element signified only by the letter "H". Which element would that be?
Q5. Professor Beaker has just asked you to name the lightest gas known, one that is colorless and has an atomic weight of 1.00793, and has given you the clue that the symbol used to indicate that element is "H". To which element is the Professor referring?

All finished? Great—check the answers on the next page to see how you did.

Q1. Hydrogen
Q2. That would be Hydrogen
Q3. That element is in fact Hydrogen
Q4. The question is referring to Hydrogen
Q5. Professor Beaker was describing an element known as Hydrogen—although it should be noted that the atomic weight is in fact 1.00794, not 1.00793 (2 extra marks if you knew this)

We might not be gifted chemistry students, but we're all going to do pretty well on that quiz. In fact, with the amount of overkill that has gone into establishing the link between "H" and "Hydrogen" in your own mind, it's now no longer something that you need to memorize. You just *know* it.

This conversion from something you are in the process of memorizing to something that you now just know is crucial. A sleight of hand here, and the student can memorize the whole lot.

Let's go back a step to see how this trick works. While we decided it's clearly impossible to memorize the whole table, we did agree that memorizing just *one* element was not only possible, but relatively straightforward. The important thing to note now is that we no longer need to memorize Hydrogen though, *because we already know it.*

This means that there is now room to memorize something else.

In this way, introducing the second element does not contravene our framework of "only one at a time". Here you are—"He" is "Helium"... And so the process continues. The only change is that from now on, before moving on to the new element each time, there will be *two* quizzes—one for the element being memorized, and a second confirmation quiz of all the elements you have already covered.

The entire process could be represented as an algorithm (Note: This spans two pages - there are SIX steps in this process!)

Stage 1:	*Select* the new unit of information to be memorized
Stage 2:	*Rehearse* that unit of information until you feel you know it thoroughly.
Stage 3:	*Test* that unit of information to see if you really know it or not.

Stage 4:	*Incorporate* that unit of information into a bigger test of all units covered so far
Stage 5:	Go back to stage 2 with any unit of information that let you down in the test
Stage 6:	Go back to stage 1

So how does this help your music students? Just as we realized that while we could not memorize the whole periodic table, but could certainly manage one symbol, even your most hardened non-memorizing students will concede that while they believe they cannot memorize a whole piece, they could certainly memorize *one measure*.

So the first challenge becomes for them to do exactly that. They rehearse the first measure of their piece until they feel they can play it without the music—and then they test it to see whether that's actually the case, by attempting to produce three error-free-and-scoreless playthroughs in a row.

No matter how difficult they find memorizing, when only confronted with a measure to memorize, they'll quickly discover that it doesn't take too much practice before they pass that test. You then put it to them that this measure no longer needs "memorizing", as they have demonstrated that they know it. (You don't have to memorize things you already know!) Which means that they now have space to memorize *one more measure*, so they can take a look at measure 2. They rehearse the new measure thoroughly, then test it when they're done.

They then need to conduct one more test that consists of the new measure, together with the measures they already know (in this case, that test would be the first two measures of the piece) If they have difficulty with any measure in that test, they should rehearse it again and retest it until it passes. If there were no problems, move on to measure three...and so on.

It's simple, it's relentless, and it works.

8.7.1 Limitations of this method, and how to compensate for them

1) This can be a blunt instrument of the most extreme type (isn't a Steamroller really a blunt instrument of the most extreme type in any case?), and while it usually does work, it can take a long time, and does not

automatically produce intelligent analysis of the score from the student. So while the Steamroller can produce some good results, it works better if it is used in conjunction with other memorization techniques.

2) The Steamroller algorithm weights practice heavily in favor of the *first* measure, while discriminating with progressive severity against subsequent measures. So in a piece consisting of 200 measures, by the time the student reaches the final measure, the first measure will have featured in 200 tests, while that final measure will have only featured in 2.

To overcome this, the student should start from *both ends of the piece.* So there will be one Steamroller going forwards that is memorizing measure 1, then 1&2, then 1,2&3...while another works in reverse memorizing measure 200, then 199 & 200, then 198, 199 & 200. In this way, every measure of the piece will receive equal attention.

3) This method is clearly not going to be practical for coping with a 90 page concerto, as the process would clearly take too long. However, it can be useful in delivering *sections* of a work that size. All the student needs to do is put a ceiling on the maximum number of bars that a section can contain, and "wrap" up sections as being complete once a test of that size has been passed.

They then treat the next set of measures almost as a separate piece, and performing the piece from memory simply becomes a question of playing the sections one after the other. (For more on this, see the next technique: "A parade of small pieces")

8.8 A parade of small pieces

This technique is designed for students who have had some success with memorizing shorter pieces, but have had trouble once the works are longer. It's more about reframing than actually practicing differently, and so can be adopted by affected students without the need for any additional practice whatsoever.

Let's assume that the student has successfully performed pieces at past recitals that were one page long, but had a couple of disasters with pieces that were three pages long. And then let's imagine that their new piece is actually *eight* pages long – a feat of memory that clearly is going to exceed their (usually self-declared) memory threshold.

The solution when practicing is for them to regard the new piece as simply being *eight pieces of one page each.* The student would memorize them in the normal way, keeping the sections quite independent of each other.

Once these mini-pieces are solid, the only thing they need to do is spend some time memorizing the "joins" between the sections – the bridge that is the final four measures of one section and the first four measures of the next.

Then, armed with the eight mini-pieces, and the means to connect them, all they need to do is play the eight pieces from memory, one after the other without a break. Students will quickly discover that the idea of only having a limited amount of brain space to remember things – like a computer with limited RAM – is a myth. The single biggest obstacle to successfully memorizing a longer piece is the *assumption* that a longer piece cannot be memorized.

That's ok. From now on, your student only has to memorize *short* pieces – even if their next piece is one hundred pages long, the most they would need to deal with at a time could still be as small as a page.

Like so much of successful practicing, winning battles with their own *perceptions* will get your student halfway to their goal.

Speeding Pieces Up

*"It is impossible to travel faster than the speed of light, and
certainly not desirable, as one's hat keeps blowing off."*

Woody Allen

The Practice Revolution: Chapter 9

• Defining the Task • The Metronome Method •
When a Section Resists Metronome Method •
The Halflight Technique • Learning on the Bike
• Rhythmic Distortions • Redefining 80% • When
All Else Fails •

9. Speeding Pieces Up

9.1 Defining the task

When pieces are brand new, even the most gung-ho of students tend to approach them fairly gingerly. Not knowing quite what to expect from each bar, they'll tiptoe through this first playthough as through they are feeling their way through a strange house in a blackout.

Everything *has* to be slowed down. Not because it's a rule, but because there is so much new information to process that it's simply impossible to work out anything meaningful if you only allow yourself fractions of a second to think between notes. And that's exactly what playing a piece at full tempo means—you only have fractions of a second.

Check the calculations for yourself. If you are playing sixteenth notes at 60bpm, you are playing four notes every beat, meaning that there is a mere 0.25 of a second between each note. This is semiquavers at a leisurely *Andante*, hardly a tempo that's going to leave your hair windswept and your audience gasping. But even at this tempo, it means that you have to come up with the correct notes four times every second. This can be tricky enough even once you've had the piece for a while, and is simply not possible for most students when the piece is still brand new.

If you are considering a more conventional fast movement—nothing too scary, just a regular *Allegro*—then the stats look even more grim. You now are now playing *ten* notes per second, every second. You would have to have figured out and played twenty notes in the time it took you to read this sentence.

Faced with impossibilities if we play fast straight away, we take the time we need to work out each note in the passage. If that means our initial tempo is only a tiny fraction of the final tempo, then so be it. At some point though, the piece has to come of age, and will have to be delivered at the tempo intended by the composer.

This chapter highlights some simple techniques students can use when it's finally time to speed things up.

9.2 The Metronome Method

Metronome Method is the most basic of all the speeding up techniques—providing a highly structured but simple to understand framework for accelerating tempos that all students can take advantage of, irrespective of how advanced they are. It also gives constant feedback on progress, with steps small enough to ensure regular feelings of success.

9.2.1 The primary goal: Countering the "Impossible" myth.

Part of the difficulty with helping students get their piece up to tempo is that they often cannot see how the final speed is attainable. You can encourage, you can praise, but if the performance tempo is 220 bpm, and they are currently struggling at a mere 80bpm, the target can seem so far out of reach that they label it as "impossible!" before a practice campaign has really even begun. These declarations of impossibility are not always said out loud. They can be silent assumptions, but can still permeate every aspect of the student's preparation, like a slow creeping rot.

It all comes back to a saying that appears several times in this book (because it's true in so many practice situations!):

"Whether you think you can, or you think you can't, you're right"

As soon as the student labels the piece as being "impossible" at full tempo, a little part of them will always remember that declaration, and not only color their attitudes towards practicing it in the short term, but undermine their ability to play it in the future.

So much of successful performing is about confidence, and it's not easy to feel confident when you are faced with something that you have already decided just can't be done. Metronome Method is specifically designed to combat these assumptions of impossibility, and it does so by side-stepping them.

9.2.2 How Metronome Method Works

The very first thing Metronome Method does is that it removes the student

195

from the world of having to deal with the target speed and it's accompanying aura of impossibility, and instead looks at the speed they *can* cope with. For our example student, despite the fact that 220 bpm was the target, even 80 bpm was a struggle.

But 60 bpm was actually fine.

That's all you need to make metronome method work. A metronome, and a speed (however slow) that the student can play the section at successfully.

What you will be taking advantage of now is the student's inability to meaningfully be able to tell the difference between 60 bpm and 62 bpm. Go and grab a metronome now to try it for yourself. Set it to 60 and allow the beat to establish itself in your mind. Then slide it up to 62 (or whatever the nearest number is). The difference is barely perceptible, and for our student with a piece to speed up, that is a very, very good thing.

It means that whatever speed they have just successfully negotiated—let's call it N—there should be no problems negotiating that speed plus a tiny bit more (say N+2), simply because there really is no difference between the two. So our student might not be able to cope with 220 yet, but if they can cope with 60, they can certainly manage 62. It's almost as though you've asked them simply to play the same piece twice in a row.

And because they can now do 62 with no problems, then 64 is not going to hold any terrors for them. And so on.

In this fashion they sneak up on the final tempo, without ever having to confront the awful reality of just how high that final tempo is until they get there. When rockclimbing, climbers are urged not to look down. When pursuing performance tempos, I always tell students not to look *up*. Just keep on climbing, one step at a time.

Sounds fairly simple. 60, 62, 64, 66, 68...all the way to 220, and your piece will be up to tempo.

Surely it can't be as easy as that? It is—once you've made some small modifications to allow for reality.

9.2.3 Ensuring that the student is ready for Metronome Method

Students can't just leap straight into metronome method. There is a prerequisite standard that their piece has to have attained before things start, otherwise the whole process can do more harm than good

For starters, metronome method is designed to speed pieces up, NOT to make your playing accurate. It gives you no feedback as to whether that note in bar four is a B flat or a B natural. All it does is ensure that whatever you were playing anyway—warts and all—is now delivered faster than it used to be.

So before the student goes hunting for their metronome, they need to have triple checked that the notes they are about to speed up are the right ones. The same also goes for rhythms, rests, fingerings and articulations. Otherwise, because there is a degree of repetition, and therefore reinforcement built into this method, they will simply be ingraining errors. You'll just end up with the same old mistakes, only faster (and harder to get rid of!).

This is why the concept of a Base Speed is important. This is the slow speed from which the whole process starts, and before metronome method can begin, the student needs to be able to *reliably* play the section through at that speed. They don't take that very first step from 60 to 62 until everything is just right at 60.

If, in the course of trying to establish a base speed, the student discovers that they cannot play the section reliably at *any* speed, then the whole notion of speeding this piece up is premature—which is a valuable thing to discover in its own right. They should probably still be working with practice techniques from "Learning the Notes" or "Making the piece Reliable".

9.2.4 Recording the maximum speeds

Even though the progression is gradual, sooner or later the student will confront a section where 130 might be fine, but 132 might be one straw too many for this particular camel. (Otherwise, extrapolating the Metronome Method Logic, we could successfully speed up pieces to 100,000,000 bpm!) The student's piece will start to rattle sooner or later, in the same way that our old car is fine at 96 km/h, but starts to shake alarmingly at 100. That's ok, and the student simply needs to be trained to look out for warning signs that the speed they just attempted was too much at the moment—such as missed notes, wild intonation or uneven rhythms. Should the student be confronted with any of these, it's just their piece telling them that this speed may be too ambitious today (which does NOT imply that it will be too ambitious tomorrow).

When this happens, the student should try that speed a couple more times, and if the passage still wobbles like an old bicycle, then they need to go back to the tempo before this one and record that number somewhere. Each section of their piece will be treated independently in this way, and will end up with its own number. I usually encourage students to write those progress numbers directly on to their scores.

Recording the maximum tempos like this has a number of advantages for the student.

First of all, it gives them a *Personal Best* to try to beat. The student will start at the same low Base Speed every time, but the maximum speed they reach before problems set in will vary each day—although will trend upwards over a longer time period. Obviously musicians should not be obsessed with Beats Per Minute in the same way that athletes are with stopwatch output, but remember that our job here was to speed the piece up—and Beats Per Minute is a tangible way of demonstrating progress.

Secondly, the creation of this Tempo Map of the piece means that you will be able to see at a glance which parts of the piece are proving difficult to speed up, and might therefore need some further attention. If the whole piece seems to be cruising at around 180-200 bpm, except for one section on page 3 that only has "110" recorded next to it, then the student knows exactly what they should be working on next. Such recalcitrant sections will probably require other speeding up practice techniques beyond simply using Metronome Method.

Thirdly, it provides an *instant structure* to the whole speeding up process. Students don't need to wonder what to do next. The Metronome Method itself is a system that quickly gains momentum for the student, and is easy to understand, while the recorded maximum speeds gives the whole story a more interesting plot—they always have a reason to be practicing, because there is always a fresh section waiting for them with a number that could be pushed a little higher today than it was yesterday.

9.2.5 Snakes and Ladder Metronome Method

One danger associated with Metronome Method is that all it takes to be propelled to the next maximum speed is *one* successful playthough at the speed you are currently attempting. This can result in the recorded Personal Best speeds being reflections of one unlikely shining moment, rather than a true indicator as to the health of the section.

A slight modification which I call 'Snakes and Ladders" Metronome Method makes allowances for this.

This time, the speed on the metronome *changes in response to the quality of the playthrough.* If the student coped with the speed with no problems at all, then it goes up a notch for the next playthrough. If there were difficulties though, the next attempted speed will actually be one notch *down.* In this way, the student will travel up and down through a series of tempos, but like a slowing pendulum, will eventually come to settle on either side of a tempo that is just right for them at the moment. Instead of starting each practice session at the Base Speed and working their way up to try to push their Personal Best, they actually start each practice session at the speed on which the previous practice session finished.

This number is a much more accurate indication of the health of the section than their Personal Best, providing an honest indicator of what performance tempo they could really cope with at the moment. (They certainly shouldn't be attempting their Personal Best as a performance tempo, because the percentages suggest that the things could get very ugly)

Given the fact that the Snakes and Ladders version is so much more accurate, why would I not recommend it automatically? Simply because some students can find the downward trips discouraging, particularly if there are several in a row. Like stock prices, the tempos will trend upwards over an extended period of time, but in the short term, can fluctuate wildly. Students who lose sight of the bigger picture may be enormously frustrated that on Monday they were playing this bit at 85 bpm, but after four more days of solid practice, it was back down to 68. Such a student would be better off starting every day at a safe 60bpm, and pushing as far as they can go, recording each new Personal Best as they occur in the traditional Metronome Method fashion.

9.2.6 The Limit of Usefulness

Sooner or later, a student will encounter a section in their piece that defies the metronome method—that no matter how many times they may use their metronome to gently try to coax the tempo upwards, the section stubbornly remains at a disappointingly safe speed. The same thing would happen when my family would try to take our fat, old Golden Retriever for a walk. It would walk a hundred metres or so, and then it would just sit. Nothing—and I mean nothing—would make it move any further.

It's not that the student now has a section that will never go fast, it's just that the Metronome Method is not quite the right tool for this particular problem—which is exactly why this, and every other section of this book, outlines many different techniques for getting the job done. Over the next few pages, we'll take a look at some alternative methods for speeding up pieces, but they're probably best used not just as alternatives, but as complementary tools—each providing a slightly different piece of the bigger puzzle.

9.3 When a section resists Metronome Method

Once the student has identified a section that is resisting the Metronome Method, it's not game over—they now need to find out *why* it resists. But before they get out the microscope to hunt for clues, there are some common causes that they should take time to rule out first.

9.3.1 Uncertainty about what the notes actually are

This problem will kill any chances of speeding up the section, no matter which "speeding things up" practice technique the student chooses. In fact most of those techniques will simply make the section worse.

The problem is that when students are uncertain about notes, they might not actually *play* the wrong note, but at the very least they will need a moment of two to figure things out. This "moment or two" is incompatible with playing fast, because by definition, playing faster actually *restricts* the amount of available thinking time.

This means that students who are unsure of notes have one of two choices. They can either play fast (and play the note on time). Or they can play the correct note. But they cannot reliably do both.

How the student can correct this:

Despite the fact that the problem may affect the student's ability to speed

200

he piece up, this is not really a speeding up problem—*it's a note security problem.* So the practice tools they use have to be specific to getting to know a new piece better, not speeding up an already secure piece.

There are drills that can help with this in the chapters entitled "Learning he Notes" or "Making the piece Reliable"—depending on how well they know he section already.

Until those drills have been completed, and the notes are rock solid, the student shouldn't even *think* about trying to speed the piece up. Otherwise all hey end up with is fast mistakes. (We've all heard plenty of those!)

9.3.2 Largo-only fingerings

One of the nasty things about bad fingering (particularly if the student is a pianist) is that sometimes the inherent badness doesn't become obvious until he student tries to play passage fast. Forged in the safe and tepid fires of Largo, some fingerings are never destined to work at any speed beyond Allegretto— but it can be difficult for a student to be able to tell this until they actually hit Allegretto for the very first time.

You can illustrate this with a simple scale. If you are playing slowly enough (and not worried about legato), you can use the most extraordinary fingering combinations for an A Major scale. You can even use the same finger over and over again if you want to. Or your phone number. Write down the awful fingering you created...and now try to make it work at Presto. Don't try for too long though, it's not worth wasting the practice time, when a well-thought out fingering might not have required any practice at all.

No amount of practice will help a student deliver a Largo-only fingering at full tempo. So the target has to be the fingering itself.

How the student can correct this:

If bad fingering seems to be the culprit, they will obviously need to experiment with some alternatives—but most importantly, they need to quickly *test each proposed fingering at a variety of different speeds*, just to see how it copes as the tempo increases. This process won't always differentiate between a good fingering and a great fingering, but it will certainly reveal any unworkable fingerings that are masquerading as easy solutions.

Once the new fingering has been selected, it can be simultaneously ingrained and sped up using Metronome Method.

9.3.3 Technical immaturity

In short, the section might actually be too *hard* for the student. It does happen, but unless you have genuinely got things wrong in selecting the piece for them in the first place, a daunting technical challenge is by no means a dead end.

But until the student has developed an approach that will allow them to cope more effectively with the section itself, trying to speed it up is a waste of time. The section will reach a point in the metronome method where it refuses to evolve any further.

How the student can correct this:

The first thing the student needs to do is identify exactly what the technical demand is in the offending section. It might be a jump, or a repeated note, or a particular arpeggio—but they have to be able to *state* the challenge with precision.

What would be ideal then is if they could find a short exercise or etude that specifically targets this technique. Odds are, they won't have one handy.

So they'll have to build it themselves.

This custom-built exercise would be filled with nothing but examples of the difficulty in question, and it would provide more exposure in one week to that difficulty than they would normally expect to see in several years of regular repertoire. So, if for example the student were having difficulty with delivering a chromatic scale at tempo, the exercise might consist of a dozen chromatic scales, starting on each of the twelve semitones. This exercise contains the elements of the problems faced in the piece, but creates demands that go well beyond the original.

Their do-it-yourself-etude is *not* designed to provide mastery simply through repetition. The aim instead is to fast-track *experience* in dealing with the type of passage in question—allowing the student to try different ways of coping with the technical problem, and discovering what works best for them. It's more useful for the thinking that it produces, than for any physical benefit.

That way, two things happen. Not only does the student get accelerated exposure to the difficulty itself, but when they return to the original piece, it suddenly feels easy by comparison.

One note of caution though—all new techniques are something that the student should have a conversation with the teacher about BEFORE launching into working with a custom-built drill. In fact for most students, the drill itself is something that the teacher should really design, together with technical pointers about how to best deliver the technique involved. Such pointers are specific not only to the passage itself, but to the instrument too, and go well beyond the scope of this book. The suggestions made here are about process, not components.

9.3.4 Accidental Doubling of the speed

It sounds obvious, but it's very easy to miss. If the student is using Metronome Method, and cannot push their 160bpm piece past 85bpm, they should quickly check to make sure that they aren't trying to fit in twice as many notes per metronome tick as they should. Life can be hard enough when you are speeding up a tough etude without trying to deliver the sixteenth notes as demisemiquavers.

A similar problem can occur if a student genuinely misreads a small passage. Suddenly everything is twice as fast as it should be, and twice as fast often means unplayable.

How the student can correct this:

This problem usually fixes itself, but the trick is spotting it in the first place. The best thing is to ensure that your students are trained to look for it as a possibility. Of all the errors, this has a big upside though—it's great news to discover that the section you were dreading so much only has to go at half the speed you imagined ☺

(There are some Chopin Etudes in which, as a student, I used to look VERY carefully for this error...hoping...)

9.4 The Halflight Technique

9.4.1 Training your autopilot to play fast for you

Sooner or later, most students become aware that the faster they want to play, the more relaxed they need to be. The problem is that people will also tell you to relax if you wake up with a giant bird-eating spider crawling across your face, but that's not easy to do either.

Like everything else, if students want to be skilled at being relaxed while they play, then they have to *practice* being relaxed while they play. Which is exactly where the Halflight Technique can help.

Here's how it works.

First your student needs to make their practice room dark enough that they can only just see their instrument. The darkness is designed to remove all visual distractions, and also to help them get into the "zone" for the exercise they are about to undertake—but it shouldn't be so dark that they cannot see what they are doing. In other words it is a veil, but not an obstacle.

They need to choose a time when their family is not going to disturb them, because—and this will sound strange—to relax as much as possible, they actually have to concentrate very hard. Your student doesn't want their little sister telling them jokes while they are trying to work.

Before they begin, they should spend a couple of minutes just taking some very deep, slow breaths—each time inhaling as far as possible, and then very slowly exhaling until there is no breath left, then inhaling slowly again and so on. I'm not promising any appointments with Nirvana here—all this is designed to do is relax them, and helping them to unclutter their mind a little from whatever thoughts are otherwise milling about. Apart from anything else, some of those thoughts can give them exactly the *wrong* signals about playing fast.

They then choose the passage they are going to play, and start playing it. But they need to play it *very* slowly. Everything should be *easy*, taking care and time to hit all the notes right in the centre, and all the while they are physically relaxing as much as they can. How little energy can the student expend and still play the passage? How small can they make their movements?

Once the student is feeling more physically relaxed, they can start to concentrate on each individual sound as though they are beautiful and fascinating moments of light in the darkness. That's easy. They *are* beautiful and fascinating moments of light in the darkness.

All the while, they need to be reminding themself how easy the passage is—it should almost float from their arms. They should actually be saying the words to themselves "Easy...relaxed...effortless...calm"

If they do this correctly, it is deliciously soothing, and they can almost forget where they actually are. (Part of the point of having the lights low or off is so that they *can* forget where they are).

9.4.2 So how can this help the student play faster?

Playing fast often works best if we don't try to supervise it too closely, and instead allow our autopilot to simply and effortlessly deliver the sequences we have rehearsed. The Halflight Technique is designed to provide some highly targeted extra training for your autopilot (or subconscious, or whatever you want to call it), and to program some particularly important messages:

1) Because the student is playing so slowly and carefully, Halflight Technique sessions are those in which the student inputs overwhelmingly *nothing but the correct information*. They are not giving their autopilot mixed messages by frequently tripping over notes, or delivering badly controlled rhythms, nor flat dynamics—everything is a snapshot of exactly how the final performance should be, only slower. Think of it as a slow motion replay (in advance!) of the performance they would love to give, similar to the technique of the same name outlined in the Preparing for Performance chapter.

2) It's not just *physical* reactions the student is training here. They are also training *assumptions*. No matter how nervous they may be in the performance itself, courtesy of plenty of Halflight Technique sessions, a part of them will be forever associating this section with "easy...relaxed... effortless...calm", together with plenty of memories of having nailed every single note, and of that act requiring very little physical energy. Our conscious mind may well be screaming at us that such things are all good and well when we are playing at half speed in the sanctuary of our practice room, but our autopilots don't work quite as analytically as that.

While this does not guarantee that you will achieve the same meditative

205

relaxation on stage that you did in the practice room, it will certainly have you less tense than you otherwise might have been—meaning that you are in better shape to cope with the demands of the full tempo.

Like all techniques outlined in this section, the Halflight Technique is designed to be used in conjunction with other tools for speeding up the piece.

9.5 Learning on the bike

Most of the practice techniques in this section are based on being *careful*. Carefully establishing a base speed to work from. Carefully using metronome method to gradually increase the speed. Carefully checking stubborn sections for common errors. Carefully constructing special drills to render the scary bits less scary.

In the middle of this festival of care, every so often the student should say "what the heck", and attempt the passage at full speed anyhow. It sounds like heresy in the light of advice elsewhere in this chapter, but there are a number of important benefits that can really only come from such occasional lapses of reason.

First of all, a full-speed playthrough allows students to see where their hard work is actually making a difference. They will be able to hear for themselves the sections that have responded well to the campaign so far, and those that are going to need some extra attention. In other words, it becomes a powerful diagnostic tool, helping the student target the next few days of practice more effectively.

Secondly, it allows students to create a feeling of progress. As long as these full speed play throughs are spaced appropriately (no more than a couple of times each week, and the student needs to have the patience not to peep more often than that), then it can be easy to see the improvements from one attempt to the next. Given that they are doing all this work on speeding the piece up, it's important for them to know that the work is yielding results, and that even though the piece is not there yet, it's heading in the right direction.

Finally, in the same way that the only effective way to learn to ride a bike is to actually ride a bike, sometimes to learn to play fast, you have to actually play fast. Like learning to ride the bike, the student will often learn more from their mistakes than their successes—if the full-speed playthrough does not work out the way the student would have liked, they will be left with impressions as to what went wrong. Perhaps it was because that new fingering is not as secure yet as they thought. Or perhaps because their hand was simply too fatigued to deal with page four after a steady stream of finger-crunching semiquavers on the first three pages.

Whatever the reasons for the problems in delivery, the student will end the session with plenty to think about—which as a teacher, is exactly what you would hope would happen. It's very difficult to just mindlessly practice when you give yourself occasional reality checks about the progress of your piece.

9.6 Rhythmic Distortions

If the student has tried the techniques outlined so far, and the piece is still lurching about awkwardly at anything more than andante, then it's time to start tweaking things a little. Changing the written relationship between notes can sometimes help students deal with technical problems in a brand new way, while also often providing unexpected insights into exactly what in the passage is causing the difficulties in the first place. Students are more likely to think outside the square if they stop thinking of the passage as being square in the first place.

Instead of delivering the notes as written, the student will deliberately distort the content, either by varying the rhythm or articulation of the original passage. The easiest way to illustrate this is with a fictional example:

Ex. 1: Original Passage

What happens to this passage now is really limited only by the imagination of the student, and every variation they practice will produce fresh insights into

207

the original. They'll come up with their own, but several useful variations have been outlined below:

9.6.1 Dots

This technique is well suited to any passages that have a flow of *equivalent note values,* such as the running sixteenth notes that dominate the example above. The idea is that instead of worrying about having to play all the notes quickly, the student only delivers *pairs* of notes at full speed. In between pairs, they pause and prepare for the next two:

Ex. 2: Dotted Rhythm

The notation above is only approximate—in reality the student would enormously exaggerate the difference between the long and the short notes, producing a double or even triple dotted effect, like a ham-acted French Overture opening. In this way, they effectively end up playing *half* the passage at full speed. To ensure that the other half is then covered, they reverse the dots (this can feel a little awkward, and don't try dancing to reverse dotted practice sessions):

Ex. 3: Reverse Dots

It's stretching the truth a little, but the principle underlying this technique is that if these two distortions were to be interpolated, *the result would be a passage that runs at full speed.* This technique is effective not so much for the improvement yielded in delivery of the passage, but for the fact that it usually reveals any pairings that the student has difficulty with. Those moments can then be isolated and targeted. If the student cannot cope with these transitions as a mere pair of notes, they have no hope of dealing with them when that pair is a part of a sequence of twenty.

9.6.2 Splurts

Having mastered the passage using both dotted and reverse-dotted rhythms at full tempo, the student can then extend this principle by gently stretching the number of notes played before having the break each time. The resulting "splurts" of fast notes are a prelude to attempting the entire passage at full tempo—the only difference between the two being the *length* of the splurts (The argument being that the passage taken as a whole is still really just a large splurt).

Ex. 4: Splurts

One of the first questions you'll be asked is how long these pauses should be, but the answer is "as long as you need". If they need thirty seconds to gather themself for the next splurt, then so be it. This gives them time to visualize exactly what is involved with the group of notes coming next—what they are, where they are, any difficult jumps or register changes, how the fingering will work. The student will *all but play the splurt while they pause*, and then the splurt itself simply becomes evidence of how clear their picture was. If their visualization is muddled, then the splurt will be too—and vice versa.

Should the splurt prove too difficult to visualize and deliver, there's no need to panic. All the student needs to do is shorten it somewhat. In the same way that Metronome Method gently stretches tempo, the student can gently stretch the length of splurts, and they should always start from a comfortable base.

9.6.3 Accents

When students are struggling with a tempo that is too hot, individual notes can get lost in a number of ways:

- by not sounding at all
- by being the wrong note
- by merging awkwardly with and "collapsing" into the next note

These problems are often not noticed by the student, because of the speed with which the note problem is hurtling past them, and because of the sheer number of notes such problems can hide amongst. Adding accents into the mix forces students to notice individual notes—they can't hide, because they are now drawing attention to themselves.

In this way, the original passage might be rendered like this:

Ex. 5: Accents on main beats

Accenting the main beats like this is a good place to start—of all the notes in the passage, these absolutely need to be delivered well. Having done that, the student can then start to highlight notes that fall between the beats:

Ex. 6: Syncopated accents

And then:

Ex. 7: Fourth semiquaver accents

You should warn the student that these offset accents can be confusing to place—they'll need to start slowly to get the hang of things. The examples above have taken care of three-quarters of the notes in the passage, and the aim is for the student eventually to highlight every note in the passage in this fashion. Which means there is one more accent still to be placed:

Ex. 8: ...and the final one

Obviously these accents should form no part of the final performance (except for the conventional marking of principal beats), but practicing in this way will force the student to confront the impact of speed upon every note in the passage in turn.

There's an additional benefit as well, although it more properly belongs in the "Making the piece reliable" chapter—students will quickly discover that if they have any doubts whatsoever about any notes in the passage, those doubts will be quickly exposed as soon as they try the heavily offset accents. These doubts not only can lead to the passage possibly collapsing under pressure, they also make it impossible for the student to play the passage quickly in the first place.

As a result, when the students use the distortion technique in response to the question "Why can't I get this section right at full tempo?!!!", they often expose the culprits behind the problem.

9.7 Redefining 80%

It's not news to music teachers that performances will often start popping springs and blowing smoke if the student plays the piece as fast as they can. This is really not very surprising—the very nature of "as fast as you can" means that it is rarely well controlled, any more than driving as fast as you can would be. (A more appropriate expression really would be "as fast as you *can't*").

As a result, the most reliable performances come when students play within themselves—at 80% instead of 100% of their fastest possible speed, and as teachers, we're usually fairly firm about insisting on such restraint.

The problem is that if "as fast as the student can" just happens to be the *same* as the recommended performance tempo, then 80% is likely to sound positively pedestrian. The student is then faced with the unpalatable choice between sounding tentative on the one hand, or engaging in something downright dangerous on the other.

The solution is to ensure that 80% of "as fast as the student can" actually *is* the performance tempo—in other words ensuring that the student can cope with *more* than the recommended tempo in the practice room. All of which means stretching "as fast as you can" well past the point at which the student would usually declare "for pity's sake, no more!"

The same logic is used by athletes, and it's a point made elsewhere in this book. If you want to be able to be able to sprint 400m without fading in the last 100, then you might ensure that you can sprint 600m if need be. That way, by comparison with your training, a mere 400m feels almost easy, helping you power all the way to the finish.

How does this change the advice contained elsewhere in this chapter? It doesn't. It just means that there is a strong case for aiming for a higher speed than the student might first have imagined. They can still Metronome Method or Halflight Technique their way to the higher tempo—and then can enjoy being able to play well within themselves on performance day.

It also means that even if they fall somewhat short of their new goal, they are no longer therefore automatically falling short of the *recommended* performance tempo. By raising the bar like this, the student might not always clear it, but they'll jump higher anyway.

Sometimes the easiest way to prepare such 125% of full speed practice tempos is to do it "blind"—in other words, not to let the student know what the performance tempo is, and that this particular flight is being deliberately overbooked. Once they come to a lesson telling you how tough the tempo you gave them for their new piece is, you can tell them the good news. You'll see them reframe their view of the difficulty of the piece instantly, providing a valuable confidence boost for a task that is often largely about confidence anyway.

9.8 When all else fails

Despite the best efforts of the student, and the most creative practice techniques you can conjure, some sections are just not destined to be played at full tempo in time for the recital.

If this is genuinely going to be the case, then the student needs to stop banging their head against this particular wall, and instead start engineering a solution which will actually see the passage work musically at a slower speed.

The previous section *"Redefining 80%"* echoed the caution many teachers give against delivering passages at a pedestrian speed—but speed alone is not the only contributor to a pedestrianesque aura. If the subspeed playthrough is also dynamically flat, lacks phrasing, has bland articulation and no regard for the relative strengths of beats, then pedestrian it is. And worse still, because there is nothing else interesting about the passage for the audience to cling to, they'll be sure to notice its other faults too. Such as the fact it's too slow.

The aim of the student should be to *distract* the audience with such musicianship and imagination that they simply don't notice in the first place that the passage should have been forty beats a minute faster—in the same way that a used car salesman with a dented car will have you focussing on the pristine and feature-packed *inside* of the car instead.

That way, the comment from any adjudicator or examiner would be referring to "an obviously highly musical performance that probably could have been a notch or two faster", rather than a performance in which "Fell apart due to technical shortcomings, with no musicianship evident". All the student needs to do is choose which comment they would rather hear, and they'll know how to practice it. (They should probably check out the chapter on "Making the piece your own")

This technique can also be used for students who *can* actually play the section up to speed, but are sacrificing all musicianship in pursuit of that end. In fact, such students should probably be carefully steered *away* from most of the techniques in this chapter. Remember, at the center of the Practice Revolution is the concept that practice techniques are only suited to the problem they have been designed to solve—and some students simply should not be trying to speed up their piece any further in the first place.

There's an unexpected side effect to all this though, even for those students who genuinely are struggling to manage the piece at tempo. Freed from the concerns of *"what if I can't play it up to speed by the time of the concert"*, they relax, and stop obsessing about the section as being a large pimple on an otherwise unblemished performance. And then, sure enough, they are then relaxed enough to be able to play the section faster than they ever dreamed possible in any case. So the "When all else" fails technique is used not just as an insurance policy against losing the battle, but as a potential tactic for actually winning the battle anyway.

Taming Tricky Bits

"Press on: nothing in the world can take the place of perseverance. Talent will not; nothing is more common than unsuccessful men with talent. Genius will not; unrewarded genius is almost a proverb. Education will not; the world is full of educated derelicts. Persistence and determination alone are omnipotent."

Calvin Coolidge

The Practice Revolution: Chapter 10

• Defining the Task • Know Your Enemy • Making things Harder to Make things Easier • Take a Break • Switch Tactics • Ten Hours, Head Down and Trust • When All Else Fails•

10. Taming Tricky Bits

10.1 Defining the task

Sometimes, despite your student's best efforts to learn, memorize, speed up, or render reliable particular sections, problems will appear that resist everything. Thumbing their noses at your student's hard work, and blowing raspberries at every practice technique they try, these problems remain as stubborn stains on the piece.

It's tempting at this point for the student to decide that their piece has a "bad bit", and that like finding yourself with a bad neighbor, there's little you can do except pull the curtains a little closer together, and hope that they move out in a few months. It's not unusual for students to head into performances with sections that they know are going to cause problems—simply because these sections always have in the past.

So what should students do when they get stuck? This chapter outlines several strategies that can help tame the savage beasts, providing alternatives to simply giving up and accepting the tough bit as a fact of life.

10.2 Know your enemy

The single most positive step a student can take towards helping problem sections is to understand *exactly* what makes the passage difficult. Many recalcitrant sections are able to safely remain in a state of disrepair, simply because the student is unable to pinpoint the nature of the difficulty, and therefore is unable to develop a strategy for combating it.

10.2.1 Stage one: Distillation

The first stage is for the student to zoom in on exactly *where* the difficulty is. It's not enough for them to simply say "This passage is hard". It's not true.

216

It's like saying "My back is itchy"—it's not as though your *whole* back is itchy. In fact, the majority of your back is probably not itchy at all. There will usually be one or two specific spots, and if someone is scratching in the wrong spot, you're going to stay itchy until you give some more specific directions. Up a bit. Down. To the left. Ahhhh! That's it, thanks.

There will be parts of that "tricky" passage that the student does not find difficult at all—in fact, just like the itchy back, it is usually the case that *the vast majority of the passage is not part of the problem.* The student needs to distill the section until only the instances that are genuinely difficult remain.

Even before the student has begun a campaign for eradicating the specific errors, this act of distillation will have produced a significant shift in their thinking—they now realize that the passage was not as bad as they first feared. That far from being twenty seconds of ugliness and embarrassment, it's simply a couple of isolated moments of trouble.

And now we're gunning for those isolated moments too.

10.2.2 Stage 2: Define the problem moments

Having established that the problem is exactly *here,* rather than blaming the entire passage, the next step is to describe exactly *what* is causing the problem. It might be an awkward fingering. It might be a difficult register change. Or a chord that the student was simply never quite sure of in the first place. Whatever the difficulty, the student has to be able to name it—the very act of naming it is an enormous step towards being able to defeat it. Sections that are difficult for no apparent reason are always more frightening than those for which the difficulty is readily explainable, because as soon as you can explain a problem, you can start to develop strategies to counter it.

10.2.3 Stage 3: Create a *range* of solutions that will target the problem

Now that the student knows exactly where the problem is, and is able to describe the essence of the difficulty itself, the next step is to design a campaign to correct the error. Because most students are not experienced enough troubleshooters to be able to recommend the perfect solution straight away, the best thing they can do is to come up with several solutions and pursue them all. This provides two advantages over the single solution approach:

First of all, the more solutions they try, the more likely they are to stumble across the solution that works best.

And secondly, sometimes a multi-pronged approach was always going to be the most powerful response in any case, working with a depth and effectiveness that no single solution could hope to match.

One example—let's imagine that the difficulty was that the student was a pianist who could not arrive at a particular chord in time. They always either arrived late at the chord, or played the wrong chord altogether. Instead of simply practicing it over and over (and thereby possibly ingraining the problem itself), they would be better served to approach it from a variety of angles:

First they might write out the chord. Then they might try to apply some sort of theory analysis to it, so that they can chunk it as a single piece of information. Then they might analyze the *shape* of the chord, and practice being able to create that shape with their hand in mid-air. They might try playing the chord on the lid of the piano. They might practice finding the chord as fast as they can by closing their eyes, putting their hands behind their back, and then having a family member yell "Go!"—at which point they need to open their eyes, and play the chord as soon as they possibly can. They might run the passage that contains the chord through the Seven Stages of Misery, so that they develop experience at finding the chord in context and under pressure. They might use the Metronome Method to gradually shrink the required thinking time to find the chord. They might have to call out the notes in the chord. Or play it as a *broken* chord from bottom to top, then top to bottom. Or play it in each octave on the piano. Or make up a tune in their left hand while they play the chord over and over in the right hand…

The point is, there is no limit to the number of approaches they could try, not only keeping their practice effective in its breadth, but making it interesting to take part in. For many students, a successful troubleshooting session can be among the most rewarding practice experiences there is, as the difference between the "Before" and "After" shots of the section can be so dramatic.

10.3 Making things harder to make things easier

A variation on this technique appeared in the "Speed the Piece Up" chapter, in which it was pointed out that athletes who are training for 400m events will often ensure that they are capable of sprinting at the same speed for 600m or more—the logic being that if they can do this as part of their preparation, then the event itself should seem easy by comparison. Your students can use a similar technique when dealing with stubborn difficult sections in their piece. All they need to do is to custom design an exercise that is built entirely from the same material as the difficult section itself, and then ensure that this new exercise makes demands of them that go well beyond those of the original passage.

It's not as difficult as it sounds, and does not require developed specialist knowledge on the part of the student beyond simply understanding the nature of the difficulty in question. If the passage was difficult because of a long held note at a particular dynamic level, then they might develop an exercise that requires them to hold twenty such notes in a row. If the difficulty was a short chromatic run that frequently changes direction, they should practice endless chromatic runs, changing direction every time they inhale or exhale. If the difficulty was that they run out of bow while holding a note for three measures, then they would practice being able to hold a note for *six* measures. If the difficulty is a scale that seems to fall apart at the required 120 bpm, then they should aim for 140 bpm when they are working to speed it up—so that the performance tempo of 120 is inside their safety zone, rather than being at the upper edge of what they can manage.

Almost every difficulty can be exaggerated, extended or repeated more often in some way to make the exercise harder than the original task. They won't always meet the demands of their draconian exercises, but merely making the attempt provides a much needed technical focus for the passage in question, and also helps the student reframe their perception of the difficulty level of the passage itself. Sitting beside the nightmare of the exercise they just cooked up, the genuine article is a mere kitten.

10.4 Take a break

If a student ever becomes really, truly stuck on a bit, they should consider stopping *all* practice on it for a couple of weeks. Down tools, turn the lights out and lock the doors. In fact, they should try not to even *think* about the section in that time. (It's not a license to stop practicing altogether, so you need to ensure that they can get on with other things!) This hint can sound a little bit like running away from a fight. It's not meant to be at all —it's simply a technique that can help students fight better on another day.

When students come back to a stubborn section after a couple of weeks off, it is almost *always* better. Maybe it's because their subconscious works on the problem in the meantime. Maybe it's because they were able to break out of the practice rut there were in and approach the section in a more effective way. Or it might simply be that after such a break, the section feels fresh and challenging again, instead of like an old and inflexible enemy. This tactic is particularly effective if the reason for the block was due to the student's negative assumptions about the section, as continuing to practice in such a case will often serve only to reinforce those assumptions.

If you want to create a genuine feeling of a fresh start, have them use a different edition of the piece. Lose the old pencil markings—the fingerings, the warnings, the reminders—so that it genuinely does feel like starting over. It's amazing what an impact a fresh score that is differently laid out can have on the perception of newness.

10.5 Switch tactics

It's been said elsewhere in this book that if you keep doing what you've been doing, you'll keep getting what you've been getting—and that is not necessarily good news. In other words, if a particular section feels like it isn't improving at all, then it's a sure sign that what the student is doing isn't working, rather than necessarily being a reflection on the section itself. And if it's not working *now*, there's little reason to assume that things will suddenly be brighter *tomorrow*, so they should stop beating their head against this particular wall and try something else.

The idea behind this is that since the student is stuck anyway, they have nothing to lose by mixing things up a little. And maybe—just maybe—a different approach might produce the breakthrough.

So whatever your student has been doing so far, they should try to change it.

If they have been practicing in the morning, they should practice in the evening instead. If they have been practicing for half an hour at a time, they should try practicing in six five-minute bursts instead. And conversely, if their practice was in short bursts, they should instead try more extended sections.

If the student is a pianist, and they have been watching their right hand when they play, they should watch their *left* instead. Or watch *neither* hand. If their practice has been mostly slow, they should try working at a faster tempo, or at a REALLY slow speed.

They can change the way they sit. They can change the relative degrees of relaxation in different parts of their arm and hand. They can try the passage with their left hand alone for longer than they might normally. Or without using the pedal at all. Or with slightly more curved fingers. Or straighter fingers. Or with a raised wrist. Or less elbow movement. Or less articulation. Or a greater focus on dynamics. Or less focus on trying to get every note right...

...if this list feels long, it's because there really is no limit to the things they can change, and all of these changes will force them to look at the passage a little differently. Most of them probably *won't* make things any better. But some will really help—your student just won't know which ones until they try.

Sometimes I tell students that there aren't really hard bits. There are just easy bits that they haven't discovered the solution for yet. It makes sense then that the more potential solutions you try, the greater your chances of stumbling across the right one.

10.6 Ten hours, head down and trust

Sometimes the feeling of being stuck is actually an illusion—all that's happening is that the student is confusing *no* progress with *slow* progress. In the same way that watched pots are always lukewarm, if a student is checking every five minutes for signs of improvement when they practice, they risk being constantly disappointed. Worse still, before long, they might begin to assume that improvement is actually impossible, and that the task is forever beyond them.

What's needed in such cases is not radical new practice techniques, but simply a change of perspective. Normally their practice process would be made up of two parts:

1) Adhering to a recommended structure of some sort, based on the problem they are trying to fix

2) Checking periodically to assess the success or otherwise of their efforts

Step 2 is normally quite important, as it stops students from wasting their time with techniques that don't work (See "Switch Tactics", above). However, some students take it to ridiculous lengths, crippling the entire practice process by not giving it time to breathe. In such a case, they need to take Step 2 out of the process completely.

You would need to tell them that for the next ten hours of practice (however many days that takes), they just have to put their head down, practice hard, and simply *trust* that their work is making a difference. They are not to worry whether or not a particular practice session seemed to yield any positive results or not, nor are they to fret over mistakes or setbacks. The only time they should assess the passage for any signs of improvement is at the *end* of the ten hours—at which point, they're not comparing it with how it sounded that afternoon, they're comparing it with how it sounded ten hours of practice ago.

One tangible way of the student doing this is for them to record the passage at the start of the ten hours, and then put that recording away until the ten hours is complete. When they then listen to the recording again, one of two things will happen, and they win either way:

1) They notice an improvement, in which case faith should have been restored in the practice process. Everyone can breathe a sigh of relief and get on with the rest of the piece. And the next time you tell them to simply have faith in the process, they will listen a little harder.

2) They notice NO improvement, in which case they now have confirmation that the practice tactics they employed in that then hours *don't work for*

them at the moment. You can head back to the drawing board with them next lesson to redesign their practice approach, and should then probably combine that with another ten hour ban on assessments as they try the second plan.

That having been said, the tactic of Ten Hours, Head Down and Trust more often than not *does* produce an improvement, helping students to understand that long lasting impacts on their playing can sometimes take a while to develop—but that they do appear if the student persists. Not a bad message for them to understand as you send them home each week to practice.

10.7 When all else fails...

When all else fails, and the battle in the practice room feels lost, the student has one more option for repairing the broken passage—and it's a powerful weapon.

You. Their teacher.

The student has to remember that their practice is not designed to solve *every* single problem in their pieces. It's designed to accelerate improvements, and for them to take their pieces as far as they possibly can by themselves. Once they reach the limit of "as far as they possibly can"—and sometimes that limit is well short of what would make for an acceptable performance—there is no shame in calling for help from the single greatest expert they have access to. In fact as teachers, we can really shine when we help students through the areas that have defeated their best solo efforts.

Students shouldn't be quick to put pieces in the "too-hard-and-my-teacher-can-sort-this-mess-out" basket, but once they have thrown every tactic they know at a passage, and it still won't yield, then it's time to take the problem to a higher authority. For this to happen effectively, they can't simply throw their hands up and get on with something else—they actually need to make a note of exactly what the difficulty is, together with what has been done so far to rectify it, and the outcome of those efforts. Armed with this information, you will be much better able to recommend help than if they simply come to you saying "I can't get page three to work".

The suggestion is for them to keep a special part of their notebook that is for Intervention Requests. You'd check this quickly each lesson, as you should probably start with whatever section was tough enough to make an appearance on that page. Alternatively, if you have your own studio website (such as is available through practicespot.com), your student could send you a help request message direct to your webpage. You can read it at your leisure, think about some solutions, and then hit the ground running next lesson. There's nothing like being able to say to a student *"I've been thinking about that problem you told me about—here are four things you might like to try"*...

Making the piece their own

"The lack of expression is perhaps the greatest enormity of all. I should prefer music to say something other than it should, rather than it should say nothing at all."

Jean-Jacques Rousseau

The Practice Revolution: Chapter 11

- Score Trawling
- Experiments
- Write the Script

11. Making the piece their own

11.1 Defining the task

No matter how reliably a student may be playing their piece, no matter how accurate, fast, or thoroughly memorized it all might be, there still remains a horrible possibility. They can get all of these things right on performance day—and still give a performance that is dull, flat, soulless, and memorable only for the fact that it was worth forgetting.

Interpretation is something that lies well outside the scope of this book, and I'm not going to start debates about how much rubato is appropriate in Bach, or whether that moment in the Debussy should be clearly veiled, or one of veiled clarity. However, students can certainly take steps in the practice room towards putting their own stamp on the piece, rather than simply turning up at the lesson as a blank slate. In that way, the lesson can be a discussion about possible ideas, rather than the student simply sitting like a newborn bird in a nest, mouth open and waiting to be fed.

This book will attract criticism from some quarters for leaving discussions about the Art in music to such a late stage in the development of a piece. My argument is that lessons about interpretation are always easier when the student is already thoroughly familiar with the work. No matter how compelling their ideas about rubato might be, if they have to interrupt a phrase every few beats while they work out what on earth the next note is, such rubato discussions are going to be a nonsense. Problems with delivery of the piece becomes a bottleneck. Similarly, students are not likely to be able to deliver compelling dynamics while they are panicking about whether the upcoming arpeggio is B or B flat.

"One thing at a time" has been a core value in The Practice Revolution, and when the time comes to discuss interpretation with a student, I want that student's mind clear of all fussing about mechanics. In other words, if they are still muddling their way through the piece, I won't insult the composer by ooking at how we can play those muddles more beautifully.

This chapter outlines practice techniques that help students get a head start
n the quest for an effective interpretation of their piece. The aim is for students
o be able to turn up to lessons with ideas already flowing—raw material if you
ike, which you can then shape at the lesson itself.

11.2 Score Trawling

Before the student gets too creative with their own version of the piece, they
really need to be familiar with what's already in the score. Traditionally
his occupies a lot of lesson time—we have to remind our students that this
ection is *piano*, and to observe the accents, and to watch for that molto rit.
n other words, the model is based on the assumption that the student will be
overlooking details, and that we need to be there to *highlight* them.

Score trawling is designed to take that process out of the studio, and into the
practice room instead. Knowing where the crescendos are in a score definitely
comes under the category of things that a student can fix for themselves...so
hey really should fix it for themselves.

Unfortunately, it's not enough to simply ask a student to "be aware of
dynamics in the score!"—there has to be a process, otherwise markings will
nevitably fall through the cracks. And anything that falls through like that will
and squarely in your lap at the next lesson.

11.2.1 The wrong person has been doing this job

We normally help students become aware of score details by *circling* those
details. It's one of the great cliches of music lessons. And the more often they
overlook something, the more circles we draw around it.

The end result is supposed to be that the circles will draw attention to a
marking that they may have missed otherwise, and that LOTS of circles around
something is meant to yell a loud reminder at them. The reality though is that
here are usually half a dozen such circles *on every page of every piece*—meaning
hat the circles fail to stand out in exactly the same way that an individual neon
ign struggles to be noticed in Las Vegas.

Worse still, sometimes these same students fall victim to the "Ignoring the

Map" practice flaw, meaning that they don't practice with the score in front of them in the first place. So you can decorate the music as much as you like, but you'll be the only one admiring your artwork.

There is a simple solution that addresses both problems.

First of all, *you shouldn't be the one making the marks.* That's your student's job. At least then you'll know that at the instant the mark was made, your student was paying attention—even if they never look at it again. Because the student has made the highlight themselves, they are much more likely to remember the point they were highlighting in the first place.

They don't do this at the lesson. They do this at home. Instead of being under instructions to please *observe* the circled score details, their job is to trawl through the score, and *create* those circles in the first place. They're not just marking those score details that they fear they might overlook in performance—they're marking *everything.* In fact, you can tell them that next lesson, you will be trying just as hard as you can to find just *one* score detail that they didn't mark. Their job is to deny you the satisfaction.

11.2.2 Solving the neon sign problem

There's still an unsolved problem. It was bad enough trying to get markings to stand out when you were only highlighting a few of them—what chance does the student have now that *every* score indication will be highlighted? Their page will just be a mass of circles, each one yelling "No! Look at ME!" in a futile attempt to fast-track their fifteen minutes of fame.

The problem lies not in the fact that they have all been marked, but in the fact that they have all been marked *in the same way.* Instead of simply using circles, it's time to start using different shapes and colors to represent different types of score details.

So for example, you might tell the student to mark everything relating to dynamics by *circling* it, but they are to draw a *box* around any details that pertain to tempo. Articulation details might get a *triangle.*

This means that straight away, the student can see whether a particular piece of information is telling them about volume, or beats per minute. It also forces them to pause for a moment and understand what information the marking is really trying convey—helping the mark to stick in their mind.

The next step then is to use *colors* to distinguish between different markings that are part of the same family. So the student might use *dark blue* circles for all the "pp" settings, with *pale blue* for "p". "mf" might be *orange*, "f" would be *light red*, "ff" would be a *dark red*. There would be similar unique indications for *crescendos*, *sforzandos* or *morendo* markings.

The student would also use different colored boxes for different tempo indications—although they have to be careful to avoid colors that have already been used. (We don't want them forever associating a particular dynamic level with a particular speed, just because they happened to share the same color... this could produce some very weird results on concert day).

Their score will then end up being covered in different colors and shapes, helping them not to see score details as an amorphous mass, but as the individual instructions that they really are. The very act of having to pigeonhole score markings like that will force the students to notice those markings in the first place, while the score itself has suddenly become a lot more fun to look at. For too long as teachers, we have insisted that markings be "pencil only"— the reality though is that if gold glitter is going to help one of my six year old students to remember to play a passage mezzo-piano, then gold glitter it is. (Teachers who honestly don't want their books defiled in this fashion can always use photocopies.)

You can then take it a step further. At the lesson itself, you can ask the student to play through the piece from memory, but to pause every time the music would have had a green circle. Or blink three times every time they would have passed a purple square. It's not about getting them to actually deliver these score details in their performance yet—it's simply about making very sure that they know where they are.

Students don't fail to play loudly because they don't know how to play loudly. Students fail to play loudly because they forget that they are supposed to. So for that reason, if I have a student in front of me, I don't want a mere *demonstration* of the appropriate dynamics for the section—any goose can do that after a reminder. I want to be told up front and without reminders what dynamic that section is supposed to be, and then will want to know every other instance of that particular dynamic in the piece.

11.2.3 Creating interpretation geography

Score indications don't just appear randomly—there are often patterns which the student can use to help make sense of the piece. For example, the crescendos and forte markings may tend to be tend to be clustered around two pages in the work. Another page might be filled with squares, indicating frequent tempo changes. In this way, the piece takes on geographical features, so instead of simply playing measures 24-43, the student will know *"I am now entering the Realm of Lots of Quiet Playing"*. They also know that this realm ends with the return of the main theme., which is the Realm of Lots of Staccato notes. And that the final page is the Realm of Lots of Ritardandos.

In this way, the student creates an understanding of the dynamic and tempo topology of the piece, helping them see how each score marking contributes to the bigger picture. Students with such a picture don't need to *remember* score indications. Armed with a thorough understanding of this type of architecture, the student can almost work them out.

So how does this translate into a practice technique? Give them a sheet of paper, and tell them to build a map of the piece. Each section of the work needs to be labelled with a summary of the prevailing musical contours. The student's job is to gradually add more and more detail as the week goes on, and then discuss their cartographical efforts with you at the next lesson.

11.3 Experiments

Score trawling is a powerful technique for assimilating what's already there, but doesn't help the student with what *isn't* there. Sometimes students will complete their score highlights, only to discover that their piece has only one dynamic marking—a solitary *"f"* at the top of the first page.

At this point, some students need to be reminded that this is *not* a request from the composer to play at exactly 98.3 decibels from start to finish. In other words, a featureless score does not imply a featureless performance. There will still be hundreds of decisions the student will need to take about phrase shapes, rubato, articulation and emphasis, balance, tone color—and dynamics. The list is limited only by their own level of musical sophistication, and the need is even more urgent when the score indications are few and far between.

In the absence of clear directions from the composer, the student is going to have to use their own imagination and discretion. The thing to remember is that as less experienced musicians, the student's instincts won't be as fine tuned as our own, and that they are unlikely to stumble upon the most compelling way of delivering a passage the first time they try it.

This wouldn't be quite so bad except that plenty of students become attached to those very first impressions, and take initial musical decisions that end up dominating their performances in three months' time. The problem is that these interpretation ideas are not representative of the *best* available ideas, but instead are merely a collection of those that the student happened to think of *first*.

The solution is to set up a practice structure that encourages students to sample much more widely before committing to any particular musical ideas. By far the easiest, most effective—and most fun—way to do this is for the student to run an *experiment*.

11.3.1 How experiments work

The principal aim of the experiment is for the student to interview a lot of possible candidates for each score detail position, create a short list of promising applicants, and then choose one as a winner.

That winner then becomes part of the performance of the piece.

So for example, they may have a scale passage heading up to the top register of the instrument, before repeating the top note several times, and then falling back down again.

What should the student do with the top notes? Should they also be the top of the phrase dynamically? Or should the student whisper them, with the scale dissolving into a somewhat ethereal pianissimo as the notes reach into the stratosphere? Should the notes be delivered in a metronomic fashion? Or should the performer take time? If so, how much? And between which notes? To what extent should the performer vary the articulation of these notes? What type of articulation is going to best complement their chosen dynamic picture? If there is to be a crescendo, what shape should it be? Should it be linear? Or should it be a little more exponential in nature, with the bulk of the crescendo taking place in a rush through the last few notes of the phrase?

Before the student begins any experimentation, they need to have a list of questions like these that they need to create answers for. They then need to actually try out each of the options. The experimenting is not just goofing around—it's a methodical system of assessing the relative merits of competing ideas.

So if the question was to work out to what extent rubato would help the performance, the student should try that same section many times, with different degrees and types of rubato each time. One playthrough, it's completely metronomic. The next, it swoons, meanders and breathes languid and self-absorbed sighs like an overacted soap opera. The next there is a conventional rit, while the playthrough after that would see the student *anticipating* the beats slightly, resulting in a feeling of quickening about the whole passage.

They shouldn't try to prejudge too much whether or not a particular approach is going to work—some of the very best solutions sometimes appear as complete surprises. So in that way, the student takes on the dual role of performer, and critic, rating each of the approaches simply by a gut reaction as to how compelling the delivery felt for them. They'll end up with a short list of possible approaches (some of which might be wildly different from each other), and they then take that list to you at the next lesson for discussion. Between the two of you, and some awareness of stylistic considerations, you can crop that shortlist until the winning option is selected.

The logic is that the greater the list of candidates they interview, the greater the chance of finding the one that is perfect for the section, as opposed to simply settling for the first one that didn't offend too much.

Apart from providing plenty of raw material for the lesson itself, such experiments will help the student understand their piece on many different levels. For example, a student who experiments with the delivery of their etude may discover that adopting a more lyrical approach not only helped them to discover hidden melodies—*it also actually made the etude easier to play.* Unless they had taken the time to ask "what if I were to play this with a warm sound, rich dynamics in each phrase and plenty of time between phrases?", they might never have discovered that this piece is more than just an endless stream of sixteenth notes.

This process doesn't just need to be limited to intermediate or advanced students—even beginners can be encouraged to experiment with different ways of playing their piece, even if all they are doing is choosing between Loud and Soft. Or Sad and Bouncy. It all helps remind the student that *how* they play the notes can completely transform a piece, and that the most exciting part of the world of music lies well beyond of Which Note is Next?

11.4 Write the Script

For students with fertile imaginations—which is just about every child you'll ever meet—sometimes the best way to make musical sense of a piece is for them to have a story to cling to while they play. Never mind fortes and pianos, what's this piece *about?* If it were the background music for a scene in a movie, what would actually be happening in that scene?

You can illustrate the impact of stories in the lesson itself. Have them imagine that it's the middle of their summer holidays, and that they are lying on an inflatable raft, eyes closed, gently bobbing up and down in the water—and then have them play their piece to suit that scene. Without having to say anything else, this little scene will produce a change in dynamics, tempo and phrasing. It's hard, for example, to imagine a student reacting to this with a staccatissimo and heavily accented approach to the passage—even if that's how they had been playing it before.

Then modify things slightly. Tell them that they are still on the raft, but this time they can feel themselves gently moving forwards—the current of the river is pulling them along, and gradually increasing their speed.

Again, you should hear this reflected in their playthrough.

And then tell them that this is no ordinary river—it's actually filled with Piranhas! In other words, they have to be very careful not to fall in, and they have reason to be afraid. No more naps on this raft.

You can throw in rapids, a waterfall, a journey into a still lake (no piranhas this time), and rain gently starting to fall. After every change to the story, their playthrough needs to reflect the change, resulting in countless minor—and sometimes significant—musical decisions.

By carefully selecting events in the story, you can engineer louder playing, longer pauses at the ends of phrases, different tempi, changes in articulation—without ever giving a musical instruction.

11.4.1 Using this as a practice technique

Scriptwriting like this in the studio has its advantages, in that you can control the content of the story, and therefore the musical impact. Instead of a piano teacher asking for "forte, more *furioso* with the beats slightly anticipated and plenty of pedal", they might simply conjure up an image of a storm. But

233

this tool comes into its own when students are able to use it for themselves at home—particularly those students who have had difficulty developing dynamic plans for their pieces in the past.

Instead of asking them to come up with their own musical elements, ask them to *make up the story that best describes the piece.* Have them bring the story to their next lesson and read it to you. This process, while not involving their musical instrument at all, provides several unique benefits:

1) Simply *hearing* the story from your student will give you a powerful insight into how they relate to this piece of music. Knowing that their story was a sad and lonely one will immediately give you clues as to how they perceive the work—and perhaps which sort of interpretation will feel most "real" to them.

On the other hand, if their story collides head on with the dynamics that you were hoping for, then there's trouble ahead—you either need to help them refashion the story, or start coming up with an entirely different set of expectations of dynamics in the first place. No matter how tranquil the piece may seem to you, if the student's story is about "the angry hornet's nest being flung about by the tornado", then you are going to have to work with that—or spend a little time helping them to discover a more tranquil tale. Simply telling them to play quietly and calmly will achieve nothing except empty compliance at best, because in their core, they felt something different entirely. If you want to reshape the *outward appearance* of the piece, the best place to start is with the student's *inner picture.* And you can't do that unless you know what the picture actually is.

2) The presence of the story as an interpretation catalyst can help the student develop a more intuitive response to the music, rather than being obsessed with the mere mechanics of playing. So instead of having dozens of instructions floating around in their head, they can carry one scene—a scene that will produce the same musical results as all those instructions in any case.

3) The very fact that you have asked for a story, and that they have the freedom to make the story about whatever they wish, reminds the student that the piece may have been written by someone else, *but the performance*

will be theirs. More than that, it lets them know that you are interested in their ideas, rather than simply expecting them to obediently recreate the ideas of others. This becomes a powerful antidote to mechanical and soulless practice, and sends your student an important message:

"I trust you, and know that you can make this work"

For the practice battles that lie ahead in the next chapter, as the student starts to prepare the piece for the performance itself, this message of trust and reassurance needs to be ringing in their ears.

Preparing for Performance

"The throwing of oranges at performers seems to have been a more or less recognized means of expressing disappointment in the eighteenth century"

Percy A. Scholes

The Practice Revolution: Chapter 12

• Defining the Task • Dress Rehearsals • Establishing a Plan B • Slow Motion Replays in Advance • Getting comfortable with Starting • Headgames • The Blitz Week

12. Preparing for Performance

12.1 Defining the task

Most teachers seem to have higher blood pressure as student recitals draw closer—and with good reason. As they look over the audience of pupils, each waiting their turn to play, they will see some students who know their pieces, but tend to fall apart on stage, sitting side by side with those who never really knew their pieces in the first place. And those rare students who know their piece and are comfortable on stage...well, they're *supposed* to play well, so we don't have much to gain there, and plenty to lose if things do go wrong.

You have to be *very* careful with the type of practice you recommend in the days leading up to a recital. It's a time in which the wrong kind of practice can actually sabotage what may otherwise have been a fine performance. But it's also a time in which some positive practice sessions can make a tremendous difference, lifting a student beyond any expectations you may have had for them previously.

This chapter is dedicated to the End Game—those final couple of weeks that culminate in the performance itself. The piece has been polished until it shines...there's only one thing left to get right.

The mental state of the student.

12.2 Dress rehearsals

This is an essential practice session that actually breaks all the conventional rules of practicing. It won't be slow and careful, it won't stop to correct mistakes, and it won't isolate difficult sections of the piece for special attention. It won't be conducted in privacy, it won't allow repetition, and if done properly, won't even give the student the usual reassuring feeling of being safe in their practice room fortress of solitude.

This is a full tempo, no stops, no second chances performance of the work, done in the presence of one or more family and friends. It aims to simulate performance conditions as closely as possible, including—if the student is taking it seriously enough—a feeling of genuine nerves.

The student would start "offstage", and would walk on and bow, just as they would for the performance itself. If they are planning on tuning while on stage in the performance, they would do that before they play—even if their instrument is already in tune. There are important differences that can never be bridged between this dress rehearsal and the real thing, but the student should otherwise have the highest expectations of themselves both in their delivery of the piece, and the authenticity of the stagecraft.

How long does this particular practice session last? Only as long as the performance itself lasts. They play it through just once, irrespective of how satisfied they may or may not have been with the final result. It's *after* the student has taken their final bow and thanked their family member(s) that the real work starts.

This practice session is not about how they played. It's about the accuracy of the post-mortem.

12.2.1 The post dress-rehearsal analysis

Ok, so that's a nicer term than "post-mortem", but it amounts to the same thing. As soon as the mock concert is complete, the student needs to record their impressions of what just happened—the good, the bad and the hideous—while those impressions are fresh. There are several questions that will need answering as part of this:

1) What happened in that performance that was unexpectedly good?

Maybe that tricky section on page two flowed better than it ever has before. Or perhaps the dynamics at the start were more compelling than is normally the case.

The aim is not only to identify positive features from the performance, but to ensure they can be *reproduced* in the future. This means that the student will also need to be clear about what they did differently during the performance to achieve the good result.

239

Perhaps that tricky section on page two flowed better than it ever has before because it was played a fraction slower than normally is the case. Or perhaps it was played with less articulation. Or *more* articulation. It's important that the student can establish a cause-effect link like this, otherwise all they can do is *hope* for a similar result in the future. These dress-rehearsal analysis sessions are not about hoping—they're about guaranteeing that the good things will happen every time.

Such a guarantee starts with a thorough understanding of how to produce the desired results, and this information can only be produced through a simulation of performance conditions. (We can all produce stellar playing when we're not being warmed by spotlights)

2) What pre-existing problems surfaced again in the performance?

In the course of preparing this piece, the student will probably have discovered a couple of sections in which they will usually think "oh no... here we go", like a nervous roller coaster passenger as they see the Loop of Death coming up. How these sections are handled can make a crucial difference to the success or otherwise of a performance—as the golf saying goes, it's not how good your good shots are, it's how effectively you recover from the bad ones.

If your student has been preparing using the techniques found elsewhere in this book, they probably will have already created a plan of attack for practicing such sections. This dress-rehearsal will allow them to assess how effective their campaign has been, and respond with modifications to their practice plans for the days ahead. In short, if the section is still not working for them, they need to change their practice approach, which is exactly why students should be equipped with knowledge of several different practice tools for each problem.

3) What *unexpected* errors arose during the performance, and what might have caused them?

Specialists who investigate car accidents have a core belief that there is no such thing as a car "accident". There's *always* a cause, and the argument is that if you identify those causes, you are half way to eliminating future instances of the disaster.

The student might not have been able to anticipate that page three was going to let them down as violently as it did in the dress-rehearsal, but there was certainly a reason that it happened. Errors don't just appear like crop circles or plagues of frogs. While the student would be unwise to make an issue of a possibly one-off error, (and thereby have it playing on their mind in the performance itself), they will want to create some reassurance that such lightning won't strike twice. The very best way to do that is for some reflection on the mechanics of the error itself:

• *Was that performance a substantially different tempo from the way I normally play it?*

• *Were there some particular thoughts that occurred to me just before the error? Some negative self-talk that proved prophetic?*

• *Was there an instant of doubt as to how two particular phrases connect, resulting in a wrong turn that caused everything to get hopelessly lost?*

• *Was there a moment of bad fingering that caused the entire passage to come crashing down?*

• *Did I take the wrong option at a repeat, and insert a replay of the exposition where the coda should have gone?*

Or simply:

• *Did I discover that under pressure, I don't know the start of page three as well as I thought I did?*

The solutions to these problems are as varied as the problems themselves, but the student has a much better chance of preventing similar problems in the future simply by having identified them. And as their teacher, it's tremendously useful for you to understand your student's take on what actually may have happened.

12.2.2 How many dress rehearsals should the student have?

The more the better, *but never more than one in a day.* This allows them to have enough dress rehearsals to become somewhat desensitized to the unfriendliness of being in the situation of having only one shot at getting their piece right, while preventing complete devaluation of the experience by allowing them to take the "once-only!" performance over and over and over.

The fact that it can only happen once in each day means that when it happens today, the student will be very focussed on what takes place, because they can't quickly erase the memory with a fresh and improved effort. The rule for having at least one audience member there is there partly to simulate playing to an audience, but also there to *prevent* the performer from having multiple attempts. (Most family instant-audiences will be delighted to hear the performance once in an afternoon, but probably will not be smiling at the student if the student makes them sit through an hour of repeated renditions.) We can all get our pieces right eventually if only we are allowed to have two dozen attempts, but this does not give any sort of realistic feedback as to what is likely to happen on concert day.

So in short, it's one shot only...until next time. And the student needs to make sure that there are plenty of well-spaced "next times".

12.2.3 How early in the preparation campaign should the dress rehearsals start, and how soon before the concert should they stop?

The first occasional dress rehearsals should really happen as soon as the student can reliably perform the piece from beginning to end. They will only be a pale shadow of how the student will be sounding once the concert actually comes, but the information they get from such play throughs can make a tremendous difference to the practice that is coming up in the weeks or months ahead.

Choosing when to *cease* such dress-rehearsals is more difficult, and depends a lot both on the preferences of the student, and the shape the program is in. Some students like to have dress-rehearsals up to, and including the day of the concert, so that the concert itself feels like a familiar challenge, and one that they are already in the zone for. Others like to leave something special for the concert itself, and abandon all dress rehearsals in the final week, ensuring that there is nothing jaded about the performance.

Many teachers recommend strongly against dress rehearsals in the forty-eight hours leading up to the concert, just in case their student discovers a problem at the last second that needs a week of practice to fix. It's a variation on "ignorance is bliss", but with confidence being such an important factor in performances, sometimes it's better for the student not to discover last minute problems that they couldn't repair in time anyway.

12.3 Establishing a Plan B

When you chat with students who are nervous before their performance, the fear seems to boil down to one thing:

"What if I mess up?"

As teachers, the temptation is to handle this fear in two ways. First of all to encourage students to practice so that they *don't* mess up, and then to follow up that by simply asserting to them that they won't. Stated as starkly as that, it's easy to see why students don't feel particularly reassured by this twin approach—even if they have done the hard work. (Leaving aside for a moment the fact that many nervous students didn't do the hard work in the first place).

Certainly we need to encourage practice techniques that *minimize* the possibility of the student losing their way while performing, but there is no magic powerful enough that can *guarantee* that a performance will be flawless throughout. (If I had the answers to that, I would not only have written a book about it already, but I would probably buy myself a nice Pacific Island with the royalties.) Given that, instead of simply living in fear of errors, students should accept them as an occasional reality of performances, and have a plan in place for dealing with them should they arise.

Don't misunderstand me. I'm not advocating that students plan on messing up their pieces. What I am suggesting is that it should be embraced

243

as a possibility, and that if something like that does happen, *the student should have a Plan B*. The default Plan B for most students is to start again, or stop while they flounder around for the right notes, or flee the stage altogether—this practice technique is designed to have them coping a little more gracefully than that.

There is an entire article at PracticeSpot (www.practicespot.com) dedicated to Saving Yourself Gracefully, where the core of the advice is hints and tricks to *bluff* your way out of trouble in such a convincing fashion that the audience never suspects that there was a mistake in the first place. In short, the less accurate the notes, the more you had better be playing beautifully, producing compelling and plausible nonsense. Purists will note that it is nonsense nonetheless, but once a breakdown in the piece strikes there is no way of avoiding weird notes—that's the essence of breakdowns. But you minimize its impact by improvising the most beautiful nonsense you can, until you can pick up from somewhere useful.

The difficulty is that maintaining composure like that, without so much as batting an eyelid in the face of a potential disaster, is not something that students can just do automatically. They have to practice it.

12.3.1 How this technique works

The first thing the student needs to do is establish a series of "safety ramps" in the piece—places that they can jump to and start from at any time. The logic is that if they get into trouble in the performance, instead of having to go right back to the start, all they need to do is jump to the nearest safety ramp and continue. Unless the audience is paying very close attention, they may not even notice that there was a problem in the first place.

It's not enough just to have defined where these safety ramps are. The student has to be able to make the jumps *instantly*, otherwise the technique doesn't work. Making instant jumps like that is not a skill the student comes pre-equipped with—they'll need to practice it.

Before the practice begins, the student will need to *number* these safety ramps, so that they can tell which one is which. They then set up a drill in which they pull a number from a hat, and then start playing from the corresponding safety ramp They're not trying to be graceful here, they're just ensuring that they can make the jump instantly if they need to. If they have to use an emergency jump like that in a performance, it is something they will want to have done many, many times in the practice room first—like a pilot who practices for emergency landing scenarios on a simulator.

12.3.2 Practicing for seamless transitions

The fact that the jumps can occur instantly is good, in that it minimizes any downtime in the performance. However, jumping like this can sound a little abrupt, and while the audience may not have picked up the error, they certainly won't be lost in the beauty of the moment either.

To rectify this, the next step is for the student to learn how to *glide* into the next safety ramp, rather than simply jumping to it. The idea is that if their piece comes unstuck, they should continue to play *something* as they head gently to the safety ramp. Anything. They don't need to be masters of improvisation, just masters of keeping a straight face. What they play can simply be a repeated note, or even just several slow held notes—but if it is played with enough conviction, with beauty in the sound and the phrasing, and imaginative and compelling dynamics, there will be plenty of people in the audience who will believe that that's how the piece actually goes. Not only has the student successfully navigated to a safe part of the piece, they have done so in a stylish and convincing fashion.

To simulate this in the practice room, the student needs to play the piece under performance conditions, but, oddly enough, will be actively *hoping* for a breakdown to occur—regarding it as an opportunity rather than an obstacle. Once the problem appears, instead of stopping and fixing it, they practice dealing with it gracefully—playing a few simple slow notes as beautifully and convincingly as they can, before commencing reality again from the nearest safety ramp. Like any other new skill, the more they do this, the better they'll get.

As they become more adept, they can start to match the key of their chosen notes to the key of the safety ramp, while advanced students may even be able to match the *style*. Beethoven may well be spinning in his grave, but the audience will be blissfully unaware of the drama that is unfolding—and being improvised—in front of them.

245

12.3.3 The true benefit of establishing a Plan B.

The immediate benefit to the student who practices this way is that the next time they ask themselves *"What if I mess up?"*, they'll have an answer.

*"I would prefer not to mess up, and will continue to practice hard to ensure that I know the piece just as well as I can— but if something **does** go wrong, it's no major problem.*

I'll simply switch to plan B, just like I've been practicing. I'll play some transition notes as beautifully as I can, and then jump to the nearest safety ramp. Simple."

But the real benefit is something else altogether. Because the student now has a plan for coping with any nasty surprises that the performance may produce, they do not fear the possibility of such surprises so much.

And because they aren't so afraid, they'll be less nervous, will play better— and probably won't even get a chance to use the Plan B skills that they have worked so hard to develop.

12.4 Slow motion replays (in advance!)

Sports stars will sometimes use slow motion replays of some of their best passages of play to motivate them. The footage is not intended to review *typical* moments from their last competition, but is a carefully filtered set of highlights of those moments in which the player could do no wrong. Watching it helps remind the athlete what is possible in the future, and gives them a glass-half-full view of the likelihood of repeating such moments in the upcoming game. They're not just being told by the coach that they are capable of great things—*they have just seen the evidence*, and they'll leave the session walking taller than when they came in.

Music performance is just as much about confidence as sports performances, and music students are subject to the same fears and disappointments as their athlete counterparts. They are also susceptible to projections of how the Big Occasion is likely to go, which means that the content of those projections is vitally important. Sometimes just telling them to "think positive" is not enough.

This next practice technique is about taking control of those projections, and ensuring that they are in fact *prophecies* of a performance that will make both you and the student proud.

12.4.1 How this works

This practice session is going to be more about what takes place in the student's *mind* than what they actually play.

The student needs to imagine that the practice session they are about to begin is going to contain nothing but slow motion replays of the upcoming performance—*replays that reflect a performance that has gone spectacularly well.* (Let's not fuss too much about how they were able to get their hands on a slow motion replay of something that hasn't happened yet. You can make up a story about time travel if they are looking worried.) In other words, they are about to produce twenty minutes of their playing at its absolute best, and will use tempo constraints to guarantee that will happen.

Before they start the replay, they need to be clear about *exactly* what it is about the performance that will be so good, whether it is engaging dynamics, beautiful legato lines, brilliant and clear semiquaver passages, or a combination of several other musical elements. Naming the elements like this will give the students a focus for the "replays" they are about to produce.

The aim now is for them to produce playthroughs of the piece which contains all those elements, save for the tempo itself—so that if all they did was take everything they had just played, and sped it up to a performance tempo, then the performance would be something they would be very proud of.

12.4.2 Rotating the focus

With several slow motion replays to be played through, the student can shift focus for each one to ensure that all musical elements are given full attention at some stage. So the first replay might be an exhibition of the finest dynamics the student can produce, in which all changes are exaggerated slightly for maximum effect. The second replay may see the student concentrate on producing flowing and legato melody lines, while the third would target the evenness and clarity of the semiquaver passages.

These musical elements are not arbitrary—they are straight from a list that the student created before they started the session began. Not only will these focussed playthroughs put these issues firmly on the agenda for the performance itself, they will help the student realize that they are not just idle wishes. They will take into the performance the memory of having made each of these elements *work* - the only difference is beats per minute.

12.4.3 Why Slow Motion Replays help, and when to use them

This technique works in reverse from most other practice methods, and as such is ideally suited to the couple of days immediately before a performance. Instead of the student playing through their piece, spotting problems, analyzing them and fixing them, this model puts the student in an environment *where problems are not likely to appear in the first place.* More than that, it puts the focus squarely on things that the student is doing *well*, while reminding them of those musical values that they most want to show off at the performance itself.

The student takes away from the practice sessions memories of the performance having gone well on a number of musical fronts, combined with the eerie assumption that underpinned all of this—that these were not just playthroughs, they actually *were* replays of what the student can expect from the concert. As a result, they are now expecting good things.

12.5 Getting comfortable with starting

For many students, the most difficult thing about performing can be delivering the first few notes. That's when they tend to be most conscious that they are actually on stage, it's when they have to establish the tempo, it's when they need to develop a feel for acoustics in the room, and it's when they are trying to establish atmosphere and stamp their authority on the performance ahead. And somewhere in there, they are also trying to play the right notes.

Given that all of this co-incides awkwardly with the moment in which they are probably feeling most nervous, it's no surprise that the opening can be overwhelming, resulting in the performance "feeling its way" for the first few phrases, until it eventually settles.

Worse still, sometimes the performance *doesn't* settle, as the stumbling opening saps their confidence and sets the pattern for what is to follow. We've all been present at performances where a bad opening for the first piece set the tone for the entire recital, and the whole process becomes like watching a ship slowly take water.

If students want their performance to seize audiences, adjudicators and examiners alike from the very first note, then they are going to have to become accustomed to coping with starting. And like anything else they want to become accustomed to, they'll have to practice it.

12.5.1 How this technique works

Because there are so many things to take care of in the first few phrases, before they practice starting it's worth the student spending some time *building a checklist of what they want the opening to achieve*. For example, they might want to use the opening to set just the right tempo— fast enough to allow the phrasing to flow naturally, but not so fast that the tricky bit on page two will come crashing down. They need to remember that although the opening is marked *pp*, they will have to ensure that the sound projects to the back of the hall. They also might need to remember that they should spend a second checking their posture, because that slouch which has been developing recently is starting to become a distraction for anyone who watches them play. And they might also need to remind themselves how much better they play when they focus on making their dynamics just as interesting as they can.

Armed with the list of Things To Do in those opening bars, it's time to practice delivering them—but when the session begins, the student should focus on these items *one at a time*. Partly to raise their awareness of them as individual issues, rather than having some get lost in the group like a quiet child in a big class. But mostly so they can experience for themselves the successful delivery of each of these issues right at the start of a performance. In other words, it is helping them to realize that a successful start is not a pipe-dream, it is achievable, and moreover has already been achieved by them many times in the past.

So they begin by nominating *one* thing that they want this opening to achieve. It might be establishing a workable tempo for the rest of the performance. They then leave the room, instrument in hand, and come back in as though they are walking on stage at the concert itself. Having bowed elegantly to the imaginary audience, they then pause for a moment, and remind themself of the job at hand...to establish a workable tempo.

Because the focus is entirely on the start, once they are underway with the piece, they should stop after a few phrases. That will be enough information for them to assess how successful or otherwise they were with their stated goal (in this case establishing an appropriate tempo), but is a short enough passage that they could practice starting many, many times in the course of fifteen minutes. The degree of experience in starting gained in half an hour would have taken a couple of years to acquire had they simply waited for performances to give them the practice they need.

Before they start the piece for the second time, they should just take a moment to reflect on how successful they were with their stated goal on the first play through. Did they establish the tempo satisfactorily, or was it clearly too fast or too slow? If there were any problems, they should start the piece again (complete with the stage walk-on) and try to correct what went wrong last time. If everything was fine, then they would simply choose a new goal for this next beginning. Switching goals like this based on outcomes ensures that they spend time on the concepts that need it, while moving quickly on from those goals that they can already deliver.

12.5.2 Combining the elements

Once the student has successfully made starts with each of the stated tasks, it's time to start *combining them* into pairs. So this time when they start, they might be establishing an appropriate tempo AND setting the scene dynamically for the dramatic entry of the main theme in bar twelve. The only change at their end is that they will probably need an extra few seconds before starting each time to process the extra goals.

By the end of the session, the aim is to have successfully combined *all* the elements into one start. The student now not only has a list of expectations for the beginning of the performance, they also know how to manage all those demands simultaneously to create a successful opening to their performance.

The audience will never know that such careful work has gone into this. All they will feel is the sense that the performance carries an air of authority right from the outset. Adjudicators, panels and examiners will notice it too, meaning that whatever first impressions actually count for, your student has just got maximum points.

12.6 Head games

Students may well practice hard and prepare their pieces thoroughly, but in the end, a huge part of the success or otherwise of a performance rides on their state of mind *while they are actually on stage.* If their confidence is low, and their body language suggests that they are anticipating a disaster, then a disaster is almost certainly on the way. The only question will be how big.

In such a case, even if the student does manage to somehow hold things together, the audience will be able to sense that something wasn't quite right from the time the student first walked on to stage, and the experience will be uncomfortable for all present. Nobody likes watching someone die up there.

By contrast, a student who is together mentally on the day can rise beyond even the most optimistic expectations you may have had of what was possible. This time the audience is at ease from the walk-on onwards, ensuring that they respond more warmly to the student *even before the first note has been struck.* Confident students will feed from this, and a loop of positive reinforcement is established. Because the student is feeling positive, the beginning of the piece goes well. Because the beginning has gone well, they are feeling even more positive for what follows—and so on.

Such an attitude can even help students who are *underprepared* pull off minor miracles. Many recitals and examinations have been rescued at the last minute by positive assumptions from the student—a fact that is borne out in tens of thousands of sporting contests every weekend, and is the reason that most professional teams have ready access to a sports psychologist.

Given the tremendous positive impact that being together mentally on the Big Day can have, it makes sense that the student should be dedicating some serious practice time to ensuring that this essential facet of their performance is in good shape. It's not simply enough for you to pat them on the head and tell them to "Be confident! Look forward to it—you'll be fine!"—they've heard it all before, and they will need to set things up in the practice room so that those sentiments won't ring as hollow encouragement.

So what can the student do in the *practice room* to ensure that they are in control of their thoughts during the *performance?*

Plenty. The one point of resistance though can be that practicing in this fashion will sometimes feel like a waste of time to the student—after all they won't be actively improving any sections of their piece, nor will they be reworking problem passages. In fact, most of the techniques below *won't even require your student to pick up their instrument.* However, they can make the difference between a great performance and a disappointment, and are well worth making time for.

12.6.1 Create a list of things that they are looking forward to showing off

Every student knows the sections of their piece that they should be *afraid* of. The tricky coda. The fast scale in bars 38-39. The extended pianissimo section in an uncomfortable register.

But most students are not armed with a similar list of sections or qualities in the piece that they are *really looking forward to* performing. So much of music lessons is about solving problems and correcting difficulties that it can be easy for negative issues to become the dominant force—not because we're negative people, but because the nature of our roles is to troubleshoot.

This means that often the only impressions students have of the challenge ahead are neutral at best, and more likely laced substantially with concerns about the things that could go wrong. I'm not suggesting that all music students are neurotic pessimists, but students don't need to dig too deep to find plenty of small reasons to be anxious in every page of music they play. Such concerns may not bring the piece to its knees, but they do change the aura of the performance, together with limiting the student's ability to deal with these problems in the first place.

Rather than dwelling on the mere *possibility* of problems, they would be much better off focusing on the list of good things that they can *guarantee* will happen, and then to see the performance as a vehicle for showing off those good things.

The first step is for the student to build a list of those positives that they have control over—musical elements that they *know* they can deliver, irrespective of nerves, memory lapses or other variables.

For example, a student could guarantee to have engaging dynamics throughout their performance. Even if the piece were filled with wrong notes from beginning to end, they can be wrong notes filled with crescendos, sforzandos and subito-pianos. The student can similarly guarantee that the slow section on page three will maintain a steady tempo. And that the Big Finish really will be a big finish, courtesy of an exaggerated ritardando and an emphatic sound. And that their playing will be legato throughout.

As the student builds this list, they will start to become aware that there a lot of positives that they can not only hope for—they can *count* on. Generating a comprehensive version of this list becomes the core of their practice, and they'll know that you will want to see a copy at the next lesson for discussion.

The second step is for the student to build a list of sections of the program in which they either play a passage particularly well, or particularly differently from other students. This becomes a list of *"Here are some great things I can do in my performance that I know most other students cannot"*. So for example, the student may have worked quite hard to produce a particular type of extreme staccato that helps the Scherzo really sound like it has a quirky sense of humor. It's not how other students usually play it, and the student knows that during that piece, whether they like it or hate it, people will be sitting up and taking notice.

Similarly, your student might also have a slow movement in a sonatina in which they play particularly even and well-crafted trills—again, something that they know other students sometimes mess up. They might also have a long held note which happens to be right in the center of their best register, providing a moment to showcase their tone at its very finest. Or a fast scale that has always just clicked with them, one that looks and feels effortless in the delivery.

Again, the student actually writes these down, and brings the list to you. The very act of spending time trawling through their piece in search of things they do unusually well will help them realize that there is actually plenty to be proud of when they are on stage this weekend—and therefore plenty to look forward to. The whole exercise also keeps their critical mind busy to such an extent that the usual self-chatter about "what if I mess up this tricky bit?" is drowned out. And besides, they now have an answer to that question—the fact that the student might mess up this tricky bit will not affect the Show-Off List one iota.

12.6.2 *Visualize* the entire experience

Armed now with a list of musical elements and passages that they are genuinely looking forward to showing off, your student can start visualizing the entire concert as a journey. But this is not an ordinary sequential trip through the piece. They don't start at the beginning and picture each bar in turn. Like a Guidebook from a tourist centre in a city, it's a carefully constructed tour, highlighting the sections and features that they have already identified as being worthy of showing off, while glossing straight past the bad bits. They don't even get a mention. The only features that will appear on this particular trip are the anticipated highlights.

So the student might begin the trip through the piece by remembering how well they bring out the melody at the start of the work. They actually hear in their mind that melody being beautifully projected, and a little part of them should be looking forward to showing off exactly that at the concert. They then jump to bar 12, which features that trill they were so proud of. Not long after that is that scale they found so easy, followed by an extended section that allows them to show off one of their strongest assets—being able to play very quietly for extended periods of time without compromising tone quality.

Page two had that great bit in which the duplets suddenly become triplets, which is a changeover that the student can now do every time without disturbing the beat at all, something they know many other student have trouble with. And a few bars after this is a section in which they have deliberately inverted the dynamics, just because it sounded better to them, meaning that the audience may well have heard this piece before, but never like *this*.

In between these highlights are probably some passages that the student struggles with. But on this tour, these black spots are nowhere to be seen, helping the student to direct their energies entirely towards making good things happen, instead of fretting about bad things. And remember, all these positive elements are not things that the student *hopes* might happen, as might be the case if you are told to "think positively"—they are all elements that the student can *guarantee* to make happen, and better still, they identified them by themselves.

This trip is best taken under circumstances similar to those outlined in the Halflight Technique (see. Speeding things up), with lights low, peace and quiet, and a chance for the student to relax and lose themselves in their positive thoughts.

12.6.3 Create flags of these highlight moments on the score

Once the features to look forward to have been defined, mapped, and the tour has taken place, the student then needs to mark them in the music itself. The aim is that the performance itself, just like the performance visualizations, will be handled as a series of short journeys from one strong bit to the next. This means that while the student is actually playing, they are always aware of *why* they are looking forward to the next section of the piece.

A smiley face will do the job nicely, and if every page on their score doesn't have several, it's not a sign that their piece is in trouble—it just means they haven't been thinking hard enough yet. The question the student needs to be able to answer as they practice is always *"what is the next highlight, and why am I looking forward to it so much?"*. Having identified that, their autopilot takes care of the section they are playing now, while their conscious mind will be looking forward to the next section like a kid in a car who knows that a playground is coming up soon.

It's a completely different place from the land of *"I hope I don't mess up this bit"*, and one that your students definitely need to dedicate some practice time to get their visa.

12.7 The Blitz Week

Most of the practice techniques in this section focus on the days immediately before a recital, and concentrate on developing awareness of *strengths* in the performance, while studiously avoiding any sort of focus on the weaker moments. However, sometimes there are sections so weak that they cannot be ignored, and no amount of reframing is going to prevent them undermining the work as a whole. Normally such sections might require a careful campaign of a couple of months to turn them around—the problem is that the student only has a couple of *weeks*.

Something drastic is called for.

The remedy is not at all gentle, and as we'll see, risks killing the patient to cure the disease. The aim is to create a week of practice in which the student takes all the passages that have been giving them a hard time, and gives *them* a hard time. A seven day blitz to turn the tigers into whimpering kittens. Not only will the students do more practice than they ever have in their lives before, *the only things they will be targeting will be their worst nightmares.* Anything that already sounds even remotely good will be conspicuous by its absence from the practice agenda.

Obviously this should not happen in the few days leading up to the concert itself—which is when students should ONLY be focussing on making their strengths shine—but instead would happen several weeks before the Big Day. You would also be very certain that the problems actually warrant this degree of attention in the first place before recommending a blitz like this. The blitz is intended to be a drug of last resort, and is certainly not designed to deal effectively with minor issues, because by giving minor issues such attention, you risk turning them into *major* issues in the student's mind. In short, unless the piece is very, very ill, a seven day blitz may actually make things worse.

With those cautions aside, here's how it works.

12.7.1 Identify the targets

Before the blitz can begin, the student needs to be very specific about exactly where the trouble spots are, together with what the nature of the problem is - similar to the analysis that was recommended in the "Taming Tricky Bits" chapter. They don't have time to waste using the wrong practice technique on the wrong problem, and they certainly don't want to be blitzing sections that don't need the help, and perhaps giving small issues big shadows in the process.

Broadly identifying the problem section can be simple enough, but filtering it so that only the essence of the difficulty has been laid bare can be a little tricker. Sometimes the problem will be that they simply don't know the notes well enough yet to make any sense of the passage. Other times they will know the notes, but will have trouble delivering them at tempo. Or perhaps they know the notes but cannot deliver them reliably from memory. Or maybe they have a fingering that is unworkable. Or maybe they don't understand the rhythm properly. Or maybe it poses technical demands that they are not yet equipped to handle.

To do this analysis may take a while (and they may need some help in the lesson itself), but once it's been done, they need to define the physical boundaries of each of the problem passages in their piece, together with a brief note as to what the problem is.

Knowing now where the bad guys are, and what makes them tick, it's going to be much easier to deal with them.

12.7.2 Commence the blitz

This book is filled with practice techniques that are specific to particular types of problems, with the view that the student will pick those that seem most effective for them. As their teacher, you also will have some specific techniques of your own.

Blitz is not a time for choosing between techniques. You state the problem, *and then you use EVERY known relevant practice tool against it in turn*. If it were a fire, you'd stamp it out, you'd put a blanket over it, use a fire extinguisher on it, you'd remove the fuel, put a lid on it, cover it with ice cubes, call in a helicopter to water-bomb it, divert a stream so it runs through it, bulldoze a mountain of dirt on top of it and then build a fire-retardant pyramid on the remains as a symbol of your complete domination over your former problem.

In short, rule out nothing, and go way, way over the top. The error in the piece will have no qualms about messing up your student's performance, so your student should show absolutely no mercy with their pre-emptive strike.

This can be very time-consuming for each problem—hence the necessity for students to be highly specific in defining the physical boundaries of problem sections (so that they are not practicing one note more than they need to), and also for them to be ready to do a lot more practice during the blitz week than they normally would. If they fail to commit to either of those two principles, then they simply won't get through everything in time.

12.7.3 Testing after the blitz

Once the student has put the trouble spot through boot camp like that, they need to construct some tests to see if it has truly learned its lesson or not, and these tests should go way beyond the demands of the concert itself. So if the problem was that they could not play their piece at the indicated 160 bpm, they should conduct tests at 180 bpm to see how it has progressed. They might not pass such a test, but for the first time, they will find themselves wishing that they could play it at "only 160 bpm". This is the first time that the word "only" has been used like that for the formerly dreaded 160, and they will view 160 differently just for having said it.

Similarly, if the problem before was that they didn't know the notes well enough to reliably play the section through without errors, then the test might demand that they play it five times without errors. In a row. And this time, if it misbehaves, it's straight back into boot camp.

12.7.4 The aim of such a blitz

A blitz isn't magic, and it's certainly not going to transform impossible sections into picnics. However it does usually give a great leap forward to the weakest parts of the upcoming performance, giving the student less to fear. In short, while the piece will not suddenly be perfect, the worst-case scenario for the concert has just got a whole lot better.

Blitz weeks also provide a focus for those students who have been putting off the toughest sections—the very suggestion of a such a week gently reminds students that they are running out of tomorrows to delay problems to. All of which leads very neatly into the next chapter.

Project Management

Time sneaks up on you like a windshield on a bug.

Jon Lithgow

The Practice Revolution: Chapter 13

• The Need for Project Management Skills
• Creating Checkpoints • Countdown Charts •
Daily Planning • Alternatives

13. Project Management

13.1 The need for project management skills

With carefully worded and effectively communicated practice instructions—a concept so important that it's had an entire chapter in this book dedicated to it—students should always go home knowing:

- Exactly what their goals are for the week
- Which practice techniques to use to reach those goals
- How to tell when those goals have been reached

In this way, the student has been given a *mission* with clear objectives, the *tools* they need to accomplish that mission, and a way of being able to tell when the mission is *complete*.

The only thing they haven't had help with yet is how to *run* the mission. What order they should tackle things in. How to tell whether they are on schedule, behind schedule, or whether they even have a schedule in the first place. How to react if a particular task proves stubborn. How to best use an unexpected five minute practice opportunity. Which tasks should take priority. And how to allocate time to ensure that everything gets done.

"Project Management" might sound overly grandiose, but consider the task for a moment from your student's point of view. They've just been given four new scales to learn, a new piece to become familiar with, two old pieces to polish, some theory homework and some sightreading to get through. All of this, and one week to complete it.

What we tend to forget is that this same student may well take an hour to get dressed in the morning, or need step-by-step instructions to do something as simple as make themself a slice of toast. And for this same student, school projects are sometimes considered to be so enormous that they become whole family affairs.

But practicing...that, they have to take care of by themselves. They disappear into the practice room, filled with lists of tactics, but no strategy.

Because of this, it's possible for them to have spent plenty of time practicing every day, to have applied all the practice techniques they have been shown, and *still* not get the whole job done—simply because they had distributed the workload inefficiently among the available practice sessions.

It's a silly reason not to be ready for lessons, because it's entirely preventable. Kids don't come to lessons pre-equipped with project management skills though, and if they're going to get this aspect of their practice right, they're going to need a little help.

This chapter looks at techniques for providing that help, both at a lesson-to-lesson level, and also as they prepare for bigger and more distant deadlines.

13.2 Creating CheckPoints

By the time students first get the awful feeling that they are not going to be ready for their lesson, it's usually too late for them to do anything about it. In fact, for many students, such a feeling often doesn't actually occur until the day of the lesson itself.

The single most effective thing you can do to help a student project manage their week of practice is to create a series of *checkpoints* during that week. These checkpoints exist to help the student answer a very important question:

"How am I doing?"

The checkpoints allow them to compare what they have *actually achieved* with *where they should be up to*. Armed with that information, they can make changes to how they are practicing (and sometimes, how much time they are setting aside for practice) before any problems become impossible to rescue. It also allows *parents* to assess how effective the practice has been for students who might be too young to otherwise assess themselves.

13.2.1 Defining the checkpoints

For most students, two checkpoints in each week are enough—the first would take place *two days after the lesson*, followed by a second checkpoint *three days after that*. So if the lesson was on Tuesday, there would be a checkpoint on Thursday, and then a follow-up checkpoint on the Sunday just prior to their next lesson.

261

Because the checkpoints are assessing lesson-readiness, they should happen under "lesson" conditions. In other words, there needs to be somebody *listening to the student*, and the student cannot have control over the order in which things are asked for. There also needs to be an expectation that unless they can demonstrate mastery over the task within the first couple of attempts, then there is an assumption from their "teacher" of no mastery at all.

The person playing the role of the teacher will be armed with a list of *what the student should have achieved by this checkpoint*. Where did they get this list from? You supplied it at the end of last lesson (we'll look at how to make such a list shortly). The "teacher" will ask the student for a demonstration of each of the items on the list.

By the end of the session—which should only take a few minutes—the student will know exactly how they are travelling, and whether or not they need to travel a little faster.

13.2.2 Checkpoint # 1: Getting the week moving early

This checkpoint is not designed to be a daunting start to the week—after all, it's only supposed to reflect two days of work. But the very fact that the student *knows* a checkpoint is coming up after only two days will ensure they kick off their week with some productive practice. Otherwise the tendency straight after a lesson can often be to relax for a few days, secure in the knowledge that their next deadline is a whole week away.

In this way—with a standard teaching year having 40 weeks—a two day checkpoint *can help reclaim 80 days of practice that might otherwise might not have taken place*. That's almost three months of practice in each year.

But aside from that bigger picture of more practice, checkpoint number one is there to make sure that the week starts with a bang, so that it doesn't have to end in a panic. If the checkpoint goes badly, the student knows that they still have five days (but only five days) to do something about it.

13.2.3 Checkpoint # 2: Getting to lesson-ready

Because the *second* checkpoint takes place quite late in the week, the list used will actually be a *full reflection of what is expected at the lesson itself*. The student will leave this checkpoint knowing exactly what still has to be done, and if need be, may have to respond by scheduling some extra practice times.

Because students will be keen NOT to have to schedule extra practice times, they will want to be ready for this checkpoint—meaning that the checkpoint will help ensure that they are lesson-ready each week *with a couple of days spare.* Those last two days can then be spent applying pressure games to each of the tasks, so that the student does not find that their hard work falls apart at the lesson itself (See the chapter on "Making the piece reliable" for a listing of such games).

13.2.4 Transforming the role of the parent

The presence of a checkpoint means that parents no longer have to adopt the traditional role of asking "How much practice have you done today?" or even *"Have* you practiced today?" The question simply is not relevant—all the parent will be checking is whether or not the student was ready for each checkpoint as it rolls around.

As a result, there's no nagging, there's no fuss. In fact, the *only* time the parent needs to intervene is if the student falls at either of the two midweek hurdles.

But even then, the conversation doesn't need to be laced with threats of allowance cuts, or demands that the television be banned for the rest of the week. All the parent needs to do is quietly ask the student *what they are planning on doing in the next few days to turn things around.* Is the extra practice going to be a couple of extra sessions, or would they prefer to simply extend the existing sessions by fifteen minutes or so? Are they also perhaps going to change the way they have been practicing? Would some alternative techniques be worth trying?

Such questions have built into them the *assumption* of extra practice, without it being a directive from the parent. In fact, the student should be left with the feeling of being the one in control. Their parent hasn't asked them to do anything—they've asked them *how* they would like to do it. So even if the child resents directives from parents, there's nothing to resent here, because there was no explicit directive in the first place.

And then, because the modified practice plan has been created by the *student,* giving them ownership over the idea, they are much more likely to adhere to it than if it had been decreed from on high, or incubated in an atmosphere of allowance-pruning threats.

13.2.5 Acknowledging the achievements

Checkpoints don't just have to be about identifying shortfalls. They're also an opportunity to celebrate *achievements*. Carefully constructed checkpoint lists will ensure that each checkpoint will be able to display plenty of evidence that the practice so far has been working, which is probably the most powerful of all incentives to keep doing more.

As a result, the parent needs to ensure that their checkpoint report *also highlights the breakthroughs that have been made*—adding steadily to the list of things that the student should be looking forward to showing off next lesson.

A quiet word from the parent before the lesson begins (or a private message from the parent if the teacher has their own studio website—there's lots more about this in the next chapter) can ensure that the teacher knows which checkpoint items have gone particularly well, so that they can create a great start to the lesson by asking for those first.

13.2.6 Building the checkpoint lists

There are two checkpoint lists, but you only need to worry about building the first one. Since the second checkpoint is simply a full check of *everything* that is expected in the lesson itself, all the parent will need is a copy of their child's to-do list for the week, and the willingness to be thorough when the time for the checkpoint arrives. You can ensure that the parent is up to speed on everything that is required from the week ahead either by clearly outlining it in the child's notebook, or posting the to-do details on the student's music lessons webpage. (Parents should always know what the job for the week ahead is in any case!)

The first of the two checkpoint lists is a little trickier to construct, as it needs to perform the dual role of giving the student a "hurry up" message for anything they are falling behind on, while also providing an early sense of achievement for the things that have gone right so far—all set against the background of the student only having had 48 hours so far to prepare. So while the content of the list will contain roughly a third of the total tasks for the week, there are two elements that absolutely need to be present in the mix:

1) *A list of several items that you are confident that the student would easily have taken care of in those first two days.* Keep the tasks small, and ensure that they work to the strengths of the student. So if they normally find learning new scales easy, make sure that the first checkpoint includes a few scales. That way you can ensure that the week begins with the student being able to give themselves plenty of ticks.

2) *Items that you are concerned may cause problems if the student **delays** targeting them.* Some jobs are tougher than others, and anything that you feel needs a full seven days of attention should feature in this first checklist. Not in its entirety, but if the task was to learn two pages from a new piece, the checkpoint might ask to hear the first half-dozen lines of page one.

This helps save students from *"I could have done this, if only I had started earlier..."*. They know they will have to have made some progress by the first CheckPoint, so the task will need to feature in their first two days of practice.

An example of all of this in action—let's imagine that the tasks for the week, together with the tests for each task, were as follows (overleaf):

Practice Instructions for the week	
Task	**Student self-test of**
• *G,D & A Major scales to be learned*	• *Must be able to play the scales twice IN A ROW with no errors, with a metronome at 80 bpm, one note per tick*
• *Learn the new minuet*	• *Must be able to play along with teacher at half tempo without needing to stop.*
• *Complete exercises 4-12 in the theory book*	• *When it's done, it's done!*
• *Fix the accidentals errors that plagued bars 23-28 of the etude.*	• *Must be able to win the Seven Stages of Misery with the passage*

Just to get things off to a good start, when we're constructing the first checkpoint list, the first thing we'll add are a few items from their to-do list that we know the student would cope with easily:

First checkpoint List—48 hours into the week.

• *Accidentals in bars 23-28 of the etude.* Must be able to play and win Tic-Tac-Toe (which is a much easier pressure game than the Seven Stages of Misery—see the chapter on "Making the piece reliable)

• *Complete exercises 4-7 in the theory book*

• *G Major scale, passing the test prescribed for next lesson*

• *D Major scale, passing the test, but without the metronome*

All of these are elements from the bigger to-do list, but scaled back somewhat to reflect the fact that they've only had 48 hours so far. Designed for a student who finds theory easy, and is enjoying scales at the moment, this is a checkpoint list so far that they probably could have been ready for after only *24* hours.

Then we move from items that are there to encourage, to items that reflect the elements *we are most worried about on the student's behalf.* Let's see—that new minuet is two pages long, in a key signature that the student pulled a face at, and is by far the toughest job for the week. So we add to the (hitherto friendly) checkpoint list:

> • *To be able to play right through the minuet from start to finish. Gaps are fine, tempo is irrelevant, but the notes need to be delivered accurately.*

In other words, we are guaranteeing that the student will at least have completed a sketch of the minuet before the week gets too old, meaning that the remaining five days of the week will be much less stressful than they might have been otherwise.

It should only take a minute or so at the end of each lesson to build these lists, and the time spent more than pays for itself in terms of the impact such a list can have on the *next* lesson.

Alternatively, if you have your own studio website, you might elect to quickly send a message to the student with their checkpoint list...but keep it a *secret* from them at the lesson itself, so that they only find out what it will contain once they actually get home and check their own lessons progress webpage. It's a sly tactic, but it will have them wondering all the way home exactly what the first checkpoint will contain. (Curiosity is a powerful weapon if you want a student's full attention).

Once they find out what the checkpoint has in store for them, they can spend a few minutes with their parents planning how they will get it all done.

13.2.7 Having students construct their own checkpoint lists

Valuable though checkpoints are, you won't need to build checkpoint lists for every student. Older and more advanced students in particular should be encouraged to *build their own.* It not only gives them control over their rate of progress during the week, it will give them valuable experience at developing short term practice campaigns.

Sometimes they will build a checkpoint list, sail through the requirements at the 48 hour check, and then *still* be underprepared for the second checkpoint—in which case, the following week, they would create a more demanding 48 hour list. Other times, they will create demands in the first checkpoint lists that were always going to be impossible to meet.

Getting this balance right will take some time, and they'll learn a lot about how they work in the process—so much so that eventually they should be able to look at a new piece, and give an accurate estimate of exactly how long it would take to learn, memorize, or get up to speed.

13.3 Countdown Charts

The checkpoint principle doesn't just apply to weekly deadlines. Students can also use it as they prepare for more distant dates such as recitals, competitions or examinations.

With a slight modification, you can turn checkpoints into *portable countdown charts for your students*—blueprints for how students can be ready for their Big Occasions on time, every time. They'll display them in their practice room at home, and then bring them to lessons, ensuring that everyone involved in the preparation knows exactly where they are up to in the campaign. They're easy to make, fun to use, and might just save your students (and your sanity!) the next time a major event looms.

So why do you need Countdown Charts in the first place? It's less to do with music, and more to do with physics. Don't let your eyes glaze over yet, as the principle outlined below affects *every* music teacher at some stage. (And it's the reason last minute panic practice occurs in the first place…)

13.3.1 Time distortions and your studio

One of the more unsettling scientific discoveries of the twentieth century is that time is *not* actually a constant. So much so that you can't count on it to act as any sort of reference point, because there are circumstances under which it can slow down, and more extreme conditions during which it could actually stop. Theoretically, of course.

Well, it's not just a theory, and you don't need to have an understanding of quantum physics or singularity theory to appreciate the point. Music teachers have *always* known that time is not a constant—not just because we have to explain the enigma of *rubato*, but because of the variable rate at which deadlines seem to approach. And through this, music teachers understand something

268

that physicists are yet to embrace; that time can also actually *speed up*.

If this all sounds a little far-fetched, consider the following:

When we first tell students about end of year concerts or exams, we'll usually give them plenty of notice. Six months is not atypical, which should give them around 180 days to prepare. That should be plenty, and they can't claim they weren't warned.

Unfortunately, the *actual* amount of time afforded by six month's warning is nowhere near 180 days. The first five months usually flies by for most students—delightful summer-holiday-lazy days of relaxed half-practice, buoyed all the while by the knowledge that the exam is still six months away.

It's not that these students are being lazy. It's the perception that throughout every one of those five months—*including* the fifth month—the exam feels as though it is *still* six months away.

Why? Because the student was once told that it is! The number sticks with all the permanence of all the other constants we memorize at school. Seven days in a week. Four weeks in a month. And six months till my performance.

So time stands still—at least for the student. No cosmetic company on the planet has been able to achieve this, but music students find themselves temporarily immune from the ravages of time whenever a deadline is in the distance. As long as they have a concert at the end of the year, they'll be Forever Young.

But of course, nature is a balance of opposite forces. The yang to this five months of indolent yings is that in the last month, time suddenly *accelerates*. Having been cocooned by the notion of the six month preparation time, the student finds out that the exam is now only four *weeks* away. Someone must have moved it.

Because a month is not long enough to get everything done, the days hurtle by with plenty of hyperventilation and arm-waving. Any notions of excellence dissolve into the pragmatic realization that simply *surviving* this exam is going to be a feat. Panic practice then sets in—the teacher telling the student that they will need to double or triple the amount of work they normally do to get through this.

As the time crisis continues to deepen, parents become involved and start shutting down everything except life-support. Televisions, gameboys, family outings…all gone, as they attempt to arrest the accelerating entropy. Like a badly scripted Star-Trek episode, the student now tries to extract the impossible from the engines, the klaxons wail and the shields go down for the last time as the performance actually begins...

....there is an explosion of accidentals and quarter notes and then...

Well who knows. Sometimes it actually goes well. But I'll tell you this much—teachers and parents are usually left panting and bloodied, staggering from the deadline like punch-drunk middleweights. Everyone's blood pressure is now permanently ten points higher than it used to be.

Things don't have to be this way.

There is something that will combat this time-distortion phenomenon, and it's really not all that hard to build.

The best way to eliminate the time distortion, and the accompanying last minute panic, is for students to *always* know exactly how far away their deadlines are. It's not enough to simply give them a date at the outset of the campaign, and then to tell them at their lesson each week that the date is getting closer. You'll end up with a studio full of ostriches, and plenty of final month grief.

Most students need a *daily* reminder of exactly how close their Big Occasion is. Not to create panic, or make them feel guilty, but to gently remind them that each day, they are a day closer. So if the concert was 73 days away yesterday, today they will know it's 72. This means that each day becomes an important and useful entity, rather than just a thing that gets bundled together with other days to form weeks.

I'm not suggesting you ring them every day at 7am to tell them how many days to go until their exam. We're going to build a countdown chart for them instead.

13.3.2 How to build the chart

First things first, you need to get a big sheet of cardboard, some colored markers and a ruler, and you need to work out exactly how many days there are to go until the Big Occasion. Not just the date—*the actual number of days is critical.* Don't round it up or down. If it's 99, remember 99, not 100.

Your sheet of cardboard is going to become a custom designed calendar, but instead of having 30 squares (as you might expect to have on a regular calendar), it will have one square for each day between now and the performance date. So there might be 25 squares, there might be 160—it all depends how far away the event is.

Using the ruler, create a grid so that you end up with enough squares.

Don't worry about multiples of seven—the focus is on how many days, not how many weeks.

Once you've done that, it's time to start labeling the squares. But don't write anything in yet.

We're going to *color code* this to make the whole thing more dynamic—and intuitive—for your student.

The idea behind color coding is to help your student perceive the approach of the deadline a little more acutely, and is also a simple psychological trick to give them fresh bursts of energy at regular intervals.

As the deadline draws nearer, the color you use to label the number of days to go will change. Pretending for a moment that the deadline is 86 days away, the colors you use to write the number might be as follows:

86-75 days to go	Light Green
75-50 days to go	Dark Green
49-35 days to go	Light Blue
34-25 days to go	Dark Blue
24-15 days to go	Purple
14-8 days to go	Orange
7-1 days to go	Red
Concert day:	Yellow

Once you have worked out your color plan, write in each of the numbers using the colors you decided on. Don't make the numbers too big—you are going to want to leave room in each square for some other things.

As your student crosses days off the chart, they will notice the color changes as landmarks. So once they hit the 75 days to go mark, and everything is suddenly dark green, they will perceive the campaign as having entered a new phase. Mindful of the change, many students will undertake a fresh burst of practice.

So your student will now be able to keep track of their approaching deadline, and won't have any illusions about its actual proximity. That's half the battle—now dates won't be as likely to sneak up and ambush your students any more.

13.3.3 Stepping Stones

The other half of the battle is helping the students project manage all of this—to take this huge deadline, and break it down into a series of smaller ones. Let's refer to these mini deadlines as "Stepping Stones" and look at how to build them into the existing countdown chart.

Let's imagine that your student has a performance exam in 100 days, at which they have to play four different pieces and some scales. To make sure that they stay on track throughout the preparation campaign, you might create the following Stepping Stones:

100 Days from now	Performance Exam!
88 Days from now	Mock exam with another teacher
80 Days from now	Mock exam with you
70 Days from now	Monster scales test (every scale listed in the syllabus for the exam, done in every imaginable way!)
60 Days from now	All pieces to be memorized
45 Days from now	All pieces learned, fingered, dynamics and phrasing worked out and polished
25 Days from now	Must be able to play through all four pieces from beginning to end
14 Days from now	Must be able to play through Etude and the Gigue slowly from beginning to end
7 Days from now	Must be able to play through the Gigue

You'll come up with your own deadlines that reflect the way in which you prefer students to prepare for pieces, but the point is, your students will know EARLY in the campaign if they are starting to slip behind. If in seven days from now, they can't play through the Gigue, it's time to get a move on.

This early notification of any lagging is a tremendous advantage for both student and teacher, as it allows both parties to react while there is still time to do something about it. They won't need to panic practice if they start to fall behind, they will just need to do a little more than usual, until they catch up.

It also means that if you do have to suddenly turn around and ask for a little extra, they will understand *why* just by looking at their chart—ensuring greater likelihood of a spirit of co-operation.

It's also worth considering allowing students to design their own stepping stones—just as some students should be encouraged to create their own checkpoints. It's much harder for a student to complain that they didn't have enough time to prepare for the Monster Scales Test when *they* were responsible for choosing the deadline.

Now that the content and dates for the stepping stones have been agreed upon, it's time to make them official—in almost a ceremonial fashion, have your student write the details on the appropriate squares of their chart.

When they look at their chart at home, they will not only be able to tell how many days there are to go till the Big Day, but they will also know at a glance whether they are ahead of schedule, behind schedule, or just cruising nicely.

13.3.4 Studiowide Countdown Chart

Once you have several students with their own countdown charts, it can start to become difficult for you to keep track of all those deadlines. This is where a studio-wide chart is essential.

It will allow you to see at a glance *all the deadlines in the studio*, together with their stepping stones, helping ensure that you have a firm grip on what is going on.

You'll build yourself a studiowide countdown chart in the same way that you constructed the charts for your students, but because your chart is for EVERYONE, it will have a lot more written on it. (So you will want each square to be a little bigger to accommodate the extra information) Be careful to label who each deadline is for—particularly stepping stones, which are likely to be different for every student. Place the chart prominently in your studio, and you'll have a clear picture of where each student is supposed to be up to, and by when.

Studio Countdown Charts also help students to feel a sense of fellowship with their peers—they will be able to see from the chart that Trial Recitals are not special tortures cooked up especially for them, but are a regular part of *any* student preparing for the end of semester concert. In fact, their own trial recital will probably be one of dozens. The knowledge that they are not alone (and being a music student can be a little insular sometimes) can be very reassuring, and for some students, oddly motivating.

13.3.5 Teaching *students* to build their own Countdown Chart

Creating a Countdown Chart for your student is only a first step towards the much bigger goal of self-sufficiency for your students, as they prepare for similar deadlines in the future. In other words, you are going to have to teach them how to make the charts for themselves.

The is best done in several stages:

1. Their first Countdown Chart: Do it ALL for them in advance, have it ready to go for their lesson

You'll have to work this way to begin with—after all, the whole idea of a Countdown Chart will be new and untested for your student, so they can hardly be expected to suddenly know how to build and use their own.

Building it in advance means that you don't have to explain two things at once. You can show them *what it's for* without having to confuse the issue by also teaching them *how to build it*. It will be ready to use straight away, like a bike that requires no assembly (which is always nice the first time you use something!)

2. Their second Countdown Chart: Build it WITH them

The second Countdown Chart you build will be a collaborative effort. Draw up the grid together, write in the days to go, fill in the date of the Big Occasion, and then talk through what the stepping stones ought to be. They'll wield the rulers and pens, you supervise and make sure it ends up being useful.

They need to understand that this Countdown Chart is every bit as legitimate as the one you made for them last time. (In fact, if anything, they will probably embrace it with greater enthusiasm, because they were part of the process of building it!)

3. Their third Countdown Chart: Let them build it *by themselves at home*, then bring it to their next lesson.

Your role now is simply to help fine tune something they have already built. Not only does this represent an important milestone in the student's quest for overall self-sufficiency, it frees you from having to build them in the future.

Most students will be quite proud of their own Countdown Chart—particularly if you make a big fuss about how much you are looking forward to seeing it, and remind them that you don't give all students permission to make their own. Finding out which stepping stones they have opted for, and when they expect those deadlines will be is always a fascinating exercise, and will give you a perspective into the mind of that student that will be useful in your other dealings with them.

Reality sometimes has a way of colliding awkwardly with the deadlines students set for themselves however. One common example: If a student has to prepare four pieces in twelve weeks, they will often allocate exactly three weeks to each piece (three times four being twelve and all...) Sounds reasonable on paper, but the reality is that some pieces are harder to prepare than others. You don't want them trying to panic cram a six week piece into 21 days, nor do you want them using up three weeks on another piece that really only needed a few days.

If this all sounds crazy, remember that some students can become quite attached to and defensive on behalf of the deadlines they create. You have to give them permission to make modifications as they go, as when they first start, they simply won't have enough experience to estimate how long jobs are really going to take. By the time they are on their fifteenth countdown chart, the alterations to their plan should only be minimal, but there still should be some. It's not unreasonable to expect that the first Countdown Chart they ever do for themselves will be almost unworkably inaccurate.

So there's one more tool students will need as well as cardboard, markers and a ruler...they will need an eraser, together with the willingness to use it occasionally.

You might want to remind them though that while stepping stones are slightly flexible, the date of the Big Day is etched in cement, and that whatever juggling they do still has to lead to them being ready on time for that. Most students will actually try to juggle as little as possible, which is probably a good thing.

Your students' Countdown Charts are powerful project management tools for them, and can also be powerful motivators—but to ensure that they are receiving the appropriate encouragement and support at home, you should ensure their parents are aware of:

• The existence of the chart, and what it is for (and where it is—whether it's on cardboard, or on their child's webpage)

• The date and the nature of the Big Occasion at the end of the chart

• Details of stepping stones

You may even find that parents like the idea so much that they want to adopt it for other Big Occasions in their child's life (Projects at school, exams or quizzes etc.) And every time they do, it will be a tangible reminder of the positive difference that music lessons make, and yet another illustration that these differences go well beyond mere notes.

13.4 Daily Planning

So far the focus has been on helping students cope with mid-to-long term deadlines:

• First of all, **checkpoints** are created to help students to understand "In order to be ready for my next lesson, where should I be up to *in two days from now?*".

• And for the bigger picture, **Countdown Charts** are designed to answer the question "In order to be ready for the concert at the end of the year, where should I be up to *in six months from now?*"

If the student is going to make such longer term goals achievable, at some stage there's one more question that needs to be asked and answered:

• "For me to be ready for my next checkpoint or Countdown Chart item, what do I have to achieve *today?"*

In other words, *they need to start each day of practice with a clear purpose.* If they don't know why they are practicing on a particular day, they really shouldn't be practicing in the first place. (See the practice flaw "Drifters" in chapter 4)

13.4.1 The Checkpoint Division

To help students work out their tasks for the day ahead, they need to apply a simple formula. They don't need to thank Newton or Euclid for this one—in fact, it's really just common sense. However, like so many other things that are "common sense", it's ignored most of the time:

*To be ready on time, every time, students should aim to divide their **work due** equally across the **number of available days.***

In other words, if the student has a checkpoint in three days' time, they really need to get a third of the job done on each day.

It sounds self-evident, but it's a calculation that most students simply don't make in the first place. As a result, there's no sense of closure or achievement with each day of practice—instead, they have to wait until the next checkpoint or lesson to find out if their hard work has actually been working. Or worse still, they simply practice for exactly thirty minutes every day, with no interest at all in outcomes.

All of this means that at the start of their week, *before they do any practice at all,* they need to ensure that those first two days of practice actually prepares them for their first checkpoint. That's the whole reason they are practicing on those two days in the first place. So in order to be ready for the checkpoint at the end of the second day, they should have completed half of the job on the *first* day.

This calculation is made so that students can answer a simple question each day, because there is nothing surer than the fact that they will *ask* it:

"Can I stop practicing yet?"

If they have sticky taped to their music stand a detailed list of everything they needed to achieve today, this question will answer itself every time.

13.4.2 The Practice Diary

Given that we're now looking at subdividing the week into checkpoints, and those checkpoints into daily tasks, it would also make sense to modify the student's practice diary to reflect this new structure. Most practice diaries simply consist of a list of the desired outcomes from the week ahead—learn this, memorize that, fix the fingering in those—all of which is great for keeping the student aware of what's needed by next lesson, but tells them nothing specifically about what to do *today*.

Once the student has performed the checkpoint division to work out their tasks for the day, they should actually write that in their practice diary under today's date: *To do today...* and then fill in the blanks. It should only take a minute or so—they don't need to decorate it or use their best handwriting.

Some students will protest that simply *thinking* about a plan for the day should be enough, without you creating extra work for them by insisting on them having to write the plan down too. Stay firm—actually writing down the Tasks for the Day like this is actually going to *save* them time:

1) Instead of the student simply reaching a vague unspoken understanding about what's involved, actually writing down the tasks for the day like this will force them to be clear about what the goals are. They'll know what they have to achieve, and they'll know when they have finished.

Their aim usually then becomes to finish it as quickly as possible, which will encourage them to practice *efficiently*. There's nothing wrong with this—it's the trade-off at the heart of the Practice Revolution.

2) Writing it down like this means that they only have to think about planning *once* in each practice session. There's no wondering what to do next—all they have to do is check their diary. Without the diary, they'll have to carry around the goals inside their head, energy which would be better spent simply getting on with the job.

3) The student will have a tangible way of demonstrating that the planning took place in the first place. If you ask students to please plan their practice each day, they'll nod and say "OK"...and then may or may not do it. The very fact that they know you will be *discussing* their diary entries with them next lesson will make it much harder for them to leap into their practice without a plan.

4) They'll be able to compare the a*ctual outcomes* of each day with the *aims*, helping them plan more effectively in the future. For example, some students work best if an entire practice session is dedicated to similar types of activities (e.g. nothing but scales) whereas others work best when they have a wider variety of tasks, but less to do with each one.

The point is, most students simply don't know, and being able to compare projected outcomes against *actual* outcomes will get them thinking about how they can do things better in the future.

You know something though...there's more to diaries than just a plan for the day ahead. There are some sneaky things that you can do in that little book that can completely transform how your students work—*if you use it in the right way.*

Come with me for a moment. I've had an idea that might just help.

14. Your student's Notebook

Everything that can be invented, has already been invented.

Director of US Patent office, 1899.

The Practice Revolution: Chapter 14

• The *Practice Revolution* Practice Planner model
• Creating lesson summaries that actually *help*
• Rating the *results* of their practice • The parent factor • Keeping track of what's coming up • "Please Prepare this": Your practice instructions • Self-assessment • Practice strategy sheets • Piece coach • Practice scheduler • 21st Century options

14. Your student's notebook

Guess what. The fact that you are *reading* about effective practice on behalf of your students is a great start, but by itself, that's not going magically transform the six days between lessons for them. My chess openings are not going to suddenly improve just because I happen to have a cousin who is reading a copy of "Spassky's Guide to Great Gambits". I either need to either read it myself, or somehow communicate with my cousin about the ideas she's been picking up.

This chapter is all about figuring out how to effectively *convey* your practice ideas to the people who need them most—without them having to sit still while you read out all 324 pages of this book.

To make that communication flow possible, we're going to need a little help from the world's most common—and badly *under*used—piece of teaching equipment. And it's not a metronome.

Whether your colleagues call it a "lesson diary", a "student notebook" or a "practice planner", the approach to using this item is the same in most studios. The student brings the book to each lesson, the teacher writes the date, some comments, and a summary of what has to be practiced this week. The student is then supposed to read it and bring it again next time.

Most of the time that's *all* it's used for though. What happened. When it happened. What's supposed to happen next.

It's a huge wasted opportunity. Remember, this book acts as your proxy—a stunt music teacher who does all the dangerous work for you in the Great Void between lessons. Used well, it has the capacity to transform your students' preparation, by supporting them when you can't.

Problem is, it's hardly ever used well—by the student or by the teacher. This chapter is about changing that, and transforming your student notebook from being a mere record-keeper into a practice powerhouse. Once your students go through the door at the end of the lesson, *for the next six days, their notebook is the best support they have*—it's time to learn to use it properly.

14.1 *The Practice Revolution Practice Planner* model

There are two different ways you can use the information in this chapter. One is to apply it to the student notebook that you **already use**, and to get your students to put in some new headings, and rule up the recommended new sections.

Alternatively you can simply switch your students to the lesson notebook that was designed specifically to complement this book. The Practice Revolution Practice Planner takes on all the functions of the notebook your students currently use, but it's also pre-equipped with sections that correspond to each of the ideas you will read in this chapter.

You can read more about this at:

www.practicerevolution.com.

Whichever solution you adopt though, things are about to change for your students at home, and some of these changes they're going to find confronting, to say the least. For you, for their parents—and ultimately for the students themselves—that's good news, and the start of a much more efficient way of preparing for each lesson.

14.2 Creating lesson summaries that actually *help...*

Music students go to great lengths to reassure us that they're listening, and don't need a written record. They *nod* at our explanations. They *smile* at our analogies. They tell us "Oh! I get it", and they say "uh huh" a lot – all helping us feel that maybe they're hearing what we say after all.

Uh huh.

Whenever you find yourself falling for any of this—and thinking that "of course they'll remember the key points from last lesson while they're practicing"—you might want to run the following experiment:

Call one of your students the day after their lesson. When you're done with "how are you?", it's time for the bombshell. You're going to ask them for a lesson summary.

"Gosh", they'll say. Like a contestant on Who Wants to be a Millionaire after a question about Tang Dynasty architecture, they'll look helplessly around the room as they wonder how many lifelines they have left.

They really shouldn't be flummoxed like this—after all, the lesson was only yesterday, and they had front row seats. What was talked about? What happened? What were the key points that they had to remember? What did they have the most trouble with? And what were they told they could do better?

And what in the heck are they doing practicing this week without being clear on those issues?

All of this brings home two important points, which I call the Practice Revolution Laws of Conservation of Communication. Forget Newton. This is the stuff you really need to know.

LAW 1: No matter how eloquently and engagingly you present your points, your students will only remember a fraction of what was said.

LAW 2: Of the points that are remembered, many will be subject to bizarre interpretations.

Given these laws, it always astonishes me when teachers indignantly tell students at lessons "But we talked about this last week!", as though the student is willfully disobeying their instructions. If the teacher was serious about a message being absorbed, they would have reinforced it, clarified it, checked for consensus on the meaning of the message—and then made sure the student has easy access to reminders.

Whether you end up using the Practice Planner that was designed specifically for this book, or your own notebook, the "Issues from Last Lesson" note has to be handled thoughtfully. Being a summary, it won't contain any specific practice instructions. *But the key issues from last lesson need to be the key issues for your student while they're practicing.* Otherwise these key issues will just end up being problems next lesson again too.

Unfortunately, it's not enough to simply *create* the summary. There are two additional battles you have to win:

1) You have to make sure that both you and your student understand the summary to mean the same thing

2) You have to make sure they actually *read* it—and remember it

Both fixable. Let's take these one at a time.

284

14.2.1 Making sure you both share the same interpretation

The best way to ensure that the student is not misinterpreting the summary is to make it *their* summary. Instead of writing something, *ask them what you should write.*

Tell them there were three big things discussed today, and ask them what they were. You can lead the witness from that point if necessary, but the explanations would be their own. That forces them to revisit key moments of the lesson while the lesson is still fresh—and then to demonstrate understanding of those points *by being able to explain them to someone else.* Any misunderstandings can be gently cleared up, and it's only once you've heard an explanation that you would be happy for them to give to another student that you can sign off on this.

And then, to make the note stick in their minds, *simply use the language they couched their explanation in.* It might not be the words you would have used, but the very fact that they chose those words means these are the phrases that hold most meaning for them. And if that means that your notebook now says "Make the opening section sound grumpy and frightening, and like it's late for something" instead of "Exposition to be *prestissimo feroce,* with a stretto-like intent", then so be it.

In this way, you're not actually recording your lesson summary at all. You're recording theirs, and they'll recognize it as such whenever they see it. Having given them ownership over the summary, and editorial control over the wording, the summary will be part of their consciousness for the practice week ahead—which is when they need it most.

14.2.2 Making sure they actually read it

Because your student created the summary, they might not actually *need* to read it to remember it. But to be sure it's part of each practice day, there are two tricks you can use.

The first is to write something in the "Issues from Last Lesson" section —*but don't show them.* Tell them it's a secret, and that they're not allowed to read it until they get home.

A secret? And they're not allowed to look? Of *course* they'll look. Consumed with curiosity, they'll probably check it out—and the other comments with it—in the car on the way home. There's a limit to how many times you can play that card though.

The second trick—and a more lasting solution—is to always start each lesson by having them tell you, from memory, *what the Issues From Last Lesson were.* Have prizes on hand if they can list everything, and make answering that question worth one of the ten points you could award for lesson readiness (see below)

14.3 Rating the *results* of their practice

Appearing straight underneath the "Issues from Last Lesson" in the Practice Planner is a "How ready I thought you were for the lesson" rating—signalling to the student that they are accountable for what their practice produces, and that they're accountable *every* week. And because it's a *number*, it provides an instant answer for curious parents as to how well prepared their child really was for the lesson:

How ready I thought you were for your lesson

The moment of truth for the student. For a full preview, go to www.practicerevolution.com

It's very simple. It takes seconds to do. But it provides a powerful incentive for the student to stay focussed on what you need from them, and then creates *springboards for conversations* that can help change their practice the following week.

One quick example. Sometimes a score of less than ten will come about because they simply didn't practice enough, but as the "Common Practice Flaws" chapter in this book illustrated, sometimes it's because the way they worked didn't work. Whatever the cause, if students are not adequately prepared, there needs to be a two part response:

1) A clear, quick-to give, easy-to-digest but non-accusatory indication that their results were below par. Your none-too-flattering score out of ten works perfectly for this.

2) An understanding as to exactly *why* the student was unprepared. Was it simply *insufficient time* spent? Was it *confusion* over what the task for the week was? Was it the *wrong practice tool* for the task at hand? Was it *ineffective allocation* of practice time? Was it the absence of *required parental help*? Or

did the student fall victim to one of the Practice Flaws outlined at the start of this book?

Be clear on one thing though. There's absolutely no point in complaining to a student about not being ready unless both of you understand *why* they weren't ready. Telling them to throw more practice at the problem is not going to help if it was their practice that was the problem in the first place.

Similarly, if your student scores a ten, it's worth knowing exactly what they did to achieve such a result. Partly so it can be duplicated in the future, but also to double check that they could not have perhaps achieved the same level of preparedness with *less* practice—if only they had practiced in a different way.

So once the outcomes for the week have been assessed, the discussion should always turn to *how* those outcomes were produced—and whether things can be done better next time.

14.3.1 Keeping your students focussed on outcomes

Because your students *know* you'll be filling this rating in each week—and because they know you'll be basing it entirely on how closely the requested practice outcomes were met—*they'll be paying much closer attention to the contents of your practice instructions in the first place.* Otherwise they'll quickly learn that it's possible to practice for hours every day, and still score a 1—if the practice is badly directed, or worse still, actively irrelevant.

It also quickly teaches them that you're not going to be impressed just because they report having completed a *lot* of practice. With your catchcry being "Show me the results!", their moment-to-moment question when practicing becomes "how will this help me get a better rating next lesson?" If they cannot answer that question, then they should be practicing differently, or something else entirely. In other words, while they're in the water, there's no point in just paddling. They need to be swimming towards their finish line for the week, which means they have to be clear on just what exactly the finish line is this time.

14.3.2 The competitive element

The fact that the rating is a *number* lends itself readily to creating competitions within the studio, as part of periodic "best practicer" awards. It also allows you to quickly *track cycles* in a student, by giving you at-a-glance information for how well prepared a student has been over a period of time. Reading back over 6 months of such ratings can be very illuminating, helping you to work better with—and even anticipate—the cyclic peaks and troughs that can occur.

You can preview the "How Ready I Thought You Were for this Lesson" feature in the Practice Planner by going to: www.practicerevolution.com.

14.4 The parent factor: Making use of "notes home"

For all the rhetoric about the practice process needing to involve parents—particularly with young students—I'm astounded how often there is *no* communication between teacher and parent over how practice should be handled. The "Notes home" section has been included in the Planner not just so you can remind parents about overdue fees. It's to help combat the fact that *many parents simply have no idea how they could be helping their child practice.*

"Please listen to the recording of the new piece - while Stacey points out the notes to you. Ask her to count out loud while she does this. Have a great week, and let me know how you go."

It's this simple. If you want parents involved in the process, you have to extend an invitation. The "Notes Home" section of the Practice Planner is designed with this in mind, and there should be a similar dedicated section in whatever lesson diary your studio chooses to use.

There's another use for this section though. The sweetest praise of all is **overheard praise**—the next time you want to give a student a pat on the back for some great practice they did, don't just tell them. Write the details in the "Notes home" section...and mention to your student that you are writing an important note for their parents. Most students will take a look at what the note says long before their parents ever see it, and will be delighted by the message.

14.5 Coming up: Ready on time, every time

Designed to stop deadlines from ambushing your students (see the Time Distortions discussion on page 268), this section allows for a clear countdown to the student's Big Occasions.

That way, time critical practice items *become time critical to the student too*—they'll be able to see for themselves that their concert is not just some distant and immovable event. It's drawing inexorably closer, and the type and intensity of the practice they do needs to change in response.

As a result, their practice is not just an endless succession of short term goals. It also allows them to prepare for the bigger picture—without waiting until they can see the whites of its eyes before they respond to it for the first time.

School talent night

27 Days to go

Guild Auditions

58 Days to go

Stop deadlines from creeping up.

14.6 "Please prepare this"...your practice instructions

This is where you can put all the advice from the Giving Better Instructions chapter of this book into action. Remember, your students will be basing everything they do this week on your instructions, so there is no room for ambiguity about the outcome you're looking for.

In fact, if your instructions are vague, there are two disasters waiting for you. First of all, you make it possible for dedicated students to prepare diligently, *but not to prepare what you needed.* And while they're busy working pointlessly hard, less motivated students will be able to use the ambiguity of *their* instructions to *shrink their target for the week,* and then still be able to demonstrate that according to the letter of the law, "this is what you asked for". Because according to the letter of the law, it was. So be careful what you write.

In short, don't let an instruction like "learn page 3" just hang there. Spell out exactly *under what circumstances* you will be hearing page three next week.

Do they have to be able to play it from memory? Are they allowed to have "gaps" while they think about the notes, or will you be asking for a performance with a metronome running? And if so, how fast will it be? Will there be a zero tolerance for misread notes? Or incorrect fingerings? Were there specific difficulties on page three that you expect to be mastered?

That way, students will be able to test the piece at home *with the same expectations that you will have of them next lesson.*

In short, if your student is to falls short of your expectations in a lesson, don't let it be because they were at all unclear as to what your expectations actually were.

---

❶ Please prepare this:

Page 4 of the new study. With the metronome at 80bpm, no interruptions ☺

❷ And this:

C,G,D,A and E Major scales. All from memory, two octaves.

Make sure they know *exactly* what you'll be asking to hear, and how it has to be delivered.

14.5.1 Keeping your promise

The "please prepare this" has a second function. It serves as a reminder to you next lesson—having set out clearly what you will be asking to hear, *you now need to actually ask for it.* No embellishments. No paraphrases. No extras. If your request at the lesson differs even slightly from your "please prepare this" note, then your student will quickly lose confidence in the instructions you give.

For both teacher and student, the buzzword is "predictability". Predictability because you know exactly what your student will be preparing. And predictability because your student knows exactly what you'll be asking for.

If either one of those elements becomes *unpredictable*, there's trouble ahead.

14.7 How ready this item is (self assessment)

Mirroring the "How ready I thought you were Lesson" rating that you give the student, this rating appears under each practice instruction, but this time is designed for the student to use. Again, it takes only a couple of seconds for the student to fill this in just before their lesson starts:

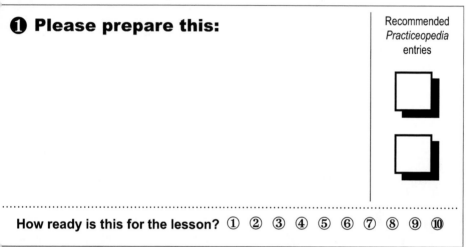

❶ **Please prepare this:**

Recommended
Practiceopedia
entries

How ready is this for the lesson? ① ② ③ ④ ⑤ ⑥ ⑦ ⑧ ⑨ ⑩

"Please prepare" paired with "How ready is this?" *self*-assessment—forcing them to honestly confront the week that was.

With the core of The Practice Revolution being a shift to outcomes-based practicing, students need to have a moment before each lesson in which they are forced to confront the effectiveness—or otherwise—of their preparation

If they give themselves a 10, the question you need to ask them then is "That's great! What happened in your practice this week so that you know this item is ready enough to get such a high score?"

At which point they'll need to outline the various tests and challenges that this section passed. The answer "Oh, I just did lots of practice on it" is not enough, and is generally a pretty good indication that *you* won't be giving the item a 10 after you hear it.

In other words, this self assessment is not just a moment where they have

291

to confront the reality of their week. It's another springboard for discussion, and can give you a window into the Week That Was even before the first note in the lesson sounds.

It's always interesting to see how closely their self-assessment matches the rating you give them. But the point is, every time a number is produced, there is potential for a short discussion as to why the number was as it was—so that the student is constantly being bombarded with assessments of outcomes.

It doesn't take much immersion in an environment like this before their practice becomes outcomes driven too.

14.8 Practice Strategies & *Practiceopedia*

The Practice Revolution outlines and discusses plenty of practice strategies, but it's really *not* a book that your students are likely to read. To save you having to explain each and every idea in this book, I've put together a huge student guide that does the job for you. 376 pages, color and fully illustrated, and packed with practice ideas, tips, tricks and traps. There are extensive previews at:

www.practiceopedia.com

Practiceopedia is not designed to be read from beginning to end, but instead is a reference that is always on hand in their practice room, and is cross referenced so they can quickly find the help they need for whatever practice problem is bugging them. It's also there for parents who supervise practice sessions, giving them a world of new options to suggest beyond just "play it until it's right".

Recommending a practice technique to a student is then as simple as noting the relevant Practiceopedia page number, and recording it in their diary. So if you want them to use the "Metronome Method" technique, refer them to the Practiceopedia entry on "Metronome Method"—it will tell them everything they need to know. If they're suffering from the "Beginners" practice flaw, then they need to head to "B" in their Practiceopedia. The chapter will then walk them through the full range of disasters that are awaiting them if they always start from the first measure whenever they work.

The A-Z format of Practiceopedia also contains a whole host of practice techniques that *don't* appear in this book—if Practice Revolution has been useful for you, you definitely should check it out.

Practiceopedia

THE MUSIC STUDENT'S

illustrated guide TO practicing

- 376 pages • Full color •
- • Cross-referenced •
- • Packed with practice ideas, strategies, tips, tricks & traps •
- • Helping you get *better results* in *less* time by working *smarter...*

The essential practice room reference
for today's busy students (and parents!)
...so that every minute counts

From the author of *The Practice Revolution*

Philip Johnston
• PracticeSpot Press •

*Practiceopedia contains all the key ideas from this
book, but in a format your students and their parents
will read—just include in your practice instructions the
relevant page numbers. Check out previews of the book
at **www.practiceopedia.com***

14.9 Piece Coach

Most pieces take much longer than a week to learn—meaning that your feedback will often be scattered through several different pages in traditional practice diaries. As a result, students tend to get a *fragmented* picture of what's important in their pieces, with the most recent issues being the most easily accessible, and therefore the highest priority.

That would be fine, except that sometimes an observation that was made three months ago is as important now as it ever was. This means that you either need to repeat the observation...or *make it easier to find in the first place*, which is where the Piece Coach cleverly comes to the rescue.

The Piece Coach allows the student to keep all the notes about one piece *in one place*. It's a special section of their Practice Planner that is sorted by title, rather than by date, so that students can instantly find all the points that were ever made about a piece they are studying.

So before a student starts a practice session on their Sonatina in F, they would turn to "Sonatina in F" section in their piece coach, and *every key issue that has ever affected that Sonatina will be there for them to see.*

Again, it's about making readily available the important points from the lesson, so that they are important points in the practice room too.

14.10 Practice Scheduler

While the Practice Revolution seeks to debunk the myth of a set amount of daily practice, if students don't actually include a practice *start* time in their daily schedule, the session probably won't happen in the first place. (See the P110 in the chapter on Why Students Don't Practice)

As outlined in that chapter, the Practice Scheduler allows students to set exactly *when* each practice session will begin, whether in terms of a time (eg. 4pm,) or an event (eg. as soon as I get home from school). In this way, they're not just understanding what needs to be done—they're committing to starting a part of the process each day.

And with the first five seconds of any practice session being the hardest to make happen, a Practice Schedule that has parents, student and teacher clear on which times belong to practicing is a powerful weapon for the week ahead.

14.11 21st Century options

If you *really* want to astound your students—and unleash a new world of practicing options—then you're going to have fun with this. It's now possible through the official PracticeSpot Press website to give your students their own practice *webpage* to work with. It means that you can boast to prospective students that your studio offers *"24 hour, 7 day a week support for students as they work at home —through the studio website"*. Obviously you won't be there 24/7. But their webpage will be, and it's packed with support for the six days between lessons.

How do you do this? The team at PracticeSpot has set all of this up *for you* already at **www.musicteaching.com**—all you have to do is move your students in.

14.1.1 Using your studio website to transform practice

Every student in your studio can have their very own webpage at your site, with their own unique address—which means that suddenly, *you are connected directly to the homes of the people you teach.*

From this simple idea, the most astonishing things are possible.

For example, the fact that you can **send messages** straight to the webpage of individual students means that you can give students a midweek "poke"—a "how are you going" message that is really reminding them to get on with it. Takes you seconds to do (in fact, you can send one en masse to all your students if you word it carefully), and usually causes a midweek burst of activity from students who might otherwise be cruising a little in that time.

If a student runs into trouble, they (or their parents) can send a **message** straight to *your* homepage, meaning that you can provide emergency support for students *between* lessons. Your reply will have them practicing harder, can transform the next lesson, the fact that you helped will have been noted by their parents—helping not just with practicing, but with retention rates. (How many studios do you know who can provide support like that?)

A built in online **Calendar** means that students can not only always see how far away deadlines are—they can actually **post new deadlines** of their own, *which then instantly updates your own calendar.* So if they find out about a talent night at school, they enter it into their own calendar, which automatically makes an entry in *your* calendar—ensuring that you can hit the ground running next lesson on this issue, and that you don't have to put up with "Oh yes, I forgot. I have a concert next week...", and the accompanying panic practice. The details will appear right there on your webpage, the instant they enter them.

Repertoire records allows you or the student to record details of every piece they ever study, and allows their parents to have an at-a-glance view of what their child has been doing. And because you can access the records of any student at any time, it makes planning for recitals easier than ever before.

Studio newsletters and inbuilt **studio policy** take the place of their paper and ink counterparts, while your own blog means that you can post your own practice advice and suggestions for the whole studio.

The studio network also means that when you list a student as "Student of the week!" in the studio newsletter, that student will know that every other student in the studio will see the details on their own homepages—in full colour, without using up your toner. You could also reward that student-of-the-week by sending them a **sticker**—choose from our image collection, type your caption, and click "send". It appears instantly in their online stickerbook, alongside all their other stickers. An infinite supply of rewards for deserving students, and a tidy way to say "thank you" to students who turn up ready to each lesson.

And if you really must still keep tabs on *how long* students spend practicing (and I'm hoping that this far into the book that it's not an issue any more!), there is built in **Practice Stats**, which allows you to see at a glance the practice records for any of your students, whether this week, or over the past twelve months. It also allows you to see just how much work it actually takes a student to produce the outcomes you've asked for, so that you can tailor future practice requests.

These highlighted tools are only a fraction of what's available at your studio website (you can also turn off any features you don't want to use)—the easiest way to discover for yourself how it can help is to set one up for yourself at:

www.musicteaching.com

There are loads of tutorials and "Ideas to Try". But best of all, if your student has a webpage of their own as their between-lesson support, the whole thing becomes a *direct and regular invitation for their parents to become involved.* All of which leads very nicely into the next chapter.

The Role of Parents

Children today are tyrants. They contradict their parents, gobble their food, and tyrannize their teachers.

Socrates, (469 BC - 399 BC)

The Practice Revolution: Chapter 15

• More than just Policing • Being Interested • Encouraging • Reflecting • Steering • Enthusing • Progress Checks • Knowing when *not* to help •

15. The Role of Parents

15.1 More than just policing

No matter how effective your tuition, no matter how engaging your analogies, nor sharp your wit, each music lesson still only occupies a mere thirty minutes of the student's week.

This means that for the rest of the week, either the parents have to provide support, or the student works completely alone. And most students really should *not* work alone, any more than they should play with power tools by themselves.

Parents are usually delighted and excited to help if they possibly can, but in many cases simply haven't got a clue how to go about it, particularly if they have no musical training of their own. In the absence of such training, they have to focus on the things they *can* understand—and of all of these issues, one screams louder than all others:

How much practice is my kid doing?

It's the dreaded question that inspired this book in the first place. Parents use the answer to this question to draw conclusions about their child's motivation, progress, and from that, *the success of lessons as a whole.* The parent's role is then reduced to that of Truant Officer, catching their kids sneaking off fishing when they should be in the practice rooms. Oh no you don't. Stop having *fun,* and turn off that computer game—this is no time for being happy. You're supposed to *practice.*

It's almost as if music lessons are simply supposed to be Character Building, like shovelling snow, or raking leaves. In the face of this, the student comes to associate a new word with music lessons:

Chore.

It becomes just one more thing that stops them from spending their free time in their own way.

Once that association becomes entrenched, you will lose that student. Maybe not this week, or even this semester. But you will lose them.

So if parents are not supposed to be fussing about how much practice their child does, how can they help?

There is plenty parents can do, even when playing Truant Officer is *not* on the list. Parents don't need any musical training whatsoever to make a tremendous difference to their child's music lessons. They need to dedicate some time to the process, they need to be patient as they work with their child in this new fashion…

…and they need to read this.

15.2 Be interested

The single best thing parents can do to help their child practice is to be *genuinely interested* in what's going on with their music lessons. To be hungry to find out what happened in the last lesson, and how their child plans on being ready for the next one. To want to know how the flute fits together, or how to apply resin to the bow, or which hand pushes those buttons on the trumpet. And what that left pedal on the piano is called. What's the highest note their child can play? How fast is that new study supposed to be? What are they most looking forward to showing off at your next lesson?

How is their child *feeling* about their next concert? What made them decide to choose to play this piece? Which scale do they hate the most and why? Which composer do they enjoy playing most? What do they mess up most often in lessons?

Such questions can happen in the car, at the dinner table, straight after lessons, while they're getting their kid dressed for school, at the checkout at the supermarket…wherever. But they should happen a lot. Parents who ask questions like this won't have to feign fascination—they'll end up with greater insights into what their child is doing, and in turn be more interested as to how things are progressing.

Most children are delighted to be the centre of their parent's attention, and will tend to view favorably any activity that thrusts them into the limelight like that. If music lessons can feature on that list of positive attention-getters, then a large part of the practice battle has been won already.

15.3 Encourage

Parents don't need to be gushing over every correct quarter note, but calculated positive feedback from parents is a great way of reinforcing behavior.

The logic is that if the parent catches their child doing something *right*, and then praises them for it, *the child is likely to want to repeat that behavior in the future.* This can be even more effective if the parent is well-versed in which issues the teacher is trying to develop, allowing for selective targeting of such praise. So if the problem for the past few months has been that the student practices too fast, the next time the parent hears a passage of slow practice—however fleeting—they should pop in and mention to the student how careful their practice is sounding.

They can also keep an ear out for when the student may be sounding frustrated with what they are doing—not so they can sweep in and fix the problem, but just so the child knows that there is someone in their corner. Depending on the situation, they can gently encourage the child to try the section a couple more times, or try it a different way, or try a different section altogether, or even to take a break for a while and come back later.

The point is that when the child battles with practicing demons, they do so with *support*, and with plenty of encouragement to persist.

15.4 Reflect

At the heart of the Practice Revolution is the need for students to understand exactly what they are trying to achieve in the week ahead—well before they start the first practice session. This means that instructions from the teacher, and feedback during the lesson are more important than ever. Parents can ensure that the communication between studio and home is complete by having the student *reflect back to them* the essential information for the week ahead.

The student should be able to explain exactly what their tasks are, together with the practice techniques that were recommended to complete them. They should also be able to answer questions about key points that were raised last lesson, together with any details of upcoming deadlines or performances.

The questions from the parent are designed to help the student cement their understanding of what's required, and are probably best conducted as soon after the lesson as possible (in the car on the way home is ideal!). It's also useful to pop into practice sessions at random and have the student outline again what their goals for the week are…that way, if the practicing has been wandering from the task at hand, the student will be gently reminded to get their eye back on the ball, without anyone having to ask.

15.5 Steer

Even when kids are completely clear on what their goals are for the week, and have a comprehensive list of practice techniques to use to pursue those goals, they can sometimes be confused as to how to organize it all. Sometimes three pieces, five scales and some theory papers can feel like a lot, and a little help from parents can go a long way.

The parents can't actually do the practice for them, but they can help the child work out how many practice sessions will happen, when they will take place, and how long will be available for each one. Once that's been done, they can build together a plan for getting everything done, as outlined in the chapter on Project Management.

Parents can also keep an eye on the practice sessions themselves, keeping a look out for any obvious appearances of the common practice flaws outlined earlier in this book. For example, if they hear the student spending twenty minutes on a section that they can already play, it's time to go in and tell the student that the section already sounds great, and that they could be done practicing sooner if they concentrated on tasks for the week that they *haven't* mastered yet.

15.6 Enthuse

While praise can be useful for reinforcing what a student is already doing, being enthusiastic can help motivate students to be excited about things *they haven't even started yet*—affecting practice sessions that may not take place for months, or even years.

So for example, the parent and child might be listening to an advanced violin sonata on the radio in the car, and the parent might turn to the child and tell them:

*"You know what's really exciting? I love **listening** to this piece, but if things keep going the way they have been, by the time you finish high school, you'll probably be able to **play** it!*

Probably only one person out of every ten thousand who start violin lessons are strong enough inside to make it that far—when I tell you I'm proud of what you did in your lesson today, I'm not kidding."

It's over the top. But it's entirely appropriate, because coming from mom or dad, words like that can ring in the child's ears long after the conversation ends.

Parents can enthuse about the new piece their kid has been given. They can enthuse about the fact that their child has almost finished their new book, and may even get through it all before the holidays. They can enthuse about the new instrument their child now has. They can enthuse about how much everyone applauded at the student concert, and how their child was one of the few to play from memory.

And the best thing about these various moments of enthusing? They don't have to be done *to* the student. They just need to be said within *earshot* of the student. (In fact, such enthusing will have its greatest credibility and impact if the child believes they were not supposed to hear what was said).

So if the parent's little aside was about how little Matthew is playing so well that it won't be long before he is playing some Beethoven, don't be surprised if little Matthew *requests* some Beethoven in a future lesson.

Why? Because being able to play Beethoven is obviously a yardstick for being musically grown up—they know, because they heard their parent say so once. As a mere teacher, no superlatives we may deliver about Beethoven would count as much as that.

15.7 Progress checks

With the practice model being based around the student having specific jobs to do, rather than practicing for a set time, knowing whether or not they are ready for their next lesson is more important for students than ever before. Students need to know *early* in the week if they are starting to fall behind, so that the lesson itself doesn't sneak up and ambush them—a week can go by awfully quickly if they're not paying attention.

One of the best ways to assess progress is with a couple of well-spaced midweek Checkpoints (as outlined in the Project Management chapter), and the parent is the perfect audience for the student to show off their work so far to. The whole process is similar to the regular inspections that take place on building sites to ensure that the job is running to schedule. So if the student's job was to learn *two pages* of music, then by half way through the week, they should be able to play *one* of them.

The check doesn't exist so that the parent can lecture the student about keeping up. Even if the session reveals that the student is behind, all the response needs to be is a discussion about how to restructure the rest of the week to still meet the deadline—no mention needs to be made about the student having been sub-par at the beginning of the week, because there is absolutely nothing anybody can do to change that now.

But there is *plenty* they can do in the remaining days to ensure that the bad start to the week simply won't matter at the lesson. If all jobs are completed, as the teacher, you shouldn't care at all that they had taken things easy for the first three days of the week—a point that this book has repeatedly stressed.

This restructuring is not just a conversation about how to fit in extra practice sessions. It should also target how the student is *planning* on practicing. Often students fall behind because the *way* they are practicing is not working, not because they are spending insufficient time in the practice room. The parent can go through the list of suggested practice techniques, and help the child look for alternatives to the one they had been using.

For those teachers who have their own studio website, midweek checks can also allow students to call for help between lessons—long before the problem grows into a big one. The thirty seconds it takes you to quickly send some advice in response to your student's help request can transform the thirty minutes of the next lesson, and will be greatly appreciated by parents.

15.8 Knowing when *not* to help

Sometimes the best help is *not to help at all.* Some students work best when they are given room to move, and will actively resent parents leaping in with solutions for every practice problem they face. Other students are undergoing temporary difficulties in their relationship with the parent concerned, and may then also undergo temporary difficulties with their music lessons too if the parent tries to involve themselves in the practice process. (The same student would probably have temporary difficulties with chocolate ice-cream if that same parent announced that they really should start eating some)

Independently of the state of the relationship between parent and child, as students become more autonomous with their practice, the parental involvement model moves gently from *helping regularly* to simply *being available* should the student need it.

But no matter how independent the practicing becomes, parents continue to set the enthusiasm levels with their own attitudes towards what is happening in music lessons. It can be as simple as eye-contact and a small nod at the end of an obviously good lesson. Parents don't need to compose a sonnet for their kids to know that they are proud. And they don't have to be sitting on the piano stool with their kids for every second of practice for the child to feel thoroughly supported, and to feel that the excitement surrounding their progress in lessons is being shared.

Towards Independence

*Never help a child with a task
at which they feel they can succeed.*

Maria Montessori

The Practice Revolution: Chapter 16

• Introduction • Choosing from the Menu • Adding New Dishes to the Menu • Choosing their own Goals • Allowing Students to Specialize • Moving to Assistance on Demand •

16. Towards Independence

16.1 Introduction

It's been said that the only certainties in life are death and taxes, but there is actually a third:

Every student that you start teaching will eventually stop having lessons.

The important thing to remember here is that it's not just those students for whom lessons didn't quite work out.

It's *everyone*—that includes your favorite students, your stars, the ones who make you smile, the ones who really listen, and those that seem to laugh loudest at your jokes.

Sometimes their family moves interstate. Sometimes their interests change. Sometimes, after years with the same teacher, it's simply *time* for a change. Sometimes the fact that you were the perfect teacher for them when they were eight means that you are exactly the *wrong* teacher for them now they are thirteen.

Whatever the reason, the single most valuable gift you can leave your student on that final day is for that student *to be able to work independently*. For this reason, when I teach students, my main aim is not to teach them pieces, theory, skills or scales—although we obviously do plenty of all four. My aim is to teach them *how to teach themselves*. To equip them with strategies that they can apply for themselves to a thousand pieces that they haven't even met yet.

So that when they pass through the studio doors for the last time, they simply don't need me any more.

In that way, music teaching is the strangest of professions. There are few careers on the planet that require you to work so hard towards your own redundancy, or leave you feeling so proud and fulfilled when that redundancy is achieved.

As teachers, most of us are well aware of this, and we already work towards independence in our students in many ways. We teach students to read. We teach them to count. We make sure that they can understand all manner of signs and terms. We teach them to regulate their own tempi, to create dynamics that work, and how to manage nerves before a performance.

But of all these skills, the one that is the most important is to teach them how to *practice*. To gently turn the six days between lessons into the *seven* days that sooner or later, won't actually feature a lesson at all.

What you've read in this book will help with this process, but it still requires *your* regular input—input that one day you won't be there to give. Here's what you've been told so far...and then we're going to add a little extra to the whole process to help students make the transformation for themselves, at which point the Practice Revolution will be complete.

16.1.1 Looking back

If the Practice Revolution achieves nothing else, it's to shift the focus on practice away from the traditional obsession with *time spent*, and towards a focus on *outcomes*. In other words, don't try to impress me with how much practice you did this week—show me what all that practice *produced.*

The student then understands that because you are no longer going to be dazzled simply by how much time they used up, if they are smart about how they work, they can actually *minimize* the amount of time they need to spend practicing in the first place. And for 21st century students who are becoming busier than ever before at a younger age than ever before, this is a very good thing.

In pursuit of this end, you clearly define the goals for the week, together with some tests that the student can self-administer so that they'll know once the goals have been reached. In other words, so that they'll know when they *don't* need to do any more practice on it.

Their mission during the week is not to do half an hour of practice every day. *It's to complete these goals*, and once they're done, they can stop. And similarly, until they're done, they can't.

You'll also equip them with a range of practice techniques—techniques which are *tailor made for the goals you set.* So if their goal is to get their piece up to tempo, you would equip them with techniques specifically dedicated to speeding pieces up, rather than giving them the general instruction to "practice hard and speed up the piece this week", and then leaving it to them to work out how.

Providing a *range* of targeted techniques means that if technique A didn't work, then technique B just might, helping the student feel a sense of hope in the face of any setbacks, and also developing an awareness of just how many different ways forward there actually are. It's much harder to be discouraged about the progress of the game when there is a steady stream of new cards to play.

To help with this, the center of this book has been dedicated to providing a wide range of highly targeted practice techniques, explanations as to why these techniques are effective, and any accompanying cautions or variations. Teachers are also encouraged to go and build their own list of techniques, and for that list to be constantly growing.

You've also been shown methods of identifying and curing common practice flaws, to save your students hundreds of hours of wasted practice in the course of each year—time which they can then spend either at leisure, or on making their music lessons move forwards even faster.

But there's one more job to be done. So far, *you need to be there for your student at every step of the way*, from the time the goal was first set, to the "week that was" review. It's time to start gently backing away, and to help them to ride this particular bike all by themselves.

16.2 Choosing from the Menu

Don't misunderstand me. We're not going to help students ride the bike by themselves by *suddenly* letting go of the bike completely. It's going to be a gentle process, and one that needs to leave the student with faith in the practice system at all times.

The least dangerous support to remove is that of the *choice* of practice techniques. Instead of telling them that they are to use these two practice techniques to memorize their piece this week, present them with a *list of half a dozen options* for memorizing the piece, and allow them to choose from that menu.

You still retain a degree of control, in the same way that a chef does at a restaurant, in that you'll only put on the menu options that you are happy for them to work with in the first place. But once that option-limiting step has been taking, the student can enjoy a feeling of autonomy as they decide for themselves which of those options they want to use. In the process, they'll learn two important lessons:

1) They will discover that they enjoy working with some techniques more than others. This means that they don't have to be condemned to working through a system that they find tedious or unrewarding—they have plenty of alternatives that they can switch to.

2) Point 1 notwithstanding, they will also discover that some techniques work more *effectively* than others. So while their early choices will probably be dictated by assessing which method is the most fun, six months down the track, they will have learned from experience which techniques are going to require the *least practice time.* And remember, "least practice time" to get the job done well is why the Practice Revolution is so attractive to students in the first place.

Whatever choices they make, at the end of the practice week, spend some time discussing their choice of techniques with them, together with assessments as to how effective they felt each technique was.

16.3 Adding new dishes to the menu

Once the student is comfortable with choosing from an *existing* list of possible techniques, it's time to start encouraging them to experiment with developing techniques of their own. While *The Practice Revolution* and the student version *Practiceopedia* spells out plenty of ideas for getting the job done, I am certainly not arrogant enough to assume that there are no more techniques possible for each of the standard practice tasks—and it just may be that your students will stumble across some that work brilliantly for them. (In which case, please email me through PracticeSpot...I would love to add such ideas to the Practice Revolution support website!)

Obviously this needs to be handled carefully though. Earlier in the book, the Practice Flaws section highlighted what sorts of disasters are possible if students just practice according to their own flights of fancy. There are two safety checks you need to build in to stop their own creative practice techniques from possibly undermining otherwise good work that they may be doing:

1) While the technique is theirs to create, they need to run the idea past you FIRST, and accept that you have the power of veto. So if their own practice technique for learning new notes is "to learn the piece without worrying about accidentals yet" (as a method of simplifying the task), you'd probably intervene and gently suggest that perhaps they should think of another method.

2) Their made-up technique is to be used in conjunction with, *not instead of*, the list of practice techniques you recommended. Students can become very enthusiastic about their own made-up practice techniques, and you need to stop them from putting all their practice eggs in a single and potentially unstable basket.

But despite your own reservations, the ultimate assessment of any new technique a student develops *is in the impact it has on their playing*. Even given all my cautions about the importance of breaking up the job, and learning things separate hands to start, I have had more than one student who learns pieces most effectively if they actually tackle the whole thing at once. While I still am not about to recommend that as an approach for my other students, I have had to accept that in those particular cases, their technique works—which means that it has permanently been added to their list of options for Learning New Pieces. The Practice Revolution is certainly about structure, but it cannot be about dogma, because students have a nasty habit of being individuals.

16.4 Choosing their own goals

In Chapter 3, a technique was outlined to give students a feeling of ownership over the goals for the week ahead by allowing them to "choose" those goals. This "choosing" was actually set against a background of the teacher steering them heavily towards their own preferred teaching goals in any case, so that the choice itself was really an illusion—like voting in one-party states.

As students become more experienced with practicing to goals, rather than to a set amount of time, you can start to *genuinely* give them control over setting those goals for the week ahead. Set the scene for them first—remind them quickly of the longer term goals they are working towards, recap the key developments in today's lesson, and then ask them what they are planning on having ready for you *next* lesson. Get out a paper and pen, and write it down, just to make it official.

The big difference between this and the previous "train tracks" approach to choosing their own goals is that this time is that *you won't be interfering at all with their choices.*

If they set a goal which is going to be absolutely impossible in only seven days, then the very best way they can learn from that is to set the goal, *and then get burned by it.* Similarly, if they set a goal which is achievable and keeps them busy, but doesn't really help move them forwards towards their more distant goals (such as an upcoming recital), then the shock of a "wasted" week might be just the shot they need to ensure that they are more careful to align their goals in the future.

All of this means that you really will have to bite your lip on occasions, because your student won't always create goals that are achievable, realistic, or useful—in fact, some of the time, their goals will be howlingly inappropriate. But after their first few weeks in the Goal Wilderness, they will have a much better understanding of what *not* to do at the very least. Messing things up, and then analyzing what went wrong becomes a more powerful learning tool for them than mere advice ever could be.

Allowing the student to set their own goals doesn't just affect their practice week. It also has implications for the next lesson. You won't have the freedom to just ask to hear the things *you* think are important—instead you need to work from the list of goals that the student set, however absurd you may privately believe those goals to have been.

In other words, if a student is allowed to set the goal for the week ahead, *then they are also effectively setting the agenda for the next lesson.* You're not abandoning all control by doing this—the lesson would need to include an analysis of the appropriateness of the stated goals from the week that was. That way, if their goals were never going to work in the first place, you can help them to understand why they were flawed, and how to set better goals next time.

And if their goals actually *were* appropriate, then it's not such a bad agenda that you need to work to in any case. Besides which, even if the agenda items proper have been dictated by the student, as the Chair of this particular meeting, the potential for "Any Other Business" remains unlimited.

16.5 Allowing students to specialize

Once students have had some experience with choosing their own practice techniques, they may start to feel confident that they can handle entire *categories* of practice tasks without help.

So, for example, they might have discovered that the practice techniques they use for memorizing pieces seem to do the job every time—meaning that whenever their task involves memorization, *they don't need any further instructions from you as to how to go about it.* All you have to do is set the goal.

In this way, the student can develop particular practice tasks that they specialize in, and will probably look forward to being given that type of task. So for our student above, you might still provide them with practice techniques for learning their new piece, or getting it up to tempo, but when the time comes to memorize, you can step back and allow them to get on with it.

16.5.1 Awarding Independence "Certificates"

One way of making tangible—and celebrating—the progress of students towards practice independence is to award them certificates to officially recognize tasks they no longer need help with. So a student who has been working towards practice independence through specializing might have the following certificate collection:

- Learning the new piece
- Preparing for performance
- Speeding up the piece
- Putting your stamp on the piece

But they still may need help with memorizing pieces, coping with stubborn sections or project management. In this way, you can save valuable lesson time by only providing assistance with practice techniques that are outside their areas of "specialty", while helping the student easily differentiate between those tasks that they should attempt for themselves, and those that still need guidance.

16.6 Moving to assistance on demand

Once the student can comfortably list *all* of the common practice tasks as being areas of specialization, lessons can move into another dimension entirely.

Because they now have a stock of half a dozen or more possible practice techniques for every common practice task they are likely to face, you don't need to spend lesson time introducing them to tools any more. *Instead the focus can be on what those tools have produced.*

In other words, at the end of the process underpinning *The Practice Revolution*—at the end of the planning and organizing, the analyzing, structuring and encouraging—more than ever before, music lessons can be about *music.*

The easiest way to provide further help - equip your students with the **Student Version** *of this book.* **Practiceopedia** *is 376 pages, color, fully illustrated - an A-Z reference of practice techniques, tricks, tips and traps written especially for music students and parents.*
Available now from www.practiceopedia.com.

Where to get more help

The Practice Revolution: Chapter 17

• The Official PracticeSpot Press Website • Some Highlights from PracticeSpot.com • Also by Philip Johnston • For more information, conference bookings etc.

17. Where to get more help

17.1 The Official PracticeSpot Press website

www.practicespot.com

The world's largest resource and idea website for music teachers and students

This book is just the beginning—it's actually completely *dwarfed* by a much larger resource that's both free and online 24 hours a day. Originally set up to provide support for *Not Until You've Done Your Practice* (my first book), PracticeSpot.com has quickly become the world's largest website for music teachers and students, offering a huge collection of resources and ideas, and attracting over two million hits every month from music studios around the world.

The content is free, and you can check it out for yourself at **www. practicespot.com,** but I've included some highlights on the next few pages so that you know why you are firing up your browser in the first place.

In short, if this book has been useful for your own teaching studio in any way, I'd love to hear from you. *The Practice Revolution* has been the first publication from PracticeSpot Press.

There are lots more coming.

17.2 Some highlights from PracticeSpot.com

17.2.1 PracticeSpot Theory Sheet Center

The Theory Sheet Center is a huge and growing collection of **free** downloadable theory sheets. Simply choose the topic you need, select the drill type, and click "print". You'll never run out—you can print a million copies of each sheet if your wish. Alternatively, you can simply give your students the address of the sheet they need to complete for homework. They can print it out at home, complete it, and bring it to the next lesson.

You'll still actually have to *teach* the theory to your students—all we've done is make sure that the workbooks you need are only ever a mouseclick away.

17.2.2 Create your own studio website.

Advertising your studio by putting up a notice in a shop window is one thing. But being able to mention on that same advertisement *"For more information, visit the studio website at..."* takes the ad to a new level entirely. Suddenly your studio feels a whole lot more real and professional, and you can include a wealth of information at a website that you could never squeeze into a shop flier.

Because most teachers don't have the time, expertise or money to set up their own studio website, PracticeSpot allows them to *instantly* create their own.

Your website can feature as much or as little information about your studio as you wish. You can then proudly refer to your new web address in your yellow pages, newspaper advertisements, letter box drops—whatever.

You don't need to know anything about webpage building to set your page up, and can easily make changes whenever you like (we know how music teachers like to fuss and fiddle).

To see such a website for yourself, you can go to our studio website information center at:

www.musicteaching.com

17.2.3 The PracticeSpot Rhythm Gym

The Rhythm Gym provides a series of carefully graded and annotated rhythm drills, designed especially for students who find reading rhythms tricky.

Students can work with the drills directly from the webpage, listen to midi files of correct performances, or you can print them out to work on in the studio.

17.2.4 The PracticeGuide

Further help for students who need to practice, but just aren't quite sure what to do. Provides many of the practice techniques outlined in this book, but aimed at students and their parents. Around 45,000 words, illustrated throughout, and one of the most popular segments at the site.

All the student has to do is look up the problem they are having (eg. "speeding my piece up"), and the Practiceguide will provide suggestions for them, much like the center chapters of this book.

17.2.5 Web's Largest Dictionary of Musical Terms

Helps your students turn obscure Italian words into something they can work with, with over 1200 musical terms, making this the most comprehensive music dictionary on the web.

Most music dictionaries can tell you what "allegro" and "pianissimo" mean. But we didn't just want to cover the basics. We wanted our visitors to get an answer on *any* term, no matter how unusual. Terms Like **"Ghiribizzoso"**. Or **"Straccicalando"**. Or **"Ungestüm"**. Simply type in the mystery term—searches take less than 0.1 seconds to find what you need.

The PracticeSpot Dictionary is also searchable in *reverse*, meaning that you can input an English word, and it will find musical equivalents, perfect for composition students.

17.2.6 Manuscript Genie

The Manuscript Genie provides an infinite supply of manuscript paper at a variety of different sizes. Simply choose the type you need, and hit "print".

17.2.7 Studio Policy Collection

Just in case you were wondering how other teachers do things, PracticeSpot has a collection of studio policies, all contributed by visitors to the site. Browse through the ideas, and then send in the policy your studio uses (We'd love to hear from you!)

17.2.8 Music Crosswords

You can solve, check or cheat your way through our collection of crosswords—all dedicated to the subject musicians know best. Crosswords also include timers, for students (or teachers!) who get competitive about these things.

17.2.9 The web's first online Music Psychologist

Because life can be complicated for musicians. Expert free advice from Lucinda Mackworth-Young, who is a leading Consultant in Psychology for Musicians. Everything from dealing with difficult parents, coping with performance anxiety to string quartets that can't get along. Also includes a link to purchase Lucinda's excellent book on the subject—"Tuning In".

17.2.10 PracticeSpot's Sightreading Central

Dedicated to students who would like to read a little better. Free printable drills, sorted by difficulty, together with tips for improving sightreading. Midi files are available for all drills so that students can hear what the playthrough was *supposed* to sound like.

17.2.11 "For Teachers" article archive

A collection of articles especially for studio music teachers. When I'm not busy writing books, I'm busy writing articles for PracticeSpot—so if The Practice Revolution has proved useful for you, then chances are you'll find plenty of articles in the "For Teachers" section that will help too. Studio promotion, finding great repertoire, motivating students, creating studio awards...offbeat solutions to common problems.

17.2.12 The Infinity Rhythm Reading Machine

Randomly generated collection of rhythm drills, and a good way for students to test themselves once they have graduated from the Rhythm Gym. Student can set the allowable elements within any rhythm (eg. rests, dots, eighth notes), and the Infinity Rhythm Reading machine does the rest. Capable of generating over 20,882,706 TRILLION unique rhythms, so it will be enough to keep you and your students busy for a while.

17.2.13 ...and lots more

There's much more at PracticeSpot that hasn't been mentioned here, and the site is being regularly added to. Teachers who want to be informed about new features or articles at the site can subscribe to the PracticeSpot Newsletter (it's free!). And as new books come out from PracticeSpot Press (I have another couple in the pipeline as you read this), details and excerpts will appear at the site.

Our aim remains to be a worldwide focal point for innovation, support and inspiration for the great career that is music teaching.

17.3 Also by Philip Johnston

The PracticeSpot Guide to Promoting your Teaching Studio

The ultimate guide for teachers who want to know how to fill the spaces in their schedule, and enjoy the hidden benefits a thriving studio brings.

This book is the single biggest collection of studio promotion techniques ever assembled - 240 pages of action you can take to build the studio you deserve.

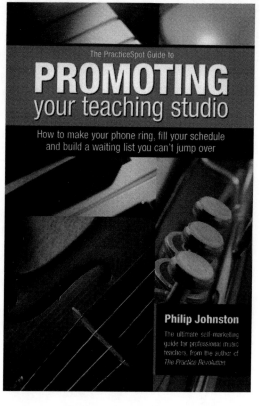

"What a great book! The author clearly explains why it is so vital to promote your teaching studio, and then provides hundreds and hundreds of great ideas that will help you to have a full studio and a full waiting list. Mr. Johnston tells you exactly how, where, and when to advertise, and offers suggestions as to other promotions...my experience was that this book paid for itself in the first week I owned it! **If you are a private music teacher (any instrument), you must own this book!** "

Review at amazon.com

About the Author

Philip Johnston is the founder of and chief writer for the world's largest website for music teachers and students at **www.practicespot. com**, while his books have stamped him as one of the world's leading experts on practicing.

Based in Australia, Philip has also recorded for Warner Music as a concert pianist in his own right, and has a Masters degree in piano performance from Indiana University. As a violin student though, he was kicked out by no fewer than six violin teachers...for not practicing.

Philip is married with three children, and juggles his time between writing, composing, performing, website development and instructing in taekwondo. His dream remains to play cricket for Australia one day, but to date, the selectors have continuously overlooked him in favour of players who are better than he is.

To book Philip for your next event:

A book can cover plenty of ground, but there's nothing quite like being able to actually *speak* to people. Philip is an infectiously enthusiastic and experienced presenter, and can be contacted at:
philipj@practicespot.com

www.recitalworks.com

New from Philip Johnston and PracticeSpot Press, Recitalworks.com is a **repertoire website** with a focus on a **new generation** of blow-the-audience-out-of-their-chairs **concert works** for piano.

Free previews of all works
So you can try before you buy, and find just the piece you need.

Early intermediate through to *international competition standard*
As your playing develops, you'll always find pieces to challenge. Easiest pieces are manageable for young students, while the hardest pieces in the collection will tax even the most accomplished concert artists.

Downloadable practice challenges
To get you from *never-seen-it-before* to *concert-ready*. Just work your way through the list, and watch your piece come together. .

Scheduled for release 2007.
But you can check out www.recitalworks.com for updates and sneak previews in the meantime. Aren't you curious?...

Made in the USA